Baseball's Greatest Streaks

Baseball's Greatest Streaks

*The Highs and Lows of
Teams, Pitchers and Hitters in
the Modern Major Leagues*

by
ALLEN LEWIS

McFarland & Company, Inc., Publishers
Jefferson, North Carolina, and London

To Mrs. Sydney Schultz for her invaluable help

and

to Research Librarians in
Clearwater, Florida
Chicago, Illinois
Cincinnati, Ohio
New York, New York
Philadelphia, Pennsylvania
St. Louis, Missouri
San Francisco, California
Tampa, Florida
Library of Congress, Washington, D.C.

British Library Cataloguing-in-Publication data are available

Library of Congress Cataloguing-in-Publication Data

Lewis, Allen
    Baseball's greatest streaks : the highs and lows of teams,
pitchers and hitters in the modern major leagues / by Allen Lewis.
        p.   cm.
    Includes index.
    ISBN 0-89950-714-X (lib. bdg. : 50# alk. paper)
    1. Baseball — United States — Records.   I. Title.
GV877.L38   1992   91-51209
                                                                CIP

Manufactured in the United States of America

McFarland & Company, Inc., Publishers
  Box 611, Jefferson, North Carolina 28640

Contents

Introduction

Each streak written up in this book is preceded by pertinent information about the team, pitcher or batter involved. Also included are the result of the game prior to the start of the streak and the team's record. The won-lost record of a pitcher beginning a streak and the average of a batter starting a streak are also given.

Each streak is a separate entity. On first mention, a player's position and first name are used but not repeated during that streak. Pitchers are identified as right-handers or left-handers. After the score by innings, the total of runs, hits and errors are given, followed by the pitchers used by the winning team and then those of the losing team, with the winning and losing pitchers in boldface. The inning in which a relief pitcher enters the game is given in parentheses after his name. In the batting streaks, the player's name beneath the line score is followed by his times at bat, runs scored, and hits in each game. These are followed by the type of hit or hits in order of value, not necessarily in the order collected by the batter.

The game in which a streak is broken follows the final game in each streak. A summary of the streak and the remainder of that season is given, and, in the case of a pitcher or batter, a summary of the rest of his career is provided.

Only twentieth century streaks have been included, all of them accomplished since the adoption of the foul-strike rule in the early 1900s, the last major rule change. Rules determining the winning and losing pitcher were not made part of the Official Baseball Rules until after the 1949 season. Some of the decisions before then remain controversial.

WINNING STREAKS BY TEAMS

26 Games • New York Giants, 1916

21 Games • Chicago Cubs, 1935

19 Games • Chicago White Sox, 1906

19 Games • New York Yankees, 1947

18 Games • New York Giants, 1904

18 Games • New York Yankees, 1953

17 Games • New York Giants, 1907

17 Games • Washington Senators, 1912

17 Games • New York Giants, 1916

17 Games • Philadelphia Athletics, 1931

Team Winning Streaks

Team	Year	Games Won	Shutouts Pitched	Yielded Two Runs or Less	Complete Games Pitched	Games Won by Relief Pitcher	Most Games Won by One Pitcher	Number of Pitchers Who Won Games	Games Won by Margin of One Run	Games Won in Final Inning*
Giants	1916	26	10	22	22	3	7	7	4	2
Cubs	1935	21	4	12	18	1	5	6	5	3
White Sox	1906	19	8	16	17	2	7	5	5	3
Yankees	1947	19	0	13	11	4	4	11	2	2
Giants	1904	18	3	12	15	0	5	4	1	1
Yankees	1953	18	2	12	6	4	4	9	2	2
Giants	1907	17	5	12	14	2	5	5	7	4
Senators	1912	17	1	7	8	2	4	6	5	2
Giants	1916	17	1	11	10	2	4	6	7	2
Athletics	1931	17	3	8	13	2	4	6	0	1

*Winning team either broke a tie or came from behind to win in final inning.

1916 New York Giants

26 Consecutive Wins

From 1901 through 1915, the New York Giants won five National League pennants—more than any other club—all under the legendary John McGraw, who managed New York for twenty-nine full seasons and parts of two others, retiring after forty games of the 1932 season.

The only time McGraw managed for a full season when his New York team finished last was in 1915. With substantially the same club in 1916, New York moved back into the first division with one of the most unusual seasons in major league history, putting together two record winning streaks. After a miserable start, New York won seventeen straight games, all on the road, then failed to break even in June, July, and August before embarking on the longest winning streak in major league history, all twenty-six games played in New York's Polo Grounds. Still, New York finished no better than fourth.

The day before the twenty-six-game winning streak began, New York played a doubleheader with Brooklyn at home, winning the opener, then losing the second game, 2–1, as left-hander Rube Marquard, former star pitcher with New York, defeated left-hander Rube Benton. The defeat gave fourth-place New York a 59–62 record and put them 13.5 games behind first-place Philadelphia, who were trying to repeat as National League champions. The record winning streak began the next afternoon.

1. Thursday, September 7

Brooklyn	010 000 000	1	2	3
New York	000 004 00x	4	6	1

WP **Schupp**; LP **Rucker**

2. Friday, September 8

Philadelphia	000 110 001	3	9	4
New York	200 020 41x	9	14	0

WP **Tesreau**; LP **Alexander**, Oeschger (8)

3. Saturday, September 9[1]

Philadelphia	000 001 000	1	4	2
New York	000 110 01x	3	10	0

WP **Perritt**; LP **Demaree**

4. Saturday, September 9[2]

Philadelphia	000 000 000	0	4	3
New York	200 000 10x	3	5	1

WP **Perritt**; LP **Bender**, Mayer (8)

5. Monday, September 11

Philadelphia	000 000 400	4	8	3
New York	010 600 11x	9	10	1

WP **Tesreau**; LP **Rixey**, Oeschger (4), Mayer (7)

6. Tuesday, September 12

Cincinnati	200 000 000	2	7	1
New York	100 110 00x	3	7	4

WP **Benton**; LP **Mitchell**

7. Wednesday, September 13[1]

Cincinnati	000 000 000	0	3	2
New York	000 003 00x	3	9	0

WP **Schupp**; LP **Toney**

8. Wednesday, September 13[2]

Cincinnati	100 102 000	4	9	1
New York	500 010 00x	6	6	2

WP **Smith**, Perritt (6); LP **Schneider**, Schulz (1), Knetzer (7)

9. Thursday, September 14

Cincinnati	000 000 010	1	7	2
New York	100 100 10x	3	8	0

WP **Tesreau**; LP **Moseley**

10. Saturday, September 16[1]

Pittsburgh	001 000 001	2	6	0
New York	210 000 50x	8	15	2

WP **Benton**; LP **Mamaux**

11. Saturday, September 16[2]

Pittsburgh	201 000 000	3	7	2
New York	000 000 022	4	6	1

WP Anderson, Smith (2), Ritter (7), **Tesreau** (9); LP **Cooper**,

12. Monday, September 18[1]

Pittsburgh	000 000 000	0	3	2
New York	000 100 01x	2	6	0

WP **Schupp**; LP **Miller**

Monday, September 18[2]

Pittsburgh	000 000 01	1	8	0
New York	000 010 00	1	3	1

P Pittsburgh, Grimes; P New York, Perritt (Tie Game—8 innings, rain)

13. Tuesday, September 19[1]

Pittsburgh	000 200 000	2	5	2
New York	300 320 10x	9	10	0

WP Anderson, **Benton** (4); LP **Jacobs**, Scott (4)

14. Tuesday, September 19[2]

Pittsburgh	000 100 000	1	7	2
New York	002 021 00x	5	11	0

WP **Tesreau**; LP **Evans**

15. Wednesday, September 20

Chicago	001 100 000	2	6	0
New York	000 200 20x	4	8	2

WP **Schupp**; LP **Lavender**, Hendrix (8)

16. Thursday, September 21

Chicago	000 000 000	0	6	1
New York	110 101 00x	4	9	0

WP **Perritt**; LP **Hendrix**

17. Friday, September 22

Chicago	000 000 000	0	7	2
New York	002 101 10x	5	10	0

WP **Sallee**; LP **Perry**, Prendergast (8)

[1]First game of a doubleheader.   [2]Second game of a doubleheader.

18. Saturday, September 23[1]

St. Louis	010 000 000	1	6	4
New York	300 012 00x	6	7	0

WP **Tesreau**; LP **Watson**, Williams (8)

19. Saturday, September 23[2]

St. Louis	000 000 0	0	3	2
New York	100 010 1	3	10	0

WP **Benton**; LP **Ames** (7 innings, rain)

20. Monday, September 25[1]

St. Louis	000 000 000	0	2	3
New York	000 100 00x	1	3	0

WP **Schupp**; LP **Meadows**

21. Monday, September 25[2]

St. Louis	000 002 000	2	6	1
New York	013 100 10x	6	6	2

WP **Perritt**; LP **Lotz**

22. Tuesday, September 26

St. Louis	000 010 000	1	8	2
New York	200 202 00x	6	15	2

WP **Sallee**; LP **Watson**, Williams (7)

23. Wednesday, September 27

St. Louis	101 000 000 0	2	10	0
New York	000 000 002 1	3	9	2

WP Anderson, Benton (3), Smith (8), **Ritter** (10); LP **Steele** (10 innings)

24. Thursday, September 28[1]

Boston	000 000 000	0	6	1
New York	000 101 00x	2	6	1

WP **Tesreau**; LP **Rudolph**

25. Thursday, September 28[2]

Boston	000 000 000	0	1	3
New York	015 000 00x	6	7	0

WP **Schupp**; LP **Ragan**, Nehf (4)

26. Saturday, September 30[1]

Boston	000 000 000	0	1	1
New York	000 000 22x	4	9	1

WP **Benton**; LP **Rudolph**

The streak ended in the second game of a doubleheader, New York's final home game of the season at the Polo Grounds:

Saturday, September 30[2]

Boston	000 200 501	8	13	3
New York	000 020 100	3	8	2

WP **Tyler**; LP **Sallee**, Tesreau (7), Anderson (7), Smith (8)

A wild throw by shortstop Art Fletcher helped Boston score two runs in the fourth, but New York tied the score in the fifth. Boston's winning five-run rally in the seventh began with a single by first baseman Ed Konetchy. Then, third baseman Red Smith and outfielder Sherry Magee homered into left-field bleachers on successive pitches, chasing left-hander Slim Sallee. Pinch-hitter Larry Chappell's single drove in the fifth

---

[1]*First game of a doubleheader.* [2]*Second game of a doubleheader.*

Long-time New York Giants Manager John McGraw with his all-time favorite
player, Hall of Fame pitcher Christy Mathewson. They were together on five
pennant-winning clubs. McGraw's teams enjoyed four winning streaks of seventeen or more games. (Courtesy of National Baseball Library, Cooperstown, New
York.)

run of inning, and the longest winning streak in major league history ended.

The pitching the Giants received during their record winning streak was almost amazing, even for the era before the lively ball. Their pitchers hurled ten shutouts, pitched six games in which the opposition scored only one run — not including the eight-inning, 1–1 tie on September 18 — and six games in which only two runs were allowed. In the other four games, New York's rivals scored three runs twice and four runs twice. In twenty-three of the twenty-six games, New York did not bat in the final inning.

Twenty-two complete games were pitched and two others in which one relief pitcher was used. The only pitcher who started, won, and did not go the route was the right-hander George Smith in Game 8. He was one of seven pitchers used as a starter in the streak. The only one of the seven who failed to win a game was right-hander Fred Anderson, who started three times and failed to last four innings in any of them.

Right-hander Jeff Tesreau was the big winner, completing all six of his starts and winning one in relief. Left-hander Ferdie Schupp won six games, left-hander Rube Benton won five and right-hander Pol Perritt won four, including both games of the September 9 doubleheader early in the streak. Sallee won two games, and right-hander Hank Ritter won the only extra-inning game in the streak by pitching one hitless inning.

During the winning streak New York outhit the opposition .277 to .176 and averaged 4.65 runs per game to 1.23. The Giants outhomered their rivals 9–5. Outfielder Benny Kauff hit four, including an inside-the-park grand slam to deep center on a 3–2 pitch in the five-run third inning of Game 25, plus one in the September 18 game that ended in a 1–1 tie. Outfielder Dave Robertson hit two, and outfielder George Burns, catcher Bill Rariden, and Tesreau each hit one. For Rariden and Tesreau, those were their only homers of the season. Fletcher led in game-winning RBIs with five and Robertson had four.

New York trailed in only six of the twenty-six games, just three times after the fourth inning. Only twice did they go into the ninth inning behind. In Game 11 (September 16, second game), Pittsburgh held a 3–0 lead when the Giants came to bat in the eighth inning. New York scored twice in the eighth on an error, a double by Burns, an infield out, and Robertson's single, then won the game with two more runs in the ninth. Fletcher doubled to left center to start the inning and was out at third on a bunt by Kauff, who stole second and took third on a wild pitch. Pirate left-hander Wilbur Cooper then walked first baseman Walter Holke and Rariden to load the bases. Kauff scored the tying run on a passed ball by catcher Bill Fischer, and, after Tesreau popped up for the second out, Burns lined a single to center to win the game.

In Game 23 (September 27), St. Louis carried a 2–0 lead into the bottom of the ninth when New York tied on a walk to catcher Lew McCarty with one out, a single to left by Burns with two out, and a triple off the right-field wall by second baseman Buck Herzog. New York took advantage of breaks to win in the tenth. After third baseman Heinie Zimmerman singled to right, Fletcher bunted and left-hander Bob Steele slipped trying to field it. Kauff then bunted, and Steele threw to third too late to get Zimmerman, loading the bases. Holke popped out to first base, but Steele then made a wild pitch over catcher Frank Snyder's head, allowing Zimmerman to score the winning run.

Only two other games were decided by the margin of one run. In Game 6 (September 12), Cincinnati scored its only two runs in the first, but the Giants scored once in the first on a single by Burns and Herzog's double to right, tied the score in the fourth when Robertson homered into the upper right-field stands, and scored the winning run in the fifth, aided by an error. Kauff led off with a single to shortstop and was safe at second when shortstop Baldy Louden dropped second baseman Heinie Groh's throw on Holke's grounder. An infield hit by McCarty loaded the bases, and Kauff scored when Benton grounded to shortstop into a double play.

In Game 20 (September 25, first game), Schupp pitched a two-hitter to win, 1–0, the Giants scoring in the fourth inning without a hit off St. Louis right-hander Lee Meadows. With one out, Robertson grounded to shortstop, and Sammy Bohne made a two-base wild throw. After Zimmerman flied out, Fletcher grounded to Bohne, who made another two-base wild throw, Robertson scoring. Outfielder Jack Smith doubled twice for the only hits off Schupp.

In addition to the four games New York won by one run, the Giants won six by two runs; four each by three runs, four runs, and five runs; three by six runs; and one by seven runs. Only the September 18 tie kept New York from sweeping eight doubleheaders.

The last three games in the streak were shutouts. In the last two Boston collected just one hit, and, strangely enough, Konetchy, the husky Boston first baseman, broke up both no-hit bids. In Game 25 (September 28, second game), Schupp allowed only two base runners. He walked catcher Earl Blackburn in the sixth, and in the seventh

Konetchy's hard grounder to second barely eluded Herzog for the only hit. The next day's game was rained out in the fourth inning with New York ahead, 1-0.

The teams considered playing a tripleheader on September 30 but decided to play only a doubleheader, and a Saturday crowd of 38,000 saw Benton extend the New York winning streak to twenty-six games in the opener, winning 4-0 and allowing only a walk to Boston catcher Hank Gowdy in the sixth and a single by Konetchy in the eighth.

The day the twenty-six-game streak ended, New York's record was 85-63, and that was only good enough for fourth place. Brooklyn led with 91-59, Philadelphia was second at 89-58, and Boston third at 85-60. In the season-ending series that followed, New York lost three of four games at Brooklyn, and Boston won four of six games at Philadelphia. Brooklyn thus finished two and one-half games ahead of Philadelphia, four in front of Boston, and seven ahead of New York.

On October 3, when New York lost a sloppy slugfest, 9-6, in Brooklyn, McGraw left the New York bench while the game was going on, later intimating that his players had not been trying to win. Some were reported to be rooting for Wilbert Robinson, who had been a popular Giants coach for three years before becoming Brooklyn's manager in 1914.

"I couldn't sit there and see what was going on without making a protest," McGraw said. "I can't stand for stuff like that."

When asked what he had seen, and for the names of the players who weren't trying, the New York manager said, "That's all I have to say. I saw some things out there I didn't like and that I couldn't stand for."

His charges made headlines and Philadelphia Manager Pat Moran demanded an investigation, but McGraw refused to amplify his remarks and nothing ever came of it, the season ending two days later.

1935 Chicago Cubs

21 Consecutive Wins

The only team that was a charter member of the National League and has remained in the same city since 1876 is the Chicago Cubs. Chicago finished first six times in the league's first eleven years and then went nineteen seasons before winning again in 1906.

That was the first of four championships in five years, but the 1918 pennant was Chicago's only one after the title in 1910 until 1929. Chicago won again in 1932, forging ahead after first baseman Charlie Grimm replaced Rogers Hornsby as manager on August 2. In a surge that began in mid–August, the Cubs won seventeen of eighteen games, including fourteen in a row at Chicago's Wrigley Field in a streak that ended in the second game of a September 3 doubleheader.

Two third-place finishes followed and Chicago, with no major additions from the year before, went into the final month of the 1935 season locked in a tight three-way race with New York and defending champion St. Louis.

Chicago had a 79–52 record after splitting a doubleheader with Cincinnati at home on September 2, losing the second game 4–2 when right-hander Gene Schott beat right-hander Bill Lee, who was done in by errors by catcher Gabby Hartnett and second baseman Billy Herman. That left Chicago in third place, two and one-half games behind first-place St. Louis and half a game in back of New York. All three teams had an off day on September 3, and the winning streak began the next afternoon at Chicago's Wrigley Field.

1. Wednesday, September 4

Philadelphia	100 000 001	2	8	0
Chicago	000 201 05x	8	8	1

WP **French**; LP **Jorgens**, Pezzullo (8), Bivin (8)

2. Thursday, September 5

Philadelphia	000 001 010 00	2	7	1
Chicago	020 000 000 01	3	7	3

WP **Root**; LP **Davis** (11 innings)

3. Friday, September 6

Philadelphia	000 000 020 0	2	11	2
Chicago	100 000 010 1	3	6	1

WP **Warneke**; LP **Bowman** (10 innings)

4. Saturday, September 7

Philadelphia	000 000 000	0	6	1
Chicago	000 021 01x	4	9	1

WP **Lee**; LP **Mulcahy**, Bivin (8)

5. Monday, September 9[1]

Boston	000 010 000	1	4	1
Chicago	000 311 00x	5	10	2

WP **Carleton**; LP **Brandt**

6. Monday, September 9[2]

Boston	000 010 000	1	9	1
Chicago	200 000 00x	2	5	1

WP **French**; LP **Frankhouse**

7. Tuesday, September 10

Boston	000 000 000	0	6	0
Chicago	000 130 00x	4	10	0

WP **Root**; LP **Cantwell**

8. Wednesday, September 11

Boston	001 101 000	3	9	4
Chicago	100 060 08x	15	19	3

WP **Lee**; LP **MacFayden**, Smith (5), Betts (6)

9. Thursday, September 12

Brooklyn	020 000 010	3	8	1
Chicago	040 270 00x	13	15	0

WP **Warneke**; LP **Benge**, Mungo (3), Green (8)

10. Friday, September 13

Brooklyn	010 000 000	1	8	1
Chicago	000 310 00x	4	10	0

WP **French**; LP **Earnshaw**, Leonard (7)

11. Saturday, September 14

Brooklyn	000 022 505	14	15	4
Chicago	251 008 20x	18	18	2

WP **Root**, Henshaw (8), Kowalik (9); LP **Babich**, Reis (1), Baker (2), Green (6), Barr (6), Munns (7), Mungo (8)

12. Sunday, September 15

Brooklyn	200 000 010	3	6	4
Chicago	220 100 10x	6	8	0

WP **Lee**; LP **Clark**

13. Monday, September 16

New York	020 001 000	3	7	1
Chicago	100 610 00x	8	12	0

WP **Warneke**; LP **Gumbert**, Gabler (4), Stout (7)

14. Tuesday, September 17

New York	000 020 010	3	11	4
Chicago	100 003 10x	5	7	1

WP **French**; LP Schumacher, **Stout** (6), Parmalee (6)

---

[1]*First game of a doubleheader.* [2]*Second game of a doubleheader.*

15. Wednesday, September 18

New York	001 100 100	3	9	4
Chicago	010 842 00x	15	20	5

WP **Root**; LP **Castleman**, Gumbert (4), Gabler (5)

16. Thursday, September 19

New York	000 000 010	1	6	0
Chicago	200 001 21x	6	13	1

WP **Lee**; LP **Hubbell**, Stout (8)

17. Saturday, September 21

Pittsburgh	000 000 012	3	8	3
Chicago	000 022 00x	4	8	1

WP **Henshaw**, Warneke (9); LP **Bush**, Birkofer (8)

18. Sunday, September 22

Pittsburgh	000 000 000	0	9	2
Chicago	100 000 01x	2	7	1

WP **French**; LP **Blanton**

19. Wednesday, September 25

Chicago	010 000 000	1	7	0
St. Louis	000 000 000	0	2	0

WP **Warneke**; LP **P. Dean**

20. Friday, September 27[1]

Chicago	002 100 111	6	13	2
St. Louis	200 000 000	2	6	3

WP **Lee**; LP **J. Dean**

21. Friday, September 27[2]

Chicago	000 000 302	5	13	2
St. Louis	000 003 000	3	4	0

WP Root, **Henshaw** (7); LP **Ryba**

The streak ended the next afternoon at Sportsman's Park, St. Louis:

Saturday, September 28

Chicago	000 020 003 00	5	13	1
St. Louis	000 302 000 02	7	12	0

WP Winford, Haines (9), **Walker** (11); LP French, **Kowalik** (8) (11 innings)

St. Louis scored three runs in the fourth on three singles, triple by outfielder Joe Medwick, a scoring fly and a wild throw, but Chicago came back with two in the fifth when outfielder Augie Galan tripled and outfielder Chuck Klein homered. Medwick hit a two-run homer in the St. Louis sixth, but Chicago tied with three runs in the ninth on singles by Klein and catcher Ken O'Dea, a triple by outfielder Frank Demaree, and a single by first baseman Phil Cavarretta before right-hander Jesse Haines relieved and got third baseman Stan Hack to ground to second into an inning-ending double play. With none out and outfielder Jack

[1]*First game of a doubleheader.* [2]*Second game of a doubleheader.*

First baseman Charlie Grimm (right) and some of his 1932 Chicago teammates. He managed the Cubs to the pennant that year and again in 1935 when a twenty-one-game winning streak was decisive. With Grimm are (left to right) right fielder Kiki Cuyler, catcher Gabby Hartnett and left fielder Riggs Stephenson. (Courtesy of National Baseball Library, Cooperstown, New York.)

Rothrock on base in the eleventh, Medwick hit his second homer of the game to end the second longest winning streak in major league history.

During the winning streak Chicago scored four or more runs in an inning ten times and scored eight or more runs in a game six times, rolling up thirteen runs in one game, fifteen runs in two games, and eighteen runs in one. The Cubs averaged 6.5 runs and 10.8 hits to 2.4 runs and 7.5 hits for the opposition, won five games by one run, three by two runs, two by three runs, five by four runs, two by five runs, one by six runs, one by ten runs and two by twelve runs.

Chicago trailed at some point in eleven games but scored the winning run after the sixth inning only three times in the streak, once in the ninth and twice in extra innings.

In Game 2 (September 5), the Cubs beat Philadelphia, 2–1, with a run in the eleventh on two walks around an error and Demaree's one-out single off right-hander Curt Davis with the bases loaded. Chicago tied the score, 2–2, in the eighth inning of Game 3 (September 6) when Herman drove in Galan, who had tripled, and won in the tenth, 3–2, on Galan's leadoff homer off Philadelphia right-hander Joe Bowman.

Chicago hammered seven Brooklyn pitchers and won, 18–14, in Game 11 (September 14) to take over the league lead for the first time since opening day. All nine Chicago starters batted in at least one run, and the Cubs had a 16–4 lead after scoring eight runs in the sixth. But the Dodgers scored five runs in the seventh and five more in the ninth before right-hander Fabian Kowalik, in his only appearance during the winning streak, struck out first baseman Johnny McCarthy, the only batter he faced, to end the game.

Chicago clinched the pennant in Game 20 (September 27) as Lee outpitched St. Louis right-hander Dizzy Dean to win, 6–2, and drove in the winning run in the fourth with a single off Dean's hand after Hack had doubled. Hack homered in the eighth to clinch Lee's twentieth victory of the season.

In their final victory in the streak, Chicago fell behind, 3–0, in the sixth inning of Game 21 (September 27), when two walks and an error loaded the bases and Medwick singled in one run before St. Louis first baseman Rip Collins doubled home two more. The Cubs tied the score in the seventh on singles by Cavarretta and Hack and doubles by pinch-hitter Johnny Gill and Galan, and won, 5–3, in the ninth with two runs on triples by Cavarretta and Hack and a single by shortstop Billy Jurges.

Chicago employed only seven pitchers during the streak and had eighteen complete games. Lee and left-hander Larry French each won five games, all complete, and right-handers Charlie Root and Lon Warneke won four games apiece, Root needing relief help in one game. Left-hander Roy Henshaw won two games, including one in relief, and right-hander Tex Carleton pitched a complete game in his only appearance during the streak. Only two starts by Root and one by Henshaw were not complete games. Lee, Root, French, and Warneke each pitched a shutout, and in twelve games the opposition scored two runs or less.

Galan was Chicago's most productive hitter, batting .360, driving in twenty-one runs and hitting five of the club's nine homers, four in the first nine games. Demaree batted .408 and drove across thirteen runs, and Herman hit .383 and knocked in fifteen runs.

The Cubs beat Philadelphia, Boston, Brooklyn, and New York four times, St. Louis three times, and Pittsburgh twice. Cincinnati was the only team Chicago did not face during the streak.

Chicago, which had a 100–52 record after its 21st straight win and a six-game lead over second-place St. Louis, lost the last two games of the season at St. Louis and finished four games ahead of the Cards. In the World Series, Chicago won the first game from Detroit, but lost the championship, four games to two.

1906 Chicago White Sox

19 Consecutive Wins

Charles Comiskey began his career in baseball as a player in the 1870s and went on to become a major league manager and owner and, after his death, a member of baseball's Hall of Fame. In his final season as a player in 1895, the "Old Roman" became the manager and owner of the St. Paul club of the Western League.

Under the tutelage of Ban Johnson, the league president, the Western League aspired to become a major league on an equal footing with the National League and changed its name to the American League in 1900, the same year it moved the St. Paul franchise to Chicago.

In 1901 the American League withdrew from the National Association and declared itself a major league, increasing its level of talent by raiding National League teams in a war that didn't end until the two leagues made peace in January 1903.

Chicago beat out Boston for the 1901 pennant under the managership of Clark Griffith, who was the club's leading pitcher with a 24–7 record. Chicago, which was owned by Comiskey and his heirs until 1959, fell to fourth place in 1902, then finished seventh, third, and second in succeeding seasons.

The White Sox, managed for the third straight season by outfielder Fielder Jones, got away to a slow start with an offense so weak it earned the club the nickname Hitless Wonders. Chicago was mired in the second division that year at the end of June, but had climbed to fourth place with a 50–43 record, seven and one-half games behind first-place Philadelphia, after losing on August 1 at home to Boston, 3–1, in a duel between left-handed pitchers Jesse Tannehill and Nick Altrock.

16

Chicago began its American League record nineteen-game winning streak the next afternoon at Chicago's South Side Park.

1. Thursday, August 2

Boston	000 000 000	0	3	1
Chicago	201 000 00x	3	5	0

WP **White**; LP **Young**

2. Friday, August 3

Boston	000 000 000	0	1	1
Chicago	010 101 01x	4	7	1

WP **Walsh**; LP **Harris**

3. Saturday, August 4

Boston	000 000 000	0	6	2
Chicago	000 000 001	1	5	0

WP **Patterson**; LP **Dinneen**

4. Sunday, August 5

Philadelphia	100 000 001	2	8	3
Chicago	100 202 05x	10	11	2

WP **White**; LP **Bender**

5. Monday, August 6

Philadelphia	100 000 100	2	7	3
Chicago	160 000 00x	7	8	3

WP **Owen**; LP **Coombs**, Coakley (3)

6. Tuesday, August 7

Philadelphia	000 000 000	0	3	0
Chicago	000 022 00x	4	6	0

WP **Walsh**; LP **Waddell**

7. Wednesday, August 8

Philadelphia	000 000 000 0	0	5	1
Chicago	000 000 000 1	1	2	0

WP **Patterson**; LP **Plank** (10 innings)

8. Thursday, August 9

Philadelphia	010 000 010 0	2	9	0
Chicago	100 000 100 1	3	9	0

WP **White**; LP **Dygert** (10 innings)

9. Friday, August 10

New York	010 000 000	1	5	0
Chicago	000 010 01x	2	8	1

WP **Walsh**; LP **Chesbro**

10. Saturday, August 11

New York	001 000 000	1	6	3
Chicago	301 000 04x	8	8	2

WP **Owen**; LP **Hogg**, Newton (1),
Clarkson (8)

11. Sunday, August 12

New York	000 000 000	0	9	2
Chicago	002 100 00x	3	7	0

WP **Walsh**; LP **Orth**

Monday, August 13

New York	000 000 000	0	3	3
Chicago	000 000 000	0	6	0

P New York, Chesbro; P Chicago, White
(Tie Game—9 innings, time limit)

12. Wednesday, August 15

Chicago	200 001 300	6	6	0
Boston	000 000 000	0	5	6

WP **Walsh**; LP **Tannehill**, Glaze (8)

13. Thursday, August 16

Chicago	312 002 100	9	14	3
Boston	000 003 010	4	7	1

WP Patterson, **Altrock** (2); LP **Harris**

14. Friday, August 17

Chicago	020 000 101	4	7	2
Boston	011 001 000	3	9	2

WP Owen, **White** (3); LP **Young**

15. Saturday, August 18

Chicago	000 000 109	10	12	1
New York	000 000 000	0	5	6

WP **Walsh**; LP **Chesbro**

16. Monday, August 20

| Chicago | 000 030 100 | 4 | 5 | 1 |
| New York | 000 000 001 | 1 | 5 | 5 |

WP **White**; LP **Orth**

18. Wednesday, August 22[2]

| Chicago | 240 000 005 | 11 | 13 | 5 |
| New York | 000 000 123 | 6 | 9 | 3 |

WP **Owen**; LP **Hogg**, Griffith (2)

17. Wednesday, August 22[1]

| Chicago | 000 204 000 | 6 | 6 | 0 |
| New York | 000 001 000 | 1 | 7 | 1 |

WP **Walsh**; LP **Chesbro**, Clarkson (7)

19. Thursday, August 23

| Chicago | 000 120 100 | 4 | 8 | 1 |
| Washington | 000 100 000 | 1 | 7 | 1 |

WP **Patterson**; LP **Falkenberg**

After rain forced a postponement, the winning streak ended the next afternoon at Washington's National Park:

Saturday, August 25[1]

| Chicago | 210 000 100 | 4 | 7 | 0 |
| Washington | 000 002 003 | 5 | 11 | 1 |

WP Hughes, **Smith** (3); LP Smith, **Walsh** (7)

Shortstop George Davis hit a two-run double in the first, and outfielder Eddie Hahn's single after two walks in the second gave Chicago a 3–0 lead. Washington scored twice in a rally in the sixth, featured by successive singles by shortstop Lave Cross and outfielders John Anderson and Charley Hickman. Chicago added a run in the seventh to take a 4–2 lead on singles by third baseman Lee Tannehill and second baseman Frank Isbell around a hit batsman. Right-hander Ed Walsh, who had allowed only two runs in sixty-three innings in the streak, took over the mound for Chicago in the seventh and pitched two hitless innings before Washington suddenly rallied for three runs in the ninth to win the game. After an infield single by Anderson, Hickman doubled, and first baseman Jake Stahl and catcher John Warner singled to tie the score. Right-hander Charlie Smith, who had relieved right-hander Long Tom Hughes in the third, then singled for the fifth straight hit to score Stahl from third base with none out to end the game and the winning streak that has never been surpassed in American League history. The defeat ended a nine-game winning streak for Walsh, the great spitball pitcher.

During the winning streak the White Sox outscored their rivals, one hundred runs to twenty-four, outbatted them .246 to .190, while

---

[1]*First game of a doubleheader.* [2]*Second game of a doubleheader.*

their pitchers hurled eight shutouts, held the opposition to one run five times, two runs three times, three runs once, four runs once, and six runs once. Chicago won five games by the margin of one run, four by three runs, two by four runs, four by five runs, and one by six runs, seven runs, eight runs, and ten runs.

Chicago trailed four times during the streak, only once as late as the sixth inning and in the eleven home games batted in the final inning just three times, winning one game in the ninth and the other two in the tenth. In the last eight games, which were all on the road, the White Sox scored the winning run in the ninth twice.

In Game 3 (August 4), Chicago was held to four hits by right-hander Bill Dinneen until the ninth, when first baseman Jiggs Donahue tripled to left center and scored with none out when outfielder Patsy Dougherty singled to right center on the next pitch to win the game, 1–0.

In Game 7 (August 8), Chicago beat Philadelphia, 1–0, in ten innings after being held to a first-inning single by Jones through nine innings, then beat left-hander Eddie Plank in the extra inning when Davis drew Chicago's third walk and scored one out later on Dougherty's triple to right center.

The other extra-inning win was in Game 8 (August 9). Philadelphia threatened to break the 2–2 tie in the tenth before catcher Ossee Schreckengost grounded into an inning-ending double play with runners on first and third. Chicago won in its tenth when Donahue tripled for his third hit and, after two intentional walks loaded the bases, infielder George Rohe batted for Tannehill and singled through the infield with one out for the 3–2 victory.

In Game 14 (August 17) at Boston, Chicago tied the score, 3–3, with a run in the seventh as Donahue scored on right-hander Cy Young's wild pitch, then won in the ninth when catcher Billy Sullivan singled, stole second, and scored on Tannehill's single to right for a 4–3 triumph. This was the only game in which the White Sox trailed after the sixth inning.

Chicago had a 6–3 lead going into the ninth inning of Game 18 (August 22), then scored five runs on errors, three singles, and doubles by Davis and right-hander Frank Owen. That rally proved decisive when New York scored three times in the last of the ninth in the 11–6 win.

Walsh led the pitchers with seven victories, including five shutouts and two wins in which he gave up only one run. Left-hander Doc White won five games, including one shutout and one win in relief of Altrock.

Fielder Jones played center field and managed the pennant-winning Chicago White Sox in 1906. Nicknamed the "Hitless Wonders," the Sox won nineteen straight games that August, then upset the Chicago Cubs in the World Series. (Courtesy of National Baseball Library, Cooperstown, New York.)

White also pitched the nine-inning scoreless tie at home on August 13 that was called to allow New York to catch a train. Right-hander Roy Patterson won three games, including two shutouts and one in which he gave up one run. Owen also won three games, and Altrock won one game after relieving Patterson.

After the nineteenth straight win, Chicago was in first place with a 69–43 record and a five-and-one-half game lead over second-place Philadelphia. The White Sox, who finished first with the lowest batting average (.230) of any pennant winner in modern major league history, had to go to the final week before clinching their second pennant, beating out New York by three games with a 93–58 record.

Owen won twenty-two games and Altrock won twenty to lead the pitchers. White won eighteen and Walsh won seventeen, including a league-leading ten shutouts. Isbell batted .279, and Davis, who knocked in eighty runs while batting .277, were the only Chicago regulars to bat as high as .260.

Heavy underdogs in the World Series against the Chicago Cubs, who had won a still-standing major league record 116 games and won the pennant by twenty games, the White Sox pulled a startling upset and won in six games.

1947 New York Yankees

19 Consecutive Wins

The New York Yankees won their first American League pennant in 1921 and won 13 more league championships through 1943. In the succeeding three years, they finished third, fourth and then third, finishing seventeen games out of first place in 1946. For 1947 the Yankees made some changes.

Veteran Bucky Harris was signed as manager; George McQuinn, released by Philadelphia, was signed to play first base; Snuffy Stirnweiss took over at second base in place of Joe Gordon, traded to Cleveland for right-hander Allie Reynolds; Billy Johnson was installed as the regular third baseman; and Johnny Lindell became the regular in left field in place of the ailing Charlie Keller. Reynolds and rookie right-hander Spec Shea were important additions to the pitching staff.

After a slow start, New York began winning consistently in June 1947. On June 29 at Washington, New York played a doubleheader and Karl Drews was beaten in the opener, 5–1, by Washington's Early Wynn in a duel of right-handers. In the fifth inning an error, a sacrifice, and singles by Wynn, third baseman Eddie Yost, and outfielder Buddy Lewis gave Washington two runs, and first baseman Mickey Vernon homered in the sixth.

That day second-place Boston lost the first game of a doubleheader at Philadelphia, and after that game was three and one-half games in back of New York, which had a 39–26 record.

The longest major league winning streak in twelve years began in the second game that afternoon at Washington's Griffith Stadium.

1. Sunday, June 29[2]

| New York | 000 020 001 | 3 | 6 | 0 |
| Washington | 010 000 000 | 1 | 6 | 0 |

WP **Johnson**, Reynolds (6); LP **Masterson**, Ferrick (8)

2. Monday, June 30

| New York | 200 010 000 | 3 | 6 | 0 |
| Boston | 001 000 000 | 1 | 4 | 1 |

WP **Shea**; LP **Dobson**, Hughson (7)

3. Wednesday, July 2

| Washington | 000 000 010 | 1 | 5 | 0 |
| New York | 103 030 01x | 8 | 11 | 1 |

WP **Reynolds**; LP **Haefner**, Pieretti (5), Candini (7)

4. Friday, July 4[1]

| Washington | 000 010 200 | 3 | 7 | 2 |
| New York | 200 300 11x | 7 | 10 | 0 |

WP **Chandler**; LP **Wynn**

5. Friday, July 4[2]

| Washington | 010 001 000 | 2 | 6 | 1 |
| New York | 000 000 22x | 4 | 9 | 0 |

WP D. **Johnson**, Drews (2), **Page** (8); LP **Masterson**

6. Saturday, July 5

| Philadelphia | 000 000 100 | 1 | 3 | 0 |
| New York | 000 500 00x | 5 | 10 | 0 |

WP **Shea**; LP **Coleman**, Fowler (8)

7. Sunday, July 6[1]

| Philadelphia | 000 200 000 | 2 | 5 | 0 |
| New York | 512 000 00x | 8 | 14 | 1 |

WP **Gumpert**, Page (6); LP **Scheib**, Flores (4), Christopher (6)

8. Sunday, July 6[2]

| Philadelphia | 000 200 000 | 2 | 6 | 1 |
| New York | 110 000 07x | 9 | 13 | 1 |

WP **Reynolds**; LP **Marchildon**, Savage (8)

9. Thursday, July 10

| New York | 000 012 001 | 4 | 9 | 3 |
| St. Louis | 011 000 100 | 3 | 11 | 0 |

WP Chandler, **Page** (7); LP Sanford, **Potter** (8)

10. Friday, July 11

| New York | 002 001 000 | 3 | 3 | 1 |
| St. Louis | 000 100 000 | 1 | 6 | 2 |

WP **Reynolds**; LP **Kinder**

11. Saturday, July 12[1]

| New York | 003 063 000 | 12 | 17 | 2 |
| St. Louis | 000 002 000 | 2 | 7 | 2 |

WP Shea, **Wensloff** (2); LP **Muncrief**, Brown (5), Zoldak (5), Swartz (9)

12. Saturday, July 12[2]

| New York | 000 120 221 | 8 | 11 | 2 |
| St. Louis | 003 000 002 | 5 | 10 | 0 |

WP Bevens, **Drews** (5), Page (7); LP **Kramer**, Moulder (7)

13. Sunday, July 13[1]

| New York | 024 210 100 | 10 | 16 | 0 |
| Chicago | 300 000 000 | 3 | 5 | 1 |

WP **Newsom**; LP **Haynes**, Maltzberger (4), Gebrian (9)

14. Sunday, July 13[2]

| New York | 040 000 002 | 6 | 10 | 0 |
| Chicago | 000 000 301 | 4 | 9 | 0 |

WP **Raschi**, Page (7), Reynolds (9); LP **Harrist**, Caldwell (2), Smith (8)

---

[1]*First game of a doubleheader.* [2]*Second game of a doubleheader.*

15. Tuesday, July 15[1]

New York	002 141 100	9	10	0
Cleveland	010 000 102	4	10	5

WP **Reynolds**; LP **Stephens**, Willis (6), Lemon (8)

16. Tuesday, July 15[2]

New York	000 100 001	2	9	0
Cleveland	000 100 000	1	6	0

WP **Bevens**; LP **Feller**

17. Wednesday, July 16

New York	301 001 003	8	14	0
Cleveland	000 002 000	2	6	0

WP **Wensloff**, Drews (6), Page (7); LP **Gettel,** Klieman (1), Lemon (7), Willis (8)

18. Thursday, July 17[1]

New York	100 200 000	3	5	0
Cleveland	000 000 100	1	9	0

WP **Newsom**; LP **Embree**, Stephens (8)

19. Thursday, July 17[2]

New York	023 001 100	7	10	1
Cleveland	000 001 010	2	6	1

WP **Raschi**; LP **Gromek**, Gettel (3), Lemon (7)

The winning streak ended the next day in a twilight game at Detroit's Briggs Stadium:

Friday, July 18

New York	000 000 000	0	2	1
Detroit	200 001 41x	8	18	0

WP **Hutchinson**; LP **Gumpert**, Drews (7)

Detroit right-hander Fred Hutchinson handed New York its first shutout loss since May 30, and the only hits off him were a single to left by outfielder Joe DiMaggio in the second inning and a safe bunt in the seventh by Stirnweiss. Hutchinson, who didn't issue a walk, faced only twenty-eight batters in his first start since June 19. Meanwhile Detroit hammered right-hander Randy Gumpert and Drews for eighteen hits, two by Hutchinson, who batted in a run with a double in the sixth, and another with a single in the four-run seventh before a crowd of 28,718. Detroit scored twice in the first when shortstop Eddie Lake singled, first baseman Roy Cullenbine walked, and outfielders Dick Wakefield and Hoot Evers hit run-scoring singles.

During the streak New York averaged 6.3 runs and 10.2 hits per game to 2.2 runs and 6.7 hits for the opposition. New York won only two games by one run, but won six by two runs; one by three runs; two

---

[1]*First game of a doubleheader.* [2]*Second game of a doubleheader.*

by four runs, five runs, and six runs; three by seven runs, and one by ten runs. The Yankees held their opponents to one run seven times, two runs six times, three runs three times, four runs twice, and five runs once. An unusual feature of the streak is that none of the wins was a shutout, the only winning streak of more than sixteen games without one in major league history.

New York trailed six times in the nineteen games, but only once as late as the seventh inning as well as once in the fifth. The Yankees won three games in their final at bat.

In Game 9 (July 10) St. Louis scored runs in the third and fourth innings, but New York scored in the fifth on a walk and singles by catcher Aaron Robinson and shortstop Phil Rizzuto and took a 3–2 lead in the sixth on singles by Stirnweiss and outfielder Tommy Henrich and a sacrifice, a wild pitch, and a double by DiMaggio. After St. Louis tied in the seventh on a single, stolen base and right-hander Spud Chandler's error, left-hander Joe Page relieved and won the game with two out in the ninth with a drive to the right-center-field roof for the second and last homer of his big-league career, 4–3.

In Game 14 (July 13) New York went into the ninth inning with a 4–3 lead and scored twice on Rizzuto's single, the second double in the game by Stirnweiss, and Henrich's two-run single. In Chicago's ninth a single and two walks loaded the bases and brought Reynolds to the relief of Page. A run scored as shortstop Luke Appling grounded into a double play, and, after a walk, first baseman Rudy York hit a foul pop to end the 6–4 game.

In Game 16 (July 15) Henrich tripled and Lindell hit a scoring fly off right-hander Bob Feller in the fourth, but shortstop Lou Boudreau, Cleveland's manager, homered in that inning to tie the score. With one out in New York's ninth, DiMaggio singled and scored with two out on Johnson's triple to the right-field corner for a 2–1 victory.

The victory in Game 19 (July 17), when the Yankees tied the American League record, came surprisingly easily. New York scored twice in the second when DiMaggio singled, took third on McQuinn's single, and came home on Johnson's infield out before Rizzuto singled home McQuinn. New York kept pecking away at three Cleveland pitchers for a 7–2 victory, Johnson batting in two more runs and Lindell, Robinson, and Stirnweiss each batting in one. Outfielder Hal Peck knocked in sixth-inning run for Cleveland, and outfielder Dale Mitchell drove home right-hander Bob Lemon in the eighth, but right-hander Vic Raschi allowed only six hits for his second victory since being recalled from Portland within the week. The doubleheader sweep was New York's sixth during its streak.

This was New York's fifth victory over Cleveland in the streak, and the Yankees, who beat every club in the league except Detroit in their surge, won four games from both Washington and St. Louis, three from Philadelphia, two from Chicago, and one from Boston.

New York outhomered its opposition 15–2, led by DiMaggio with four and Henrich with three. Rizzuto hit the streak's only grand-slam homer in the streak in Game 13.

Eleven pitchers won games, led by Reynolds, who won four of the eleven complete games pitched. Shea, right-handers Bobo Newsom, Raschi, and Butch Wensloff, as well as Page, each won two games, and right-hander Don Johnson, Chandler, Gumpert, Bill Bevens, and Drews won one apiece. Page won his two in relief, while Wensloff and Drews won one in relief.

After its nineteenth win, New York was in first place with a 58–26 record and had an eleven-and-one-half-game lead over second-place Detroit. The Yankees won only eight more games than they lost the rest of the season, but won the pennant with a 97–57 record and a twelve-game margin over runner-up Detroit and then beat Brooklyn in a seven-game World Series.

New York led the league in batting (.271), runs (794), home runs (115), and pitching (3.39) and was second in fielding (.981). Reynolds won nineteen games, and Shea and Page won fourteen each, but no other Yankee won more than nine games. DiMaggio was the team leader in batting (.315) and in home runs (20), and his ninety-seven runs batted in were one less than Henrich had.

New York finished third in 1948, then won an unprecedented fourteen pennants in the next sixteen years.

1904 New York Giants

18 Consecutive Wins

The New York Giants won National League pennants in 1888 and 1889, then finished as high as second place only twice in the next fourteen years before winning their third flag in 1904. In 1902 New York had three managers, Horace Fogel, Heinie Smith, and John McGraw, who took over in mid–July and who went on to become one of the game's great managers.

New York made no significant immediate improvement under McGraw, who had managed Baltimore of the National League in 1899 and Baltimore of the new American League in 1901 and 1902 before jumping back to the National League with the Giants. In fact, New York finished last in 1902 but moved up to second in 1903 with a team that featured a pair of right-handed, thirty-game-winning pitchers in Joe McGinnity and Christy Mathewson, two future Hall of Famers.

In 1904 Chicago and New York dueled for the National League lead for the first two months of the season. On June 15 McGinnity, his twelve-game winning streak snapped four days before, lost to St. Louis, 5–2, on a four-run sixth-inning rally that featured a walk, two singles, and a two-out single to right field by outfielder Homer Smoot that went through outfielder George Browne for a costly error.

That defeat gave New York a 30–16 record, good enough for a half game lead in the standings over second-place Chicago. The winning streak began the next afternoon at New York's Polo Grounds.

1. Thursday, June 16							2. Friday, June 17					
St. Louis	000 110 010	3	7	3			Brooklyn	000 000 000	0	4	4
New York	020 001 001	4	6	2			New York	200 000 00x	2	5	1
WP **Mathewson**; LP **O'Neill**							WP **Taylor**; LP **Poole**					

3. Saturday, June 18

Brooklyn	000 010 000	1	7	2
New York	200 200 10x	5	9	1

WP **McGinnity**; LP **Garvin**

4. Sunday, June 19

New York	002 304 020 11	18	0
Brooklyn	000 000 000 0	3	4

WP **Wiltse**; LP **Jones**, Cronin (7)

5. Monday, June 20

Brooklyn	200 101 000	4	10	8
New York	310 114 20x	12	13	2

WP **Mathewson**; LP **Poole**, Reidy (7)

6. Tuesday, June 21

New York	020 010 003	6	12	1
Boston	000 001 001	2	12	4

WP **McGinnity**; LP **Willis**

7. Wednesday, June 22

New York	201 102 103	10	14	1
Boston	001 000 000	1	3	0

WP **Wiltse**; LP **Fisher**

8. Thursday, June 23

New York	001 104 000	6	11	3
Boston	010 000 010	2	9	5

WP **Mathewson**; LP **Pittinger**

9. Friday, June 24

New York	000 210 002	5	10	2
Boston	000 000 003	3	3	1

WP **McGinnity**; LP **Wilhelm**

10. Saturday, June 25

Philadelphia	100 100 004	6	13	2
New York	300 321 00x	9	12	5

WP **Wiltse**, McGinnity (6); LP **McPherson**

11. Monday, June 27

Philadelphia	020 000 000	2	4	2
New York	010 202 14x	10	10	3

WP **Taylor**; LP **Fraser**

12. Tuesday, June 28

Philadelphia	000 102 030	6	12	3
New York	403 002 00x	9	7	2

WP **Wiltse**; LP **Duggleby**, McPherson (2)

13. Wednesday, June 29

Boston	001 000 000	1	5	2
New York	011 101 00x	4	8	4

WP **McGinnity**; LP **Willis**

14. Thursday, June 30

Boston	000 000 000	0	7	3
New York	000 001 02x	3	8	0

WP **Mathewson**; LP **Pittinger**

15. Friday, July 1

Boston	100 000 000	1	6	1
New York	120 220 00x	7	10	4

WP **Taylor**; LP **Wilhelm**

16. Saturday, July 2

Boston	000 000 001	1	8	9
New York	021 123 50x	14	16	0

WP **McGinnity**, Wiltse (6); LP **Willis**

17. Monday, July 4[1]

Philadelphia	000 010 000	1	10	1
New York	202 000 00x	4	8	2

WP **Taylor**; LP **Sparks** (morning game)

18. Monday, July 4[2]

Philadelphia	000 001 002	3	4	5
New York	211 200 50x	11	18	1

WP **Mathewson**, Ames (8); LP **Mitchell** (afternoon game)

---

[1]*First game of a doubleheader.* [2]*Second game of a doubleheader.*

The winning streak ended the next afternoon when the two teams moved to Philadelphia.

Tuesday, July 5

New York   011 101 001 0   5 12 1
Philadelphia   000 103 100 1   6 13 1
WP Duggleby, **Fraser**; LP McGinnity,
Taylor (9) (10 innings)

A misplay by third baseman Bob Hall, an error by right-hander Bill Duggleby, and a misjudged fly to left by outfielder Sherry Magee helped New York score three of its first four runs. Second baseman Kid Gleason scored for Philadelphia in the fourth, in the three-run sixth, and again in the seventh, when the home team went ahead, 5–4. New York tied in a ninth-inning rally that saw Duggleby hit both second baseman Billy Gilbert and catcher John Warner with pitches with two out. McGraw ran for Warner, and Moose McCormick, batting for McGinnity, doubled off the right-field screen to score Gilbert with the tying run, but McGraw was thrown out at the plate on the play.

New York went out in order in the tenth; Philadelphia scored the winning run with two out. After first baseman Jack Doyle flied to center, catcher Red Dooin got an infield single for his third hit and took second on Magee's grounder to first. Hall then hit a short fly that fell among three Giants in short left center for the hit that scored Dooin to win the game, 6–5, and end what was then the longest major league winning streak since Providence won twenty in a row in 1884.

After winning its eighteenth straight game, New York was in first place with a 48–16 record and a ten-and-a-half-game lead over second-place Cincinnati and third-place Chicago. In the eighteen games, New York averaged 7.3 runs and 10.8 hits to 2.1 runs and 7.1 hits for the opposition. In six of the games, New York scored ten or more runs and committed only thirty-four errors to fifty-nine by its rivals. The Giants won only one game by one run, two games by two runs, five by three runs, three by four runs, one by six runs, three by eight runs, and one each by nine runs, eleven runs, and thirteen runs.

Mathewson and McGinnity each won five games, four complete games. Right-hander Dummy Taylor won four games, all complete, and left-hander Hooks Wiltse won four, three complete. Right-hander Red Ames was the only other pitcher New York used in the streak, working only two innings in relief. McGinnity and Wiltse each relieved in one game, both pitching four innings. Taylor, Wiltse, and Mathewson each pitched one shutout. The Giants beat Boston seven times, Philadelphia five times, Brooklyn four times, and St. Louis once.

New York trailed in only five of the eighteen games, just once after the third inning. In Game 11 (June 27) against Philadelphia, an error, a single by outfielder John Titus, a long fly by Hall on which a run scored, a muffed third strike, and right-hander Chick Fraser's run-scoring force-play grounder gave Philadelphia a 2–0 lead in the second. New York scored once in the second and went ahead with two runs in the fourth when third baseman Art Devlin tripled home a run. The Giants went on to win, 10–2.

The only game New York won in its final time at bat was Game 1 (June 16) at home. St. Louis tied the game at 3–3 in the eighth when catcher Frank Bowerman dropped a throw at the plate. New York won, 4–3, with two out in the ninth. With runners on first and third, outfielder Roger Bresnahan grounded to shortstop and Danny Shay's throw to second baseman Dave Brain was dropped, allowing shortstop Bill Dahlen to score the winning run.

After New York set the all-time record by winning twenty-six games in a row in 1916, Mathewson, then managing Cincinnati, recalled the 1904 streak of eighteen, but his memory wasn't perfect.

Referring to Providence's record of twenty straight wins in 1884, Mathewson said, "I think the Giants might have turned the trick [broken Providence's record] some years ago when I was a member of the team had it not been a slip by Joe McGinnity.

"Joe was pitching great ball in those days, but he had an agreement whereby he twirled for a team of semiprofessionals on Sundays. I think we had won eighteen games [in a row] when we struck Philadelphia. McGinnity was listed to pitch against the Phillies on Monday. But the day before, Sunday, he had a hard game with the semipro team that he occasionally twirled for. When he faced the Phillies the following day we lost." Actually, it was two days later.

After the winning streak ended, New York won seven of its next nine games and went on to win the pennant easily with 106 victories, still a club record, and 47 defeats, finishing thirteen games in front of second-place Chicago.

McGinnity had a 35–8 record that year, leading the league in wins, winning percentage (.813), earned run average (1.61) and shutouts (9). Mathewson had a 33–12 record and led the league in strikeouts (212). First baseman Dan McGann led the team in batting with a .288 average, and Dahlen led the league in runs batted in (80).

1953 New York Yankees

18 Consecutive Wins

New York joined the American League in 1903, won its first pennant in 1921, and won its nineteenth in 1952 in an unprecedented run of success. In 1953 the Yankees sought to become the first major league team to win five consecutive pennants.

The only major addition for New York in 1953 from the team Casey Stengel managed to the pennant by a two-game margin over the second-place Cleveland Indians in 1952 was left-hander Whitey Ford, who returned after two seasons in the army following his successful rookie year in 1950.

By the end of April 1953, New York had an 11–3 record but then split even in the first twelve games in May before winning six of the next seven games. Then, at home on May 25, the Yankees were outscored, 14–10, in a slugfest that saw the Boston Red Sox pound out twenty hits.

That defeat, only the fifth home loss of the season for the Yankees, gave them a 23–11 record and a three-game lead over Cleveland. After an open date on May 26, New York began an eighteen-game winning streak the next afternoon at Yankee Stadium, a streak that still stands as the second longest in the history of both the Yankees and the American League.

1. Wednesday, May 27

Washington	100 000 000	1	3	1
New York	101 100 00x	3	8	1

WP **Lopat**; LP **Masterson**, Stobbs (8)

2. Thursday, May 28

Washington	100 000 010	2	5	1
New York	000 025 00x	7	9	1

WP **Ford**; LP **Porterfield**, Sima (6), Dixon (8)

3. Friday, May 29

New York	035	201	100	12	12	1
Philadelphia	400	000	102	7	11	0

WP Raschi, **Scarborough** (1); LP **Byrd**, Rozek (3)

4. Sunday, May 31

Philadelphia	000	000	100	1	6	0
New York	002	104	00x	7	13	0

WP **Sain**; LP **Kellner**, Scheib (6), Martin (8)

5. Tuesday, June 2

New York	002	100	001	4	8	1
Chicago	000	101	010	3	10	0

WP **Lopat**, Reynolds (9); LP Fornieles, Aloma (6), Bearden (6), **Dorish** (8)

6. Wednesday, June 3

New York	320	514	210	18	19	0
Chicago	000	110	000	2	11	3

WP **Ford**, Miller (8); LP **Keegan**, Dobson (2), Consuegra (4), Kretlow (8)

7. Thursday, June 4

New York	113	000	000 4	9	11	0
Chicago	000	011	120 0	5	9	1

WP Raschi, **Reynolds** (8); LP Pierce, Fornieles (6), Dorish (8), **Bearden** (9) (10 innings)

8. Friday, June 5

New York	011	030	000	5	9	1
St. Louis	000	000	000	0	5	5

WP **Sain**; LP **Holloman**, Lanier (5)

9. Saturday, June 6

New York	200	003	100	6	8	1
St. Louis	000	020	000	2	6	0

WP **Scarborough**, Kuzava (6), Reynolds (6); LP **Blyzka**, Paige (6), Holloman (8)

10. Sunday, June 7[1]

New York	100	001	502	9	15	1
St. Louis	010	010	000	2	6	0

WP **Lopat**; LP **Littlefield**, Paige (7), Stuart (8), Cain (9)

11. Sunday, June 7[2]

New York	000	007	000	7	12	1
St. Louis	110	000	000	2	7	0

WP **Ford**, Reynolds (7); LP **Brecheen**, Trucks (6), Stuart (8)

12. Tuesday, June 9

New York	200	001	000	3	7	2
Detroit	000	200	000	2	8	0

WP Raschi, **Gorman** (4); LP **Gray**

13. Wednesday, June 10

New York	001	007	012	11	15	1
Detroit	000	400	000	4	8	2

WP **Sain**, Scarborough (6); LP **Hoeft**, Madison (6), Wight (7), Erickson (8), Herbert (9)

14. Thursday, June 11

New York	011	100	300	6	13	2
Detroit	000	000	210	3	9	0

WP **McDonald**, Reynolds (9); LP **Houtteman**, Harrist (8)

15. Friday, June 12

New York	000	000	301	4	7	0
Cleveland	000	010	001	2	6	0

WP **Ford**, Reynolds (7); LP **Wynn**, Brissie (7), Hooper (8)

16. Saturday, June 13

New York	010	412	010	9	10	0
Cleveland	000	010	102	4	8	0

WP **Lopat**, Scarborough (8); LP **Feller**, Hoskins (4), Brissie (7), Chakales (8)

[1]*First game of a doubleheader.* [2]*Second game of a doubleheader.*

17. Sunday, June 14[1]					
New York	000 000 132	6	13	1
Cleveland	000 200 000	2	8	1

WP Sain, **Kuzava** (7), Reynolds (8); LP **Lemon**, Brissie (9)

18. Sunday, June 14[2]					
New York	000 300 000	3	7	2
Cleveland	000 000 000	0	3	1

WP **Raschi**; LP **Garcia**

After an open date, the winning streak ended in first game of home stand at Yankee Stadium.

Tuesday, June 16

St. Louis	010 020 000	3	8	0
New York	000 010 000	1	6	1

WP **Pillette**, Paige (8); LP **Ford**, Scarborough (6), Gorman (9)

Seventh-place St. Louis, ending the longest losing streak in the major leagues in 1953 at fourteen games, took advantage of three of Ford's four walks to hand the New York southpaw his first big-league loss as a starting pitcher after he had won sixteen in a row and lost one in relief in 1950. In the St. Louis second, Ford walked catcher Les Moss and right-hander Duane Pillette before outfielder Johnny Groth hit a two-out, run-scoring single. In the fifth Ford walked outfielder Jim Dyck before outfielder Vic Wertz homered into the the right-field stands.

New York scored its lone run in the fifth when outfielder Gene Woodling walked, third baseman Gil McDougald singled, and first baseman Johnny Mize, batting for shortstop Phil Rizzuto, lined a run-scoring single to right for his two-thousandth major league hit.

Right-hander Satchel Paige relieved in the eighth and allowed only a two-out ninth-inning single by Woodling before McDougald fouled out to third, ending the game and New York's chance to tie the American League record of nineteen straight wins.

After the eighteenth consecutive victory, New York was in first place with a 41–11 record and had a ten-and-one-half-game lead over second-place Cleveland. During the streak New York won two games by one run, two by two runs, two by three runs, three by four runs, five by five runs, one by six runs, two by seven runs, and one by sixteen runs. New York scored seven runs in an inning twice, had four five-run innings and six four-run innings, and averaged 7.2 runs and 10.9 hits per game to 2.4 runs and 7.2 hits for the opposition.

---

[1]*First game of a doubleheader.* [2]*Second game of a doubleheader.*

Ten different pitchers were used by the Yankees in the streak, and nine won at least one game. Left-hander Ed Lopat and Ford won four each; right-hander Johnny Sain won three; right-hander Ray Scarborough won two, including one in relief, and right-handers Jim McDonald, Vic Raschi, Allie Reynolds, and Tom Gorman and left-hander Bob Kuzava won one apiece, the last three in relief. Sain and Raschi pitched the only two shutouts.

New York trailed in eight of the eighteen games, five of them past midgame, and won two games in its last time at bat. Only three of the eighteen victories were at home.

The biggest deficit the Yankees overcame was 4–0 in Game 3 (May 29) at Philadelphia, and they did it quickly. Three of the Athletics' four first-inning runs scored on a home run by outfielder Guz Zernial off Raschi. Scarborough relieved and hit the only homer of his big-league career in the second inning with two men on base. The big blow in New York's five-run third was a three-run homer by McDougald, and New York went on to win, 12–7.

The first game New York won in its last time at bat was Game 5 (June 2) at Chicago. First baseman Joe Collins hit a two-run homer in New York's third, and McDougald singled in a run in the fourth for a 3–0 lead. Chicago outfielder Minnie Minoso doubled and scored in the fourth, first baseman Ferris Fain singled and scored on Minoso's double and an infield out in the sixth, and Minoso's third double and a double by outfielder Sam Mele tied the score in the eighth. New York won in the ninth, 4–3, when Collins homered again with two out.

The only extra-inning win was in Game 7 (June 4) at Chicago. New York took a 5–0 lead after three innings, but Chicago scored single runs in the fifth, sixth, and seventh and tied at 5–5 in the eighth on a single, two walks, third baseman Rocky Krsnich's scoring fly, and a pinch-hit single by left-hander Gene Bearden. The Yankees scored four runs off Bearden in the tenth to win, 9–5, on outfielder Mickey Mantle's single, McDougald's homer, and two walks and an error by Bearden, who dropped a throw at first base to allow the last two runs to score.

In Game 13 (June 10) at Detroit, the Tigers scored four runs in the fourth for a 4–1 lead, but New York exploded for seven runs in the sixth on runs batted in by catcher Yogi Berra and Mize as pinch-hitters, by second baseman Billy Martin, Mantle, outfielder Hank Bauer, and Woodling. Collins hit a two-run homer in the ninth to cap the 11–4 victory.

Raschi pitched a brilliant three-hitter in Game 18 (June 14) to complete a doubleheader sweep before a crowd of 74,708 at Cleveland. Singles by Collins and Mantle, Berra's triple, and Woodling's double produced the three New York runs in the fourth inning for the 3–0 win.

Although New York started a nine-game losing streak five days after the winning streak ended, the Yankees went on to win the pennant with a 91–52 record and finished eight and one-half games ahead of runner-up Cleveland. New York finished first in the league in batting (.273), first in pitching (3.20) and third in fielding (.979). Ford was the team's top pitcher with an 18–6 record, Woodling led in batting (.306), and Berra topped the team in homers (27) and runs batted in (108).

New York capped its season by winning the six-game World Series against Brooklyn for its sixteenth world championship and fifth in succession for a record that still stands.

1907 New York Giants

17 Consecutive Wins

The New York Giants won two National League pennants before 1890 and, after the arrival of John McGraw as manager in mid–July 1902, in 1904 and 1905. McGraw's team finished a distant second to the Chicago Cubs in 1906 and made only one important change for 1907, veteran Tommy Corcoran and then rookie Larry Doyle taking over at second base in place of veteran Billy Gilbert.

New York got away to a good start in 1907, winning seven of its first nine games, and then lost at Philadelphia, 3–1, on Wednesday, April 24, with left-hander Johnny Lush outpitching right-hander Dummy Taylor, who gave up two runs in the first inning on a walk and doubles by outfielder Sherry Magee and first baseman Kitty Bransfield.

After that loss New York was in third place with a 7–3 record, only half a game behind first-place Chicago and in a virtual tie with second-place Philadelphia. The next afternoon New York began its seventeen-game winning streak, still the third longest in the club's history.

1. Thursday, April 25

New York	003 120 000	6	9	2
Philadelphia	002 000 010	3	10	4

WP **McGinnity**; LP **Corridon**, Moren (6)

2. Friday, April 26

New York	012 001 10	5	14	1
Philadelphia	001 000 30	4	11	0

WP **Mathewson**; LP **Sparks**, McCloskey (7) (8 innings, rain)

3. Saturday, April 27

New York	000 000 002	2	5	0
Brooklyn	000 001 000	1	7	2

WP **Wiltse**; LP **Stricklett**

4. Monday, April 29

Boston	000 100 000	1	4	3
New York	000 100 11x	3	3	1

WP **Ames**; LP **Pfeffer**

36

5. Wednesday, May 1

Boston	100 000 030	4	5	1
New York	200 110 03x	7	11	2

WP **McGinnity**; LP **Dorner**

6. Thursday, May 2

Boston	000 000 100	1	5	2
New York	130 000 00x	4	7	2

WP **Taylor**; LP **Flaherty**

7. Friday, May 3

Brooklyn	000 000 000	0	2	0
New York	000 010 00x	1	3	1

WP **Mathewson**; LP **Stricklett**

8. Saturday, May 4

Brooklyn	000 000 000	0	2	5
New York	213 201 01x	10	13	1

WP **Wiltse**, H. Mathewson (9); LP **Pastorius**, McIntire (2)

9. Tuesday, May 7

Brooklyn	000 000 010	1	5	0
New York	000 100 10x	2	6	0

WP **Ames**; LP **Bell**

10. Wednesday, May 8

Pittsburgh	000 000 000	0	4	1
New York	002 011 00x	4	9	1

WP **Mathewson**; LP **Leifield**

11. Saturday, May 11

Pittsburgh	200 020 101	6	6	1
New York	221 000 40x	9	10	6

WP McGinnity, Wiltse (3), **Mathewson** (7); LP Willis, **Lynch** (2), Phillippe (8)

12. Monday, May 13

Cincinnati	000 000 000 000	0	5	0
New York	000 000 000 001	1	7	0

WP **McGinnity**; LP **Mason** (12 innings)

13. Tuesday, May 14

Cincinnati	010 000 001	2	6	4
New York	000 221 00x	5	5	1

WP **Taylor**; LP **Ewing**

14. Wednesday, May 15

Cincinnati	001 000 200	3	5	2
New York	000 000 202	4	6	4

WP Ames, **Wiltse** (8); LP **Minahan**

15. Friday, May 17[1]

St. Louis	000 010 000 000	1	3	1
New York	000 010 000 001	2	9	1

WP **Mathewson**; LP **Beebe** (12 innings)

16. Friday, May 17[2]

St. Louis	000 000 000	0	3	3
New York	000 202 00x	4	11	1

WP **McGinnity**; LP **Karger**

17. Saturday, May 18

St. Louis	000 000 011	2	8	4
New York	030 001 02x	6	11	3

WP **Wiltse**; LP **McGlynn**

After an open date, the seventeen-game winning streak ended at New York's Polo Grounds.

[1]*First game of a doubleheader.* [2]*Second game of a doubleheader.*

Monday, May 20

St. Louis   000 020 040   6   9   2
New York   200 000 110   4 10   4
WP **Brown**; LP **Taylor**, Ames (8),
Ferguson (9)

New York took a 2–0 lead in first inning on a walk, third baseman Art Devlin's single, outfielder Cy Seymour's grounder to first that went through Jake Beckley for two bases, another walk, and a wild pitch. St. Louis tied in the fifth on singles by outfielder Al Burch and right-hander Buster Brown and a wild throw by catcher Roger Bresnahan. Outfielder Sammy Strang homered for a 3–2 New York lead in the seventh, but St. Louis exploded for four runs in the eighth to win. In the rally second baseman Pug Bennett singled, outfielder Red Murray doubled, and Beckley hit a two-run single to right and continued to third on Strang's error. Right-hander Red Ames replaced Taylor and walked third baseman Bobby Byrne, who stole second. One out later, outfielder John Kelly beat out an infield hit, scoring Beckley, and while New York players argued the close play at first, Byrne also came home. New York's last run scored in the eighth when first baseman Dan McGann walked, took third on a wild throw by Byrne trying for a double play after catching shortstop Bill Dahlen's fly, and scored on second baseman Danny Shay's long fly to right.

The seventeen-game winning streak put New York in the National League lead with a 24–4 record and a one-game lead over second-place Chicago. During the streak the Giants averaged 4.4 runs and 8.2 hits to 1.7 runs and 5.4 hits for their opposition. The Giants won seven games by a one-run margin, one by two runs, five by three runs, three by four runs, and one by ten runs.

McGraw used six pitchers in the streak and five won games, led by right-hander Christy Mathewson with five. Right-hander Joe McGinnity and left-hander Hooks Wiltse won four each, and right-handers Ames and Dummy Taylor won two apiece. Mathewson and Wiltse each won one game in relief, but fourteen of the other fifteen were complete games. Mathewson and McGinnity, who both pitched four complete games, each pitched two shutouts, and Wiltse was the winning pitcher in the fifth shutout, 10–0, with right-hander Henry Mathewson, Christy's younger brother, pitching the ninth inning in his only appearance of the season.

New York trailed in seven of the seventeen games, only twice after the fifth inning, and won five games in its last time at bat, two of them in extra innings.

In Game 3 (April 27), New York trailed, 1–0, until the ninth, when Brooklyn right-hander Elmer Stricklett hit two batters in succession, Seymour sacrificed, and Bresnahan hit a two-run single to center. With runners on first and third in the Brooklyn ninth, Wiltse struck out outfielder John Hummel and retired shortstop Phil Lewis on a fly to left to end the game.

An error helped the Giants win Game 4 (April 29). With the score tied, 1–1, in the seventh, Boston shortstop Al Bridwell fumbled McGann's grounder and Dahlen doubled in the winning run.

Boston scored three runs in the eighth inning of Game 5 (May 1) to tie the score on a two-run double by outfielder Johnny Bates and a run-scoring single by first baseman Fred Tenney, but New York came back with three runs in the home eighth to win the game, 7–4. Out-fielder George Browne's single, a stolen base, and a run-scoring single by Seymour put the Giants ahead, and Bresnahan then hit a changeup over the right-field fence for a home run.

The only run scored in Game 7 (May 3), when Bresnahan walked in the fifth, reached third on two sacrifices, and scored on Corcoran's single to right as Mathewson shut out Brooklyn on two hits. Brooklyn got only two hits in Game 8 (May 4) and finally scored in the eighth inning of Game 9 (May 7) but suffered its eleventh straight loss in a twelve-game losing streak when New York scored on a single, two sacrifices, and a passed ball in the fourth and on Bresnahan's bunt, a wild pitch, and a single by first baseman Frank Bowerman in the seventh.

The first extra-inning victory was in Game 12 (May 13) as New York scored in the twelfth when Bowerman led off with a single to left, McGann sacrificed, Dahlen smashed a single off Cincinnati right-hander Del Mason, and Corcoran beat out an infield hit to drive in the game's only run.

The Giants trailed, 3–2, in Game 14 (May 15) until the home ninth, when they rallied. Right-hander Cotton Minahan, pitching the only complete game of his brief major league career, walked Dahlen, who stole second before pinch-hitter Browne walked. Outfielder Spike Shannon then walked to load the bases, Strang's long fly to center scored the tying run, and Devlin singled past third to score Browne with the run that beat the Reds, 4–3.

In the second extra-inning game in the streak, Game 15 (May 17), both St. Louis and New York scored in the fifth on run-producing fly balls. New York scored the winning run in the twelfth, when Corcoran doubled to left with one out and Mathewson — who struck out eleven in posting his sixth victory of the season without defeat — followed with a single to right to win the game.

Starting with the defeat that ended what was then the second longest winning streak in the history of the Giants, New York lost ten of its next fourteen games, and never recovered. New York finished the season in fourth place, twenty-five and one-half games behind first-place Chicago and four games in back of third-place Philadelphia. Despite Mathewson's league-leading twenty-four wins, the Giants finished sixth in pitching with a 2.45 earned run average. Seymour was the team's top hitter with seventy-five runs batted in, thirty-six extra-base hits, and a .294 average.

1912 Washington Senators

17 Consecutive Wins

The Washington Senators joined the American League in its first season of 1901, but sixth place was their highest finish in their first eleven years. Former pitcher Clark Griffith, who managed the Chicago White Sox in 1901 and 1902, the New York Americans from 1903 through part of the 1908 season, and then piloted the Cincinnati Reds from 1909 through 1911, became manager of the Senators after the 1911 season.

Washington finished a distant seventh in 1911, even with a twenty-five game winner in right-hander Walter Johnson. Griffith traded away catcher Gabby Street and several other veterans and revamped his infield. First baseman Chick Gandil, purchased from Montreal in late May, was a key acquisition, and he made his debut with the Senators in the May 30 morning game at Boston.

Washington lost that game, 3–2, as right-hander Hugh Bedient defeated right-hander Joe Engel, with Boston overcoming a 2–1 deficit in the eighth inning on an error by second baseman John Knight, a triple by third baseman Larry Gardner, and a sacrifice fly by first baseman Hugh Bradley. After that morning loss, Washington was in sixth place with a 17–19 record, eight and one-half games behind first-place Boston but only one and one-half games in back of third-place Detroit. Washington's seventeen-game winning streak, the longest in the club's history, began that afternoon at Boston's Fenway Park.

1. Thursday, May 30					**2. Saturday, June 1**				
Washington	002 110 100	5	12	0	Washington	102 000 113	8	12	3
Boston	000 000 000	0	5	2	St. Louis	000 001 020	3	12	0
WP **Johnson**; LP **O'Brien** (afternoon game)					WP **Hughes**; LP **Nelson**, Hamilton (3)				

3. Sunday, June 2

| Washington | 000 110 400 | 6 | 9 | 2 |
| St. Louis | 200 000 001 | 3 | 6 | 4 |

WP **Groom**; LP **Lake**, Brown (7)

4. Monday, June 3

| Washington | 001 023 007 | 13 | 17 | 3 |
| St. Louis | 100 200 010 | 4 | 8 | 2 |

WP **Engel**, Hughes (8); LP **Baumgardner**,
Brown (6)

5. Tuesday, June 4

| Washington | 020 100 000 | 3 | 8 | 2 |
| St. Louis | 000 100 010 | 2 | 6 | 0 |

WP **Johnson**; LP **Powell**

6. Wednesday, June 5

| Washington | 003 131 000 | 8 | 10 | 0 |
| Chicago | 110 011 000 | 4 | 9 | 5 |

WP **Hughes**; LP **Benz**, Mogridge (5),
Peters (6), White (8)

7. Thursday, June 6

| Washington | 101 000 304 | 9 | 9 | 1 |
| Chicago | 000 001 000 | 1 | 3 | 4 |

WP **Musser**, Johnson (6); LP **Walsh**,
Mogridge (7), Peters (9)

8. Friday, June 7

| Washington | 000 000 202 | 4 | 6 | 0 |
| Chicago | 001 000 001 | 2 | 5 | 2 |

WP **Groom**; LP **Lange**

9. Saturday, June 8

| Washington | 050 100 001 | 7 | 13 | 2 |
| Chicago | 001 000 000 | 1 | 7 | 1 |

WP **Johnson**; LP **White**

10. Sunday, June 9

| Washington | 011 200 000 | 4 | 7 | 1 |
| Detroit | 110 001 000 | 3 | 9 | 3 |

WP Musser, **Hughes** (3); LP **Willett**

11. Monday, June 10

| Washington | 101 020 300 | 7 | 12 | 0 |
| Detroit | 100 000 200 | 3 | 9 | 2 |

WP **Engel**, Cashion (7); LP **Mullin**

12. Tuesday, June 11

| Washington | 000 000 003 | 3 | 5 | 2 |
| Detroit | 010 010 000 | 2 | 7 | 1 |

WP Groom, **Cashion** (2), Johnson (9); LP
Dubuc

13. Wednesday, June 12

| Washington | 100 101 110 | 5 | 8 | 2 |
| Detroit | 000 100 000 | 1 | 3 | 3 |

WP **Johnson**; LP **Covington**, Works (9)

14. Thursday, June 13

| Washington | 020 020 200 | 6 | 13 | 2 |
| Cleveland | 000 002 001 | 3 | 7 | 0 |

WP **Groom**; LP **George**, Blanding (9)

15. Friday, June 14

| Washington | 010 332 400 | 13 | 20 | 4 |
| Cleveland | 004 022 000 | 8 | 13 | 3 |

WP **Hughes**; LP **Blanding**, Steen (5),
Kahler (6), Baskette (8)

16. Saturday, June 15

| Washington | 000 240 000 | 6 | 13 | 0 |
| Cleveland | 003 010 100 | 5 | 12 | 1 |

WP **Cashion**, Groom (8); LP **Mitchell**,
Steen (5), Kahler (9)

17. Tuesday, June 18

| Philadelphia | 000 000 301 | 4 | 12 | 2 |
| Washington | 100 010 201 | 5 | 9 | 1 |

WP **Groom**; LP Morgan, Houck (7), **Pennock** (9)

After Washington finished seventh in 1911, Clark Griffith was hired as manager and guided the Senators to second place, aided by a seventeen-game winning streak. (Courtesy of National Baseball Library, Cooperstown, New York.)

The winning streak ended the next afternoon at Philadelphia's Shibe Park.

Wednesday, June 19[1]

Washington	000 001 000 0	1	5	2
Philadelphia	000 000 001 1	2	7	1

WP **Coombs**; LP **Hughes** (10 innings)

A crowd of 20,000 saw Washington score in the sixth on shortstop George McBride's leadoff single, catcher John Henry's sacrifice, and a double to left by right-hander Long Tom Hughes. The 1–0 lead lasted until there were two out in the home ninth. Then third baseman Frank Baker foul-tipped a three-two pitch that Henry dropped, after which Baker homered over the right-field wall to tie the score. Philadelphia won in the tenth when shortstop Jack Barry singled with one out and

[1]*First game of a doubleheader.*

catcher Jack Lapp followed with a double to right. Outfielder Danny Moeller fielded the ball and threw to second baseman Ray Morgan, who relayed the ball home. Henry had the plate blocked, but Barry slid home safely on a very close play to win the game.

The winning streak enabled Washington to jump right into the American League pennant race. After the seventeenth win in a row, the Senators were in second place, only one and one-half games in back of first-place Boston. Later they fell back.

Washington averaged 6.6 runs and 10.8 hits during the streak to 2.9 runs and 7.8 hits for the opposition. The Senators won five games by a one-run margin, one by two runs, two by three runs, three each by four runs and five runs, and one each by six runs, eight runs, and nine runs. Only the first game was a shutout, and none was decided in extra innings.

Griffith used six pitchers during the streak and nineteen during the season, although only seven pitched in more than nine games. Johnson, Hughes and right-hander Bob Groom won four games each, Engel and right-hander Carl Cashion won two each and right-hander Paul Musser won one. Johnson and Groom pitched four complete games each, while Hughes pitched three complete games and won one in relief. The only other relief win was by Cashion.

Washington trailed in ten of the seventeen games, but in only three after the fifth inning. Two games were won in Washington's last time at bat, and the first sixteen wins were road games, still the American League record.

The Senators trailed in Game 8 (June 7) until the seventh inning, after Chicago scored in the third on a walk and right-hander Frank Lange's double. Washington took a 2–1 lead in the seventh when third baseman Eddie Foster tripled, held third on an infield hit by outfielder Clyde Milan, who stole second, and came home on a grounder by outfielder Howard Shanks. Milan scored when catcher Bruno Block made a wild throw trying to pick him off third. In the ninth Gandil singled home what proved to be the winning run, advanced on an error, and scored from second on a wild pitch.

In Game 12 (June 11), Detroit scored a run in the second inning on a close play that resulted in Groom's ejection for arguing the decision. Cashion relieved and gave up a run in the Detroit fifth on a walk, sacrifice, and single by outfielder Davy Jones. Held to three hits by right-hander Jean Dubuc for eight innings, Washington scored three times in the ninth to win. A walk to Foster and singles by Milan and

Gandil produced one run with the runners advancing to second and third on the late throw. A long fly by Shanks enabled Milan to score and Gandil to take third after the catch, and Morgan's fly to short left brought in Gandil with the winning run.

In Washington's seventeenth straight win, a capacity crowd of 15,561, including President William Howard Taft, turned out at National Park for the first home game in the streak. Washington scored in the first inning on Gandil's single and in the fifth on Barry's wild throw. Philadelphia scored three times in the seventh on singles by first baseman Stuffy McInnis and Barry, Lapp's pinch-hit triple, and outfielder Bris Lord's single.

In the home seventh, Washington scored on Milan's single, Gandil's double, and a wild relay throw to the plate for a 4–3 lead, but Philadelphia tied in the ninth when Barry walked and catcher Ben Egan tripled. In the home ninth, Philadelphia left-hander Herb Pennock walked Moeller, who advanced to third on two infield outs and came home on a two-strike single to right by Gandil for a 5–4 victory.

Washington lost four straight and six of eight games after the winning streak. The Senators finished the season in second place with a 91–61 record, fourteen games behind pennant-winning Boston. Johnson won thirty-two games and lost twelve, and Groom had a 24–13 record as Washington led the league in earned run average (2.69). Milan, who broke Ty Cobb's stolen-base record with 88, led the club in batting (.306), while Gandil hit .305, but the Senators were sixth in batting (.256) and fourth in fielding (.954).

1916 New York Giants

17 Consecutive Wins

The New York Giants won five National League pennants within a span of ten years early in this century but fell all the way from second to eighth in 1915, the only time they finished last when John McGraw was their manager for a full season. McGraw, who managed New York from mid–July 1902 until early June of 1932, made some important additions after that disappointing season, all from the disbanded Federal League. Bill McKecknie replaced Hans Lobert as the regular third baseman, Benny Kauff took over for traded center fielder Fred Snodgrass, and Bill Rariden replaced Chief Meyers, who had been the regular New York catcher for six seasons.

Despite the changes, New York started slowly in 1916, winning only one game in April and owning a 2–13 record after losing on May 8 to Boston, 6–2, as right-hander Pat Ragan beat New York left-hander Emilio Palmero. After that defeat New York was in last place, eight and one-half games behind first-place Brooklyn, and four games in back of seventh-place Pittsburgh. That game ended what was called the most disastrous home stand the Giants had had in many years.

The seventeen-game winning streak began the next afternoon when New York opened a six-city road trip at Pittsburgh's Forbes Field. That streak is still the longest winning streak compiled entirely on the road in major league history.

1. Tuesday, May 9

New York	011 006 401	13	16	1
Pittsburgh	021 010 001	5	8	3

WP **Tesreau**, Benton (6), Mathewson (6);
LP **Harmon**, Jacobs (6), Hill (7)

2. Wednesday, May 10

New York	300 310 000	7	13	0
Pittsburgh	000 010 000	1	3	3

WP **Anderson**; LP **Adams**, Cooper (1),
Jacobs (6)

3. Thursday, May 11

New York	000 000 300	3	7	2
Pittsburgh	000 002 000	2	3	3

WP **Perritt**, Stroud (7); LP **Kantlehner**

4. Friday, May 12

New York	000 000 011 1	3	7	0
Pittsburgh	000 002 000 0	2	6	0

WP Mathewson, Benton (7), **Schauer** (9);
LP **Mamaux** (10 innings)

5. Sunday, May 14

New York	103 010 100	6	9	0
Chicago	002 000 011	4	13	3

WP **Tesreau**, Benton (9); LP **McConnell**,
Packard (5)

6. Monday, May 15

New York	011 001 000	3	9	2
Chicago	020 000 000	2	6	4

WP **Perritt**; LP **Vaughn**

7. Wednesday, May 17

New York	014 300 010	9	15	1
St. Louis	000 001 002	3	8	5

WP **Anderson**; LP **Doak**, Meadows (3),
Steele (3)

8. Thursday, May 18

New York	002 100 000	3	8	2
St. Louis	000 000 000	0	6	2

WP **Benton**; LP **Ames**

9. Friday, May 19

New York	004 000 010	5	11	1
St. Louis	100 030 000	4	12	0

WP Stroud, Tesreau (3), **Perritt** (5); LP
Sallee, Williams (9)

10. Saturday, May 20

New York	010 000 030	4	8	0
St. Louis	000 000 001	1	6	2

WP **Mathewson**; LP **Jasper**, Williams (9)

11. Sunday, May 21

New York	300 000 440	11	16	2
Cincinnati	000 000 100	1	6	3

WP **Anderson**; LP **Knetzer**, Dale (4),
Moseley (9)

12. Tuesday, May 23

New York	001 000 300	4	10	1
Cincinnati	000 000 012	3	10	3

WP **Benton**, Tesreau (9), Mathewson (9);
LP **Schneider**, Knetzer (9)

13. Wednesday, May 24

New York	000 200 004	6	10	1
Cincinnati	000 000 010	1	11	4

WP **Perritt**; LP **Schulz**

14. Friday, May 26

New York	102 020 214	12	14	1
Boston	010 000 000	1	7	3

WP **Tesreau**, Stroud (3); LP **Tyler**

15. Saturday, May 27[1]

New York	110 100 001	4	12	4
Boston	100 000 020	3	6	1

WP **Anderson**; LP Allen, **Hughes** (9)

16. Saturday, May 27[2]

New York	100 100 000	2	5	0
Boston	000 000 010	1	9	0

WP **Benton**; LP **Ragan**

17. Monday, May 29

New York	100 000 020	3	7	2
Boston	000 000 000	0	4	3

WP **Mathewson**; LP **Rudolph**

[1]*First game of a doubleheader.* [2]*Second game of a doubleheader.*

The streak ended in the Memorial Day morning game at Philadelphia's Baker Bowl.

Tuesday, May 30

New York	000 000 001	1	6	1
Philadelphia	000 000 05x	5	7	1

WP **Demaree**; LP **Perritt** (morning game)

The pitching duel between Philadelphia right-hander Al Demaree and New York right-hander Pol Perritt was decided in the eighth inning, when the Phillies ended the scoreless deadlock with five runs. Key hits in the rally were second baseman Bert Niehoff's two-run triple and outfielder Gavvy Cravath's two-run homer after shortstop Dave Bancroft's bunt single scored pinch-runner Oscar Dugey with the game's first run. Kauff scored from first base on Demaree's wild pickoff throw in the ninth inning for New York's lone run.

After the seventeenth consecutive victory, New York was in second place with a 19–13 record, one and one-half games behind Brooklyn. During the streak, the Giants averaged 5.8 runs and 10.4 hits to 2.0 runs and 7.4 hits for the opposition. New York won seven games by one run, one by two runs, three by three runs, one by five runs, two by six runs, and one each by eight runs, ten runs, and eleven runs. In eleven of the seventeen games, the rivals scored two runs or less.

McGraw used seven pitchers during the streak and six of them won games. Right-hander Fred Anderson won four games, all complete, while Perritt won four games, two complete. Right-hander Jeff Tesreau and left-hander Rube Benton each won three games; right-hander Christy Mathewson won two, and right-hander Rube Schauer won one. Schauer's win and one of Perritt's were in relief. Ten of the seventeen wins were complete games, Benton and Mathewson pitched the only two shutouts, and there was just one extra-inning game.

The Giants trailed in five of the seventeen games, three after the fourth inning, and won only two games in their last time at bat.

New York's biggest inning during the streak was the sixth inning of Game 1 (May 9). Pittsburgh had a 4–2 lead through five innings before the Giants put together an error, a walk, and singles by pinch-hitter Edd Roush and outfielders George Burns and Dave Robertson to bring on right-hander Elmer Jacobs in relief. A hit batsman and two more hits completed the six-run rally.

In Game 3 (May 11), left-hander Erv Kantlehner's triple, an error, a stolen base, and a single by outfielder Bill Hinchman gave Pittsburgh a 2–0 lead in the sixth. New York won with three runs in the seventh when catcher Red Dooin singled, Burns was safe on an error, Robertson singled, and outfielder Max Carey dropped second baseman Larry Doyle's fly to left.

The only extra-inning victory was in Game 4 (May 12), and again Pittsburgh took a 2–0 lead in the sixth, this time on hits by first baseman Doc Johnston and outfielder Dan Costello and an error by shortstop Art Fletcher. New York scored in the eighth on Robertson's homer and tied the score in the ninth on a walk, Rariden's single, a sacrifice, and a sacrifice fly by Burns. In the tenth doubles by Kauff and Fletcher gave the Giants a 3–2 win.

New York tied Chicago, 2–2, on a run-scoring single by McKechnie in the second inning and another by Doyle in the third inning of Game 6 (May 15). The Giants won, 3–2, with a run in the sixth on McKechnie's single, a forceout, and a single by Burns.

In Game 9 (May 19), New York scored four runs in the third inning, three in a homer by Robertson, but St. Louis tied, 4–4, with three runs in the fifth when outfielder Jack Smith hit a two-run triple off the right-field wall and scored on a single by second baseman Bruno Betzel. The Giants untied it in the eighth and won, 5–4, on Robertson's single, an infield out, and Fletcher's single through the shortstop.

Mathewson saved Game 12 (May 23) at Cincinnati after New York had gained a 4–0 lead with three runs in the seventh on a two-run single by Benton and a run-scoring single by Robertson. The Reds scored once in the eighth, and Tesreau relieved in the ninth after three singles produced one run. A single by pinch-hitter Ivy Wingo batted in another tally, and Matty then relieved with runners on first and third. He retired third baseman Heinie Groh and outfielder Greasy Neale to end the game.

After Boston scored twice in the eighth inning of Game 15 (May 27) on two singles, a sacrifice, and a wild throw past Anderson at first by first baseman Fred Merkle, the Giants won in the ninth, 4–3, when Robertson's single to center was fumbled and, after an out and an intentional walk, Fletcher singled to left.

Fletcher doubled home both runs in New York's 2–1 win over Boston in Game 16 (May 27), Benton getting out of a bases-loaded jam in the eighth inning when outfielder Ed Fitzpatrick grounded into a double play as the only opposition run scored.

Mathewson pitched the eightieth and last shutout of his great career in Game 17 (May 29), allowing four singles and no walks. He was helped by three double plays, starting one with a barehanded catch of Boston third baseman Red Smith's line drive and throwing to first to double first baseman Ed Konetchy off the bag.

Despite this winning streak in May and their all-time record twenty-six-game winning streak four months later in September, the New York Giants did not have an outstanding season because between the two streaks they won only forty games while losing forty-nine. They finished the season in fourth place with an 86–66 record, seven games behind first-place Brooklyn and three games in back of third-place Boston.

For only the second time in McGraw's fourteen full seasons as manager of the Giants, and for the second year in a row, New York did not have a twenty-game winning pitcher. Perritt and Tesreau were the top winners with eighteen victories each, while Benton won sixteen. Robertson was the team's only .300 hitter with a .307 average and led the league in home runs with twelve.

1931 Philadelphia Athletics

17 Consecutive Wins

The first fourteen years the Philadelphia Athletics were in the American League they won six pennants. They finished last for the next seven years and did not reach the first division again until 1925.

By then Manager Connie Mack's rebuilding program was starting to get results, and the A's won their first pennant since 1914 in 1929. They also won in 1930 and 1931, and that team is generally regarded as one of the great teams of all time.

Philadelphia won those three consecutive pennants by large margins, and won the World Series in both 1929 and 1930. Half a dozen future Hall of Famers wore Athletics uniforms in those years, including Mack, who managed the A's for their first fifty years; third-base coach Eddie Collins, catcher Mickey Cochrane, first baseman Jimmie Foxx, left fielder Al Simmons, and pitcher Bob ("Lefty") Grove.

Despite their great success in 1929 and 1930, the Athletics started slowly in 1931. They had only a 5–6 record in April, won their first two games in May, then lost the opener of a three-game series at home to the Boston Red Sox, 7–5, on May 4. A solo homer by second baseman Jack Rothrock and a three-run homer by third baseman Urban Pickering snapped a 2–2 tie in the four-run fifth inning and chased right-hander Bill Shores, who had relieved right-handed starter Hank McDonald in the second.

That defeat gave the A's a 7–7 record and put them in a three-way tie for fourth place, two and one-half games behind first-place Cleveland. The longest winning streak in the history of the Athletics franchise began the next afternoon at Philadelphia's Shibe Park.

1. Tuesday, May 5

Boston   000 000 100   1   6   0
Philadelphia   100 000 12x   4   11   0
WP **Earnshaw**; LP **Durham**, Kline (8),
Moore (8)

2. Wednesday, May 6

Boston   100 011 000   3   11   0
Philadelphia   021 131 02x   10   18   1
WP **Rommel**; LP **Russell**, Lisenbee (5),
Kline (7)

3. Saturday, May 9

Philadelphia   000 010 050   6   6   0
St. Louis   101 010 100   4   12   2
WP **Walberg**, Grove (8); LP **Gray**,
Kimsey (9)

4. Tuesday, May 12

Philadelphia   112 000 001   5   9   1
Chicago   000 200 000   2   4   1
WP **Grove**; LP **Caraway**

5. Wednesday, May 13

Philadelphia   010 020 011 02   7 11 1
Chicago   200 102 000 00   5   9 2
WP **Earnshaw**; LP Thomas, **Faber** (11) (11
innings)

6. Thursday, May 14

Philadelphia   000 221 000   5   9   0
Chicago   000 002 000   2   7   1
WP **Walberg**; LP **Frasier**, Lyons (6)

7. Friday, May 15

Philadelphia   000 000 121   4   9   0
Cleveland   000 000 000   0   9   4
WP **Rommel**; LP **Brown**, Harder (9)

8. Saturday, May 16

Philadelphia   000 003 063 12 20   1
Cleveland   101 002 001   5 12   2
WP **Grove**; LP Hudlin, **Thomas** (6),
Harder (8), Bean (8), Crawford (9)

9. Sunday, May 17

Philadelphia   320 023 023 15 18   2
Cleveland   150 210 100 10 16   3
WP Earnshaw, **McDonald** (5), Grove (9);
LP Ferrell, **Jablonowski** (6), Brown (8)

10. Monday, May 18

Philadelphia   000 203 041 10 13   1
Cleveland   021 000 220   7 12   1
WP **Walberg**, Grove (8); LP Miller,
Hudlin (6), Bean (8)

11. Tuesday, May 19

Philadelphia   201 000 110   5   9   0
Detroit   000 000 000   0   2   2
WP **Earnshaw**; LP **Hoyt**

12. Wednesday, May 20

Philadelphia   001 101 000   3   9   0
Detroit   000 000 000   0   3   0
WP **Grove**; LP **Uhle**

13. Thursday, May 21

Philadelphia   200 012 232 12 18   1
Detroit   100 001 300   5 14   1
WP Rommel, **Mahaffey** (2), Walberg (7);
LP **Bridges**, Sullivan (7), Sorrell (8), Herr-
ing (9)

14. Saturday, May 23

Boston   000 000 100   1   4   0
Philadelphia   420 100 00x   7 10   1
WP **Earnshaw**; LP **Durham**, Lisenbee (1),
Brillheart (8)

15. Sunday, May 24

Philadelphia   010 302 001   7 10   0
New York   000 002 010   3 11   0
WP **Walberg**; LP **Ruffing**, Pipgras (4),
Weinert (9)

16. Monday, May 25[1]

New York   020 000 000   2   8   0
Philadelphia   003 000 01x   4   8   0
WP **Grove**; LP **Johnson**

[1]*First game of a doubleheader.*

17. Monday, May 25[2]

New York	000 000 013	4 6 1
Philadelphia	900 250 00x	16 15 0

WP **Mahaffey**; LP **Sherid**, McEvoy (1),
Weaver (5)

The winning streak ended the next afternoon, two games shy of the American League record.

Tuesday, May 26

New York	030 002 010	6 10 0
Philadelphia	001 000 001	2 7 1

WP **Gomez**; LP **Rommel**, McDonald (3),
Shores (8)

New York never trailed and jumped off to a 3–0 lead in the second inning when catcher Bill Dickey tripled in two runs, and scored on an infield out by Lefty Gomez, and then singled across another run in the sixth when outfielder Babe Ruth homered. Philadelphia, scoring fewer runs than in any game during the streak, tallied once in the third when shortstop Joe Boley doubled and came home on a single by outfielder Mule Haas, and once in the ninth when Simmons hit a home run over the left-field roof.

After the seventeenth win in a row, Philadelphia was in first place with a 24–7 record, five games in front of second-place Washington.

Although the Athletics came from behind to win seven times during the streak, they trailed only three times after the seventh inning, never batted in the bottom of the ninth and only once — in the lone extra-inning game — did they win a game in the final inning. The A's never trailed in any game by more than three runs.

Of the fifteen teams which won sixteen or more consecutive games in major league history, Philadelphia is the only one that failed to win a game by a one-run margin. It won three games by two runs, five by three runs, two each by four runs, and by five runs, one by six runs, three by seven runs, and one by twelve runs.

Philadelphia employed only seven pitchers during the streak, and six won at least one game. Grove, right-hander George Earnshaw, and

---

[2]*Second game of a doubleheader.*

Connie Mack, who managed good and bad Philadelphia Athletics teams for fifty years, poses with catcher Mickey Cochrane and pitcher Lefty Grove. These were two of Mack's stars when the A's won seventeen straight games en route to a third pennant in a row in 1931. (Courtesy of National Baseball Library, Cooperstown, New York.)

left-hander Rube Walberg each won four games, right-handers Eddie Rommel and Roy Mahaffey won two apiece, and McDonald won one. Grove and Earnshaw pitched four complete games, Walberg and Rommel completed two, and Mahaffey, who won one game in relief, completed one. McDonald's win was in relief of a start made by Earnshaw. Grove's relief pitching saved two of Walberg's victories. Rommel, Earnshaw, and Grove pitched the only shutouts.

During the streak Philadelphia did not face Washington and beat Cleveland four times; Boston, Chicago, Detroit, and New York three times; and St. Louis once. Twelve of the seventeen wins were on the road. Philadelphia averaged 7.8 runs and 11.9 hits to 3.2 runs and 8.4 hits for the opposition.

The streak's first shutout was in Game 7 (May 15) when Rommel scattered seven singles and two doubles while walking one to win, 4–0, at Cleveland. It was his first shutout in four years and the last of his thirteen-year major league career. A run-scoring single by third baseman Jimmy Dykes snapped a scoreless tie in the seventh inning.

In Game 11 (May 19), Earnshaw faced only twenty-nine batters as outfielders John Stone and Frank Doljack both singled in the second inning and were the only Detroit base runners in the 5–0 victory, in which Foxx batted in three runs.

The next day in Game 12 (May 20), Grove beat Detroit, 3–0, allowing only singles by Stone, third baseman Marty McManus, and Doljack, and, like Earnshaw, he did not issue a walk. Haas singled in one run, and Foxx and outfielder Bing Miller homered for the other two runs.

The first come-from-behind win was in Game 3 (May 9). St. Louis right-hander Sam Gray had a two-hitter and a 4–1 lead until an error paved the way for a five-run rally in the eighth, the big hit in the 6–4 victory being a three-run homer by Foxx that landed on top of the center-field stands.

In Game 5 (May 13) Chicago had a 5–3 lead after seven innings before solo homers by Cochrane in the eighth and Miller in the ninth tied the score. Philadelphia won with two runs in the eleventh, 7–5, one run scoring when Miller doubled and came in on a sacrifice fly by Earnshaw, with an insurance run scoring on a double steal.

Although the A's left thirteen men on base, they overcame a 4–3 deficit with a six-run rally in the eighth to win, 12–5, in Game 8 (May 16). Second baseman Max Bishop, Cochrane, Simmons, and Miller each had three hits to lead the twenty-hit attack on five Cleveland pitchers.

In Game 9 (May 17) Simmons hit a three-run homer in the Philadelphia first, but Cleveland took a 6–5 lead in the second and led, 9–7, after the fifth. Homers by Foxx in the three-run sixth and by Cochrane in the three-run ninth helped the A's win, 15–10.

Philadelphia came from behind for the third straight day in Game 10 (May 18) and won, 10–7, on Foxx's hitting, handing Cleveland its tenth loss in a club record losing streak that reached twelve.

New York scored twice in the second inning on outfielder Ben Chapman's homer and Dickey's scoring fly in Game 16 (May 25). Philadelphia scored three times in the third on a two-out walk to Bishop, a triple by Haas, a double by Cochrane, and a single by Simmons and went on to win, 4–2.

The Athletics delighted the capacity crowd of 32,000 in the second game that day, scoring nine runs in the first inning of Game 17 (May 25) on the way to a 16–4 rout of New York. Cochrane's two-run triple and Boley's three-run three-bagger were the big blows in Philadelphia's biggest inning during the streak.

Later in the season Philadelphia won every home game from July 15 through August 31 to set a league record of twenty-two straight home victories. When the season ended, the A's had a 107–45 record and finished thirteen and a half games ahead of second-place New York. Grove won thirty-one games, including sixteen in a row, and lost only four; Earnshaw won twenty-one games and Walberg, twenty. Grove led the league in wins, winning percentage (.886), earned run average (2.06), complete games (27), shutouts (4) and strikeouts (175). Simmons won his second straight batting title with a .390 average and batted in 128 runs. Cochrane batted .349 and Haas hit .323, while Foxx hit thirty homers and batted in 120 runs.

That fall Philadelphia lost the World Series to St. Louis in seven games, the A's last in Philadelphia. The A's finished second in 1932, third in 1933, then would up in the second division nineteen times in the next twenty-one seasons before moving to Kansas City when the Mack family sold the club after the 1954 season.

LOSING STREAKS
BY TEAMS

23 Games • Philadelphia Phillies, 1961

21 Games • Baltimore Orioles, 1988

20 Games • Boston Red Sox, 1906

20 Games • Philadelphia Athletics, 1916

20 Games • Philadelphia Athletics, 1943

20 Games • Montreal Expos, 1969

19 Games • Boston Braves, 1906

19 Games • Cincinnati Reds, 1914

19 Games • Detroit Tigers, 1975

Team Losing Streaks

Team	Year	Games Lost	Games Lost by Shutout	Losers Scored Two Runs or Less	Complete Games Pitched by Losers	Games Lost by Relief Pitchers	Most Games Lost by One Pitcher	Number of Pitchers Who Lost Games	Games Lost by Margin of One Run	Games Lost in Final Inning
Phillies	1961	23	4	20	1	1	4	9	8	2
Orioles	1988	21	3	14	2	3	5	8	5	3
Red Sox	1906	20	2	11	15	0	5	6	5	2
Athletics	1916	20	4	15	13	2	5	7	3	1
Athletics	1943	20	3	10	13	2	4	8	8	5
Expos	1969	20	2	10	1	6	5	7	3	2
Braves	1906	19	9	14	14	0	6	4	6	1
Reds	1914	19	2	14	8	4	5	6	8	5
Tigers	1975	19	4	12	6	5	4	9	7	4

1961 Philadelphia Phillies

23 Consecutive Losses

The Philadelphia Phillies won their first National League pennant in 1915. Four years after that first championship they were in the cellar and finished in the second division from 1918 through 1931. They won their second pennant in 1950 and eight years later fell to the bottom and finished last each year from 1958 through 1961.

The Phillies were in their second season under Manager Gene Mauch in 1961, and nothing had improved. Despite a trade with the Los Angeles Dodgers that added third baseman Charley Smith and outfielder Don Demeter to the regular lineup, a disastrous May, in which the Phillies won only six games, dropped them into eighth place to stay. There were no noticeable changes in June or July.

In the second game of a twilight-night doubleheader at home on July 28, the Phillies beat San Francisco, 4–3, to end a five-game losing streak. Right-hander John Buzhardt went the route to win his third game against ten defeats, winning when second baseman Bobby Malkmus hit a seventh-inning home run into the lower left-field stands to snap a 3–3 tie. That victory gave the last-place Phillies a 30–64 record, twenty-nine games behind first-place Cincinnati and ten games in back of seventh-place Chicago.

The twenty-three game losing streak, still the longest in modern major league history, began the next night at Philadelphia's Connie Mack Stadium.

1. Saturday, July 29			
San Francisco	400 000 000	4 7 0
Philadelphia	000 201 000	3 10 1

WP **McCormick**; LP **Ferrarese**

2. Sunday, July 30			
San Francisco	011 012 000	5 13 1
Philadelphia	200 000 000	2 8 1

WP **Sanford**; LP **Owens**, Baldschun (5), Brown (6), Short (8), Sullivan (9)

3. Wednesday, August 2[1]

Philadelphia	001 000 100	2	10	0
Cincinnati	000 202 00x	4	10	0

WP **O'Toole**, Henry (9); LP **Mahaffey**, Sullivan (6), Baldschun (7)

4. Wednesday, August 2[2]

Philadelphia	001 010 000	2	11	0
Cincinnati	012 000 00x	3	6	2

WP **Jay**, Jones (6); LP **Short**, Baldschun (4)

5. Thursday, August 3

Philadelphia	010 000 000	1	9	1
Cincinnati	020 122 00x	7	15	0

WP **Johnson**; LP **Buzhardt**, Sullivan (5), Owens (6), Lehman (8)

6. Friday, August 4

Philadelphia	300 010 301	8	14	2
St. Louis	304 001 10x	9	12	2

WP **Broglio**, Anderson (7), Bauta (8); LP **Ferrarese**, Mahaffey (3), Short (7), Baldschun (7)

7. Saturday, August 5

Philadelphia	000 000 000	0	8	1
St. Louis	100 060 00x	7	13	1

WP **Simmons**; LP **Brown**, Lehman (5)

8. Sunday, August 6[1]

Philadelphia	000 000 001	1	4	1
St. Louis	030 000 00x	3	5	1

WP **Sadecki**; LP **Sullivan**, Baldschun (8)

9. Sunday, August 6[2]

Philadelphia	200 000 000	2	6	2
St. Louis	000 000 201	3	7	1

WP **Gibson**; LP **Owens**, Baldschun (9)

10. Monday, August 7

Pittsburgh	110 000 100	3	10	0
Philadelphia	000 001 000	1	4	0

WP **Friend**; LP **Buzhardt**, Baldschun (9)

11. Tuesday, August 8[1]

Pittsburgh	010 011 052	10	13	1
Philadelphia	000 010 100	2	8	0

WP **Haddix**; LP **Mahaffey**, Baldschun (8), Brown (9)

12. Tuesday, August 8[2]

Pittsburgh	100 001 010	3	10	0
Philadelphia	000 100 010	2	7	0

WP **Sturdivant**; LP **Short**, Baldschun (9)

13. Wednesday, August 9

Cincinnati	001 120 001	5	9	0
Philadelphia	000 000 000	0	6	1

WP **Jay**; LP **Ferrarese**, Sullivan (5), Lehman (6), Baldschun (9)

14. Friday, August 11

Philadelphia	000 000 0	0	5	0
Pittsburgh	501 000 x	6	10	0

WP **Friend**; LP **Roberts**, Lehman (5) (7 innings, rain)

15. Saturday, August 12

Philadelphia	000 000 000	0	5	0
Pittsburgh	001 200 01x	4	7	1

WP **Mizell**; LP **Owens**, Ferrarese (8)

16. Sunday, August 13

Philadelphia	000 120 001	4	13	4
Pittsburgh	302 008 00x	13	16	0

WP **Sturdivant**; LP **Buzhardt**, Short (4), Baldschun (6), Green (6)

[1]*First game of a doubleheader.* [2]*Second game of a doubleheader.*

17. Monday, August 14

Philadelphia	010 100 000	2	6	2
Chicago	220 050 00x	9	9	2

WP **Ellsworth**; LP **Sullivan**, Ferrarese (5), Baldschun (7)

18. Tuesday, August 15

Philadelphia	102 001 010	5	12	1
Chicago	402 000 00x	6	7	1

WP **Curtis**, Schultz (8), Anderson (9); LP **Mahaffey**, Lehman (3), Buzhardt (4), Baldschun (8)

19. Wednesday, August 16

Philadelphia	101 000 210	5	13	0
Chicago	040 003 11x	9	13	0

WP **Cardwell**; LP **Short**, Sullivan (2), Green (3), Baldschun (8)

20. Thursday, August 17

Philadelphia	030 000 300 00	6	9	2
Milwaukee	210 010 020 01	7	12	3

WP Buhl, McMahon (9), **Nottebart** (11); LP Roberts, Mahaffey (2), Ferrarese (9), **Baldschun** (9) (11 innings)

21. Friday, August 18

Philadelphia	000 000 100	1	6	0
Milwaukee	210 100 00x	4	8	0

WP **Burdette**; LP **Owens**, Lehman (5), Green (8)

22. Saturday, August 19

Philadelphia	000 110 001	3	12	0
Milwaukee	004 000 00x	4	7	0

WP **Cloninger**, McMahon (9); LP **Sullivan**, Ferrarese (6)

23. Sunday, August 20[1]

Philadelphia	020 000 000	2	5	0
Milwaukee	000 230 00x	5	7	0

WP **Spahn**; LP **Short**, Baldschun (5), Green (7)

The losing streak ended in the second game of the doubleheader that afternoon at Milwaukee's County Stadium.

Sunday, August 20[2]

Philadelphia	000 201 040	7	13	1
Milwaukee	001 000 111	4	9	0

WP **Buzhardt**; LP **Willey**, Hendley (7), Nottebart (8), Antonelli (9)

Milwaukee took a 1–0 lead in the third inning when shortstop Roy McMillan hit his fifth homer against the left-field foul pole, but Philadelphia went ahead to stay in fourth when outfielder Wes Covington hit his third homer over the right-field fence and third baseman Lee Walls doubled and scored on catcher Clay Dalrymple's ground single to center. Singles by Walls and Dalrymple and a sacrifice fly by Malkmus

---

[1]*First game of a doubleheader.* [2]*Second game of a doubleheader.*

Gene Mauch managed the Philadelphia Phillies during an all-time record twenty-three-game losing streak in 1961. He also guided the Montreal Expos in 1969 when they dropped twenty straight games. (Courtesy of National Baseball Library, Cooperstown, New York.)

made it 3–1 in the sixth, and Philadelphia added four runs in the eighth to clinch the victory. Demeter singled to open the rally, outfielder Ken Walters batted for Covington and singled, and, after a force-out, Dalrymple walked to load the bases. Right-hander Don Nottebart relieved and Malkmus singled to right for one run, Buzhardt's squeeze bunt brought in another, and second baseman Tony Taylor's two-run single to right capped the rally.

Milwaukee scored its second run in the seventh on singles by outfielder Hank Aaron and first baseman Joe Adcock and a force-out hit into by outfielder Frank Thomas. A walk, an infield out, and outfielder Lee Maye's single added a run in the eighth, and Adcock led off the bottom of the ninth with his twenty-sixth homer over the fence in right center. Two outs later, shortstop Felix Mantilla singled, but pinch-hitter Gino Cimoli grounded to second into a force-out to end the game and the longest losing streak in modern major league history. The win was Buzhardt's fourth of the season against thirteen defeats and was the first win for the Phillies since Buzhardt won the game the night before the losing streak began.

After the games of August 20, Philadelphia was in last place with a 31–87 record, forty-two games behind first-place Cincinnati and nineteen and one-half games in back of seventh-place Chicago. During the losing streak, the opposition averaged 5.8 runs and 9.8 hits to 2.3 runs and 8.3 hits for Philadelphia. Four of the defeats were shutouts, and only one game went more than nine innings and one less. The opposition hit twenty-three home runs by nineteen different players and the Phillies hit twelve by eight players.

Nine different pitchers lost games, with right-hander Jim Owens and left-hander Chris Short losing four each, left-hander Don Ferrarese and right-handers Art Mahaffey, Buzhardt and Frank Sullivan three apiece. Right-handers Paul Brown, Robin Roberts, and Jack Baldschun lost the other three. Roberts was the only pitcher who didn't lose a game he started, and the only game a rival starting pitcher failed to win was the eleven-inning game.

The Phillies lost to every team in the league except Los Angeles and were beaten six times by Pittsburgh. Eight of the defeats were by one run, three by both two and three runs, two by four runs, one by five runs, two each by six runs and seven runs, one by eight runs, and one by nine runs. At one point they went scoreless for twenty-nine innings.

Philadelphia led in nine games, but only twice after the fourth inning and both those games were decided in the last inning.

One was in Game 9 (August 6) at St. Louis. The Phillies scored twice in the first inning when outfielder John Callison homered and C. Smith singled after a walk and two infield outs. A grounder that went through C. Smith's legs at third and pinch-hitter Carl Sawatski's homer to the right-field roof tied the score in the St. Louis seventh.

St. Louis won in the ninth on third baseman Ken Boyer's single, a force-out, two wild pitches, an intentional walk, another walk and, after Baldschun relieved, a single to center by Sawatski that ended the 3–2 game.

The other was in Game 20 (August 17) at Milwaukee in the streak's only extra-inning game. Philadelphia took a 6–4 lead with three runs in the seventh on singles by Covington and Walls, a sacrifice, a two-run single by Malkmus, a sacrifice and Taylor's grounder that went through third baseman Eddie Mathews for an error.

Milwaukee tied in the eighth on a walk to Aaron and Adcock's twenty-fifth homer over the center-field fence. In the eleventh two walks around an error on a sacrifice loaded the bases, and Baldschun struck out Aaron for the first out, but outfielder Al Spangler singled to center to win the game, 7–6.

After snapping the losing streak, Philadelphia returned home and extended its longest winning streak of the season to four games with two wins over Chicago and one over Milwaukee. One of the wins was a one-hit, 6–0 victory over Chicago by Mahaffey. Philadelphia dropped twenty of the thirty-three remaining games, however, and finished eighth with a 47–107 record, forty-six games behind pennant-winning Cincinnati and seventeen in back of seventh-place Chicago.

Demeter led the club in home runs with twenty and runs batted in with sixty-eight, while outfielder Tony Gonzalez led the regulars in batting with a .277 average. Mahaffey won eleven games, and no other pitcher won more than six, but he also tied for the league lead in losses with nineteen. The Phillies were last in batting at .243 and last in pitching with a 4.61 earned run average.

1988 Baltimore Orioles
21 Consecutive Losses

The high-flying Baltimore Orioles, a remarkable success story for more than a quarter century, suddenly fell on hard times in the mid–1980s. They hit bottom in 1988 when they began the season with a historic losing streak. Baltimore lost twenty-one straight games in 1988 before scoring its first win of the season, setting a major league record for the most consecutive losses at the start of the season, setting an all-time American League record for consecutive defeats, and coming within two of the modern major league record for most losses in succession, a mark set by the 1961 Philadelphia Phillies.

Baltimore's first major league team played in the American Association from 1882 through 1891. The city had a National League team from 1892 through 1899 and an American League club in 1901 and 1902. In addition there was a team in the Union Association, which was in existence only in 1884. Six of those nineteen teams finished in last place, but the Birds won National League pennants from 1894 through 1896, and established a reputation as one of the best and smartest baseball teams in history.

Baltimore had only minor league baseball from 1903 until the St. Louis Browns, a ragtag team in the American League, switched their franchise to Baltimore for the 1954 season. It took until 1960 for the Orioles to reach the first division, but from then on they have been a baseball power. In fact, despite finishing seventh and last in the American League's Eastern Division in 1986 and sixth in 1988, Baltimore's record for the thirty-one years from 1957 through 1987 is the best for winning percentage in the big leagues. The Orioles won six pennants and three world championships from 1966 through 1983.

Baltimore's sudden descent from the World Series victory in 1983 to the role of an also-ran was unexpected. The Orioles had done well in the fourteen and one-half years they were managed by Earl Weaver (1968–82). Joe Altobelli managed the Birds to the world championship in 1983, then was replaced in 1985 when Weaver returned. Cal Ripken, long-time minor league manager and coach with Baltimore, was named manager for 1987, but was replaced by Hall of Famer Frank Robinson after the club lost its first six games in 1988.

The hard times Baltimore ran into were surprising because it had the nucleus of a respectable team with first baseman Eddie Murray, second baseman Billy Ripken and the other son of the manager, shortstop Cal Ripken, Jr., outfielder Fred Lynn, and catcher Terry Kennedy. The pitching, however, was ineffective, and the staff earned run average in 1987 was an inflated 5.01, next to the worst in the American League.

1. Monday, April 4

Milwaukee	000 220 260	12	16	0
Baltimore	000 000 000	0	5	2

WP **Higuera**, Clear (8), Plesac (9); LP **Boddicker**, Peraza (6), Schmidt (8), Sisk (8)

2. Wednesday, April 6

Milwaukee	000 003 000	3	6	0
Baltimore	010 000 000	1	5	0

WP **Bosio**; LP **Morgan**

3. Friday, April 8

Baltimore	000 000 000	0	3	0
Cleveland	000 000 30x	3	8	2

WP **Bailes**; LP **Thurmond**, Sisk (7)

4. Saturday, April 9

Baltimore	000 000 001	1	8	3
Cleveland	054 111 00x	12	20	0

WP **Candiotti**; LP **Boddicker**, Williamson (2), Bautista (3), Peraza (7), Niedenfuer (8)

5. Sunday, April 10

Baltimore	000 010 200	3	9	1
Cleveland	010 401 00x	6	9	2

WP **Yett**, Codiroli (7), Schatzeder (7); LP **McGregor**, Schmidt (4)

6. Monday, April 11

Baltimore	000 020 000	2	8	0
Cleveland	000 202 30x	7	9	1

WP **Swindell**; LP **Morgan**, Sisk (7)

7. Tuesday, April 12

Kansas City	000 330 000	6	8	0
Baltimore	100 000 000	1	2	0

WP **Gubicza**, Quisenberry (8); LP **Peraza**, Williamson (5), Niedenfuer (8), Sisk (9)

8. Wednesday, April 13

Kansas City	102 302 100	9	18	1
Baltimore	000 011 010	3	4	1

WP **Bannister**, Farr (7), Garber (9); LP **Thurmond**, Bautista (4)

9. Thursday, April 14

```
Kansas City    012 000 001   4  5  1
Baltimore      000 012 000   3  8  3
```
WP **Saberhagen**, Black (9), Garber (9); LP
Boddicker

10. Friday, April 15

```
Cleveland      010 000 020   3  8  1
Baltimore      020 000 000   2  7  0
```
WP **Yett**, Jones (8); LP **McGregor**, Sisk
(8)

11. Saturday, April 16

```
Cleveland      000 000 000 01   1 3 0
Baltimore      000 000 000 00   0 8 0
```
WP **Swindell**, Jones (11); LP Morgan,
Schmidt (10) (11 innings)

12. Sunday, April 17

```
Cleveland      010 200 100   4 10  0
Baltimore      001 000 000   1  5  1
```
WP **Farrell**, Schatzeder (9); LP **Peraza**,
Williamson (5), Niedenfuer (9)

13. Tuesday, April 19

```
Baltimore      301 001 000   5  8  4
Milwaukee      230 030 10x   9 14  0
```
WP **Nieves**, Crim (6); LP **Thurmond**,
Schmidt (2), Sisk (5), Bautista (8)

14. Wednesday, April 20

```
Baltimore      003 110 010   6 12  0
Milwaukee      030 041 00x   8 15  0
```
WP **Wegman**, Stapleton (6), Plesac (8); LP
Boddicker, Williamson (5), Thurmond (7),
Niedenfuer (8)

15. Thursday, April 21

```
Baltimore      000 000 010   1  8  0
Milwaukee      006 100 00x   7 10  1
```
WP **Bosio**; LP **McGregor**, Peraza (3),
Bautista (7)

16. Friday, April 22

```
Baltimore      000 010 000   1  3  2
Kansas City    900 001 12x  13 19  2
```
WP **Gubicza**; LP **Morgan**, Schmidt (1),
Sisk (5), Niedenfuer (7), Bautista (8)

17. Saturday, April 23

```
Baltimore      100 110 000   3  7  0
Kansas City    001 101 001   4 10  1
```
WP Bannister, **Power** (6); LP Williamson,
Sisk (8)

18. Sunday, April 24

```
Baltimore      000 000 001   1  6  0
Kansas City    000 012 00x   3  9  0
```
WP **Saberhagen**; LP **Thurmond**, Peraza
(6), Bautista (6)

19. Tuesday, April 26

```
Baltimore      101 000 000   2  3  1
Minnesota      000 003 01x   4  8  0
```
WP **Viola**, Reardon (8); LP **Morgan**,
Schmidt (7), Scherrer (8), Sisk (8)

20. Wednesday, April 27

```
Baltimore      310 000 002   6 11  1
Minnesota      210 100 03x   7 13  0
```
WP Blyleven, **Berenguer** (7), Atherton (9);
LP McGregor, Bautista (4), **Scherrer** (8),
Sisk (8)

21. Thursday, April 28

```
Baltimore      100 000 100   2  6  2
Minnesota      000 202 00x   4  6  0
```
WP **Anderson**, Mason (7), Portugal (7);
LP **Boddicker**, Niedenfuer (8)

American League's longest losing streak ended the next night at Chicago's Comiskey Park.

Friday, April 29

Baltimore	200	010	402	9	11	0
Chicago	000	000	000	0	4	1

WP **Williamson**, Schmidt (7); LP **McDowell**, John Davis (7), Long (8), Thigpen (9)

Excellent pitching by right-handers Mark Williamson and Dave Schmidt and some timely hitting finally produced Baltimore's first victory of the season. For the fourth game in a row, Baltimore scored in the first inning as Murray hit his second homer of the season with a mate aboard. In the fifth, Baltimore added a run when outfielder Pete Stanicek, playing his first big-league game of the season, singled to center, stole second, took third on B. Ripken's fly to right, and scored on a wild pitch by right-hander Jack McDowell. The Orioles clinched the win with four runs in the seventh when Stanicek doubled in a run and Kennedy hit a sacrifice fly. C. Ripken hit his third homer of the season in the two-run ninth. Meanwhile Williamson allowed three singles in six innings and Schmidt one in the final three, with neither pitcher issuing a walk.

During its losing streak, Baltimore averaged 2.1 runs and 6.3 hits per game to 6.01 runs and 10.8 hits for the opposition. The Orioles faced only four different teams, losing seven times to Cleveland, six to Kansas City, five to Milwaukee, and three to Minnesota, and thirteen of the losses were on the road. They lost to sixteen different pitchers, five of them beating them twice. Only two relief pitchers were winners.

Eight different Baltimore pitchers suffered at least one loss, with right-hander Mike Boddicker suffering five defeats and right-hander Mike Morgan and left-hander Mark Thurmond losing four each. Left-hander Scott McGregor lost three and right-hander Ossie Peraza two, while left-hander Bill Scherrer and right-handers Doug Sisk and Schmidt each lost one, and those three were the only defeats in relief.

Only three of the games were lost in the opposition's final time at bat. In the ninth game in the streak (April 14), the Orioles came back from a 3–0 deficit to tie at 3–3, one of the runs coming on Lynn's first homer of the season. Kansas City won in the top of the ninth when designated hitter Jim Eisenrich scored from first base when left fielder

Jeff Stone lost second baseman Frank White's single in the lights and the ball rolled to the wall.

In the eleventh game (April 16), Cleveland scored the game's only run in the top of the eleventh when outfielder Cory Snyder walked, took second on a passed ball by catcher Carl Nichols, and scored two outs later when first baseman Cecil Upshaw singled, only the third hit of the game for Cleveland.

In the seventeenth game (April 23), with one out in the ninth, Kansas City outfielder Bo Jackson tripled off the top of the right-field wall and, after an intentional walk, scored when shortstop Kurt Stillwell hit the first pitch up the middle for a single.

Baltimore lost five games by one run, five by two runs, three by three runs, one by four, two by both five and six runs, one by eleven runs, and one by twelve runs.

After the twenty-first straight defeat, the Orioles trailed Cleveland by sixteen games in the Eastern Division.

The most losses at the start of a season previously were thirteen. The 1904 Washington Senators and the 1920 Detroit Tigers lost thirteen in the American League, and the Atlanta Braves lost the first thirteen in 1982.

1906 Boston Red Sox

20 Consecutive Losses

The Boston Red Sox won American League pennants in 1903 and 1904, fell down to fourth place in 1905, and dropped all the way to last place in 1906, although they still had the nucleus of their pennant-winning teams on their roster.

Boston's three top pitchers in 1904 — left-hander Jesse Tannehill and right-handers Cy Young and Bill Dinneen — each won more than twenty games that year, and they were the three top starters in 1906. In addition, the double play combination of second baseman Hobe Ferris and shortstop Freddy Parent, as well as center fielder Chick Stahl, were also on both clubs.

In 1906 Boston, also known as the Puritans, won only two home games in April and finished that first month of the season with a 6–7 record in a three-way tie for fifth place, two games behind first-place Philadelphia.

On April 30 at New York, Boston pounded out twenty-three hits off right-hander Jack Chesbro and left-hander Doc Newton to bury the home club, 13–4, scoring nine runs in the ninth inning. Tannehill and right-hander George Winter, who relieved in the sixth after Boston had taken a 4–3 lead, held New York to seven hits, although five of the seven were extra-base hits.

The losing streak began the next day at New York's Hilltop Park and then continued for nineteen more games, all in Boston, for the longest losing streak at home in major league history. Instead of the expected climb in the standings that lasted from May 2 through June 2, Boston became the first major league team in the twentieth century to lose more than fifteen games in succession.

1. Tuesday, May 1

| Boston | 000 000 000 | 0 | 1 | 1 |
| New York | 010 021 22x | 8 | 9 | 3 |

WP **Hogg**; LP **Gibson**

2. Wednesday, May 2

| Washington | 200 000 010 | 3 | 9 | 1 |
| Boston | 000 100 001 | 2 | 9 | 1 |

WP **Patten**; LP **Young**, Winter (9)

3. Thursday, May 3

| Washington | 003 030 000 | 6 | 9 | 1 |
| Boston | 010 100 110 | 4 | 8 | 3 |

WP **Kitson**; LP **Winter**, Harris (6)

4. Friday, May 4

| Washington | 102 000 010 | 4 | 9 | 4 |
| Boston | 000 020 000 | 2 | 8 | 1 |

WP **Hughes**; LP **Dinneen**

5. Monday, May 7

| Philadelphia | 100 111 000 | 4 | 8 | 2 |
| Boston | 000 000 000 | 0 | 7 | 1 |

WP **Waddell**; LP **Winter**

6. Tuesday, May 8

| Philadelphia | 000 012 107 | 11 | 20 | 3 |
| Boston | 000 100 030 | 4 | 8 | 2 |

WP **Coakley**; LP **Tannehill**

7. Wednesday, May 9

| Philadelphia | 100 040 400 | 9 | 13 | 3 |
| Boston | 100 002 210 | 6 | 12 | 2 |

WP **Plank**; LP **Young**

8. Thursday, May 10

| Philadelphia | 001 200 020 | 5 | 9 | 0 |
| Boston | 000 001 000 | 1 | 10 | 5 |

WP **Bender**; LP **Harris**

9. Friday, May 11

| St. Louis | 010 000 421 | 8 | 9 | 1 |
| Boston | 001 010 100 | 3 | 6 | 4 |

WP **Smith**; LP **Dinneen**

10. Saturday, May 12

| St. Louis | 210 000 060 | 9 | 11 | 1 |
| Boston | 100 000 000 | 1 | 5 | 2 |

WP **Glade**; LP **Gibson**, Winter (2)

11. Monday, May 14

| St. Louis | 003 110 303 | 11 | 15 | 2 |
| Boston | 000 000 100 | 1 | 6 | 3 |

WP **Howell**; LP **Young**

12. Tuesday, May 15

| St. Louis | 202 010 022 | 9 | 15 | 2 |
| Boston | 000 410 000 | 5 | 10 | 3 |

WP **Jacobson**; LP **Tannehill**

13. Wednesday, May 16

| Cleveland | 000 060 100 | 7 | 7 | 1 |
| Boston | 001 000 122 | 6 | 10 | 2 |

WP **Rhoads**; LP **Winter**

14. Thursday, May 17

| Cleveland | 010 000 033 | 7 | 12 | 0 |
| Boston | 020 110 000 | 4 | 9 | 2 |

WP **Hess**; LP **Harris**

15. Friday, May 18

| Cleveland | 260 000 051 | 14 | 21 | 1 |
| Boston | 000 000 100 | 1 | 5 | 5 |

WP **Joss**; LP **Dinneen**, Gibson (2), Hughes (3)

16. Saturday, May 19

| Cleveland | 000 002 001 | 3 | 10 | 0 |
| Boston | 000 000 200 | 2 | 5 | 3 |

WP **Bernhard**; LP **Young**

17. Monday, May 21

Detroit	110 000 000	2	9	3
Boston	000 001 000	1	6	3

WP **Mullin**; LP **Winter**

18. Tuesday, May 22

Detroit	010 100 112	6	9	2
Boston	000 100 020	3	10	3

WP **Siever**; LP **Harris**

19. Wednesday, May 23

Detroit	002 010 000	3	8	2
Boston	110 000 000	2	9	2

WP **Killian**; LP **Dinneen**

20. Thursday, May 24

Chicago	400 000 300	7	12	4
Boston	001 001 210	5	9	2

WP **Altrock**; LP **Young**, Winter (1)

The losing streak ended the next afternoon at Boston's Huntington Avenue Grounds.

Friday, May 25

Chicago	000 000 000	0	3	2
Boston	010 200 00x	3	4	3

WP **Tannehill**; LP **White**

Tannehill, the last pitcher to win for Boston, pitched a brilliant one-walk three-hitter for his second and last shutout of the season. Chicago's only hits were singles by first baseman Jiggs Donahue and second baseman Frank Isbell, and a double by outfielder Bill O'Neill, who was out trying for a triple in the third. Catcher Bob Peterson, who batted in only nine runs for the season, knocked in the three Boston runs in this game. He singled between shortstop and third base to score third baseman John Godwin after two errors in the second, and singled through the same hole after a leadoff single by first baseman Moose Grimshaw, a two-out single by outfielder Buck Freeman, and a walk to Ferris had loaded the bases.

After the twentieth loss in a row, Boston was in eighth place with a 6–27 record, eight games behind seventh-place Washington and sixteen games in back of first-place Philadelphia.

During the losing streak, the opposition averaged 6.8 runs and 11.2 hits to 2.7 runs and 7.1 hits for Boston. The Red Sox, shut out only twice, lost five games by one run; three by two, three, and four runs; one by five runs; one by seven runs; two by eight runs; one by ten runs; and one by thirteen runs.

Six pitchers lost games in the streak, with Young losing five, Dinneen and Winter four each, right-hander Joe Harris three, and right-

Hall of Fame third baseman Jimmy Collins, who managed the Boston Red Sox in their first six seasons, was replaced late in the 1906 season, three months after the club lost a record twenty straight games. (Courtesy of National Baseball Library, Cooperstown, New York.)

hander Norwood Gibson and Tannehill two apiece. Boston lost to every team in the league, including four times to Philadelphia, St. Louis and Cleveland, three times to Washington and Detroit, and once to New York and pennant-bound Chicago.

The first game in the streak saw Boston get only one hit in an 8–0 loss on May 1 at New York. Parent's single to center with one out in the seventh prevented a no-hitter by right-hander Bill Hogg, who walked two in his 8–0 victory.

Boston led in six of the twenty games, two after the fifth inning, and lost three games in the ninth inning.

In Game 6 (May 8) at Boston, the Red Sox scored once in the fourth and three times in the eighth to tie, 4–4. Right-hander Chief Bender, who went to left field when Topsy Hartsel was injured by a foul tip, homered for Philadelphia's fourth run in the seventh and homered again as the visitors rallied for seven runs in the ninth inning to win, 11–4.

In Game 14 (May 17) at Boston, the Red Sox took a 4–1 lead in the fifth, helped by a two-run homer by Ferris in the second. Cleveland tied with three runs in the eighth on three singles and an error and an infield out, and won, 7–4, with three runs in the ninth on singles by left-hander Otto Hess and outfielder Elmer Flick, a fumbled grounder by third baseman Jimmy Collins, Boston's manager, shortstop Terry Turner's two-run single, and a single by first baseman Claude Rossman.

In Game 16 (May 19) at Boston, Cleveland scored twice in the sixth, and the Red Sox tied in the seventh on two walks, a sacrifice, and outfielder Kip Selbach's two-run single to left. Cleveland won, 3–2, in ninth on first baseman George Stovall's leadoff single, a sacrifice, and third baseman Bill Bradley's line single to center.

Boston improved only slightly for the rest of the season and Collins, who had managed the Red Sox since their inception in 1901, was replaced in the waning weeks of the season by Stahl, who managed the club for the final eighteen games, then committed suicide the next March.

Boston finished last with a 49–105 record, eight games behind seventh-place Washington and forty-five and one-half games in back of pennant-winning Chicago. Boston was last in pitching and fielding and sixth in batting. Grimshaw led the team with a .290 batting average, and Tannehill was the only pitcher with a winning record (13–11). Young also had thirteen wins, and he and Harris led the league in defeats with twenty-one. Six years later, Boston was back on top of the American League.

1916 Philadelphia Athletics
20 Consecutive Losses

Under Manager Connie Mack, the Philadelphia Athletics won six pennants in the first fourteen years of the American League, and four of them were in a five-year span from 1910 through 1914. After trading away several stars and losing some others to raids by the Federal League, Philadelphia fell all the way from first to last place in 1915.

Things went from bad to worse in 1916. By the middle of June, Philadelphia was in eighth place to stay. On July 11, right-hander Bullet Joe Bush shut out St. Louis, 3–0, in the second game of a home double-header to end a twelve-game losing streak by Philadelphia. The Athletics lost the next nine games in a row before Bush pitched a three-hit shutout to beat Cleveland, 2–0, in a second game of a July 20 home doubleheader. The two runs scored in the sixth on a two-base error, a run-scoring double to center field by outfielder Amos Strunk, an infield hit and a squeeze bunt by first baseman Stuffy McInnis.

After that victory, Philadelphia was in last place with a 19–60 record, fifteen games behind seventh-place St. Louis and twenty-seven and one-half games in back of first-place New York. The next afternoon at Philadelphia's Shibe Park, the Athletics began the twenty-game losing streak that tied the American League record. That streak has been exceeded only twice in post-1900 major league history.

1. Friday, July 21

Cleveland	042 000 010	7	11	0
Philadelphia	010 000 001	2	7	4

WP **Coumbe**; LP **Nabors**

2. Tuesday, July 25

Philadelphia	000 002 001	3	10	1
St. Louis	060 020 00x	8	14	0

WP **Koob**; LP **Lanning**, Sheehan (2)

3. Wednesday, July 26[1]

Philadelphia	000	000	000	0	10	0
St. Louis	100	100	03x	5	6	0

WP **Weilman**; LP **Myers**

4. Wednesday, July 26[2]

Philadelphia	000	000	100	1	6	1
St. Louis	210	020	00x	5	7	3

WP **Davenport**; LP **Bush**, Lanning (2)

5. Thursday, July 27

Philadelphia	000	001	010	2	11	1
St. Louis	001	000	02x	3	6	1

WP **Hamilton**, Groom (9); LP **Nabors**

6. Friday, July 28

Philadelphia	000	200	004	6	11	5
St. Louis	240	200	00x	8	7	2

WP **Groom**, Koob (9); LP **Sheehan**

7. Saturday, July 29[1]

Philadelphia	000	001	000	1	6	5
Chicago	221	001	00x	6	5	0

WP **Faber**; LP **Myers**

8. Saturday, July 29[2]

Philadelphia	000	000	013	4	5	2
Chicago	201	000	03x	6	9	2

WP **Benz**, Russell (9), Cicotte (9); LP **Bush**

9. Sunday, July 30[1]

Philadelphia	100	000	000	1	6	1
Chicago	052	002	10x	10	19	0

WP **Cicotte**; LP **Lanning**

10. Sunday, July 30[2]

Philadelphia	000	000	000	0	7	0
Chicago	100	006	00x	7	7	0

WP **Wolfgang**; LP **Williams**

11. Monday, July 31

Philadelphia	000	000	030	00	3 8 2
Chicago	000	200	100	01	4 10 0

WP Williams, **Faber** (8); LP Sheehan, **Bush** (8) (11 innings)

12. Tuesday, August 1[1]

Philadelphia	000	000	000	0	6	1
Chicago	001	000	02x	3	7	4

WP **Russell**; LP **Nabors**

13. Tuesday, August 1[2]

Philadelphia	000	100	100	2	9	0
Chicago	000	021	00x	3	7	4

WP Scott, **Danforth** (4); LP **Myers**

14. Wednesday, August 2

Philadelphia	100	100	000	2	7	0
Chicago	000	205	01x	8	13	1

WP Cicotte, **Benz** (5); LP **Johnson**, Williams (5), Lanning (7)

15. Thursday, August 3

Philadelphia	000	000	001	1	7	1
Cleveland	002	000	01x	3	6	1

WP **Bagby**; LP **Bush**

16. Friday, August 4

Philadelphia	000	100	010	2	9	1
Cleveland	040	000	01x	5	9	1

WP **Beebe**; LP **Sheehan**, Williams (3)

17. Saturday, August 5

Philadelphia	000	120	000	3	9	1
Cleveland	211	411	20x	12	16	1

WP **Coveleski**, Lambeth (6); LP **Johnson**, Lanning (4), Sheehan (5)

18. Sunday, August 6

Philadelphia	000	002	000	2	9	2
Cleveland	000	120	11x	5	11	0

WP **Morton**, Klepfer (8); LP **Nabors**, **Myers** (4), Bush (7)

---

[1]*First game of a doubleheader.* [2]*Second game of a doubleheader.*

19. Monday, August 7				
Philadelphia	100 000 100	2	6	2
Detroit	020 002 00x	4	5	1

WP **Coveleski**; LP **Myers**

20. Tuesday, August 8				
Philadelphia	000 000 000	0	6	2
Detroit	120 010 32x	9	17	0

WP **Boland**; LP **Nabors**

The losing streak ended the next afternoon at Detroit's Navin Field.

Wednesday, August 9

Philadelphia	104 000 110	7	8	2
Detroit	000 000 001	1	4	2

WP **Bush**; LP **Dubuc**, Cunningham (4), Mitchell (8)

Philadelphia won its first game of the season in the West as Bush, who posted the only three A's victories in a stretch of forty-four games through this win, pitched a brilliant game. He held Detroit to two hits, both by outfielder Ty Cobb, until the ninth, when second baseman Pep Young bunted safely, catcher Red McKee hit a fly ball to right, and outfielder Jimmy Walsh fell down starting for the ball, which rolled away for a triple, preventing a shutout. For Philadelphia, second baseman Nap Lajoie singled across a run in the first, and in the four-run third, shortstop Whitey Witt tripled, Walsh and Strunk walked, and Detroit contributed some sloppy fielding. Witt walked and scored on a wild pitch in the seventh, and catcher Pat Haley doubled across an eighth-inning run.

After the twentieth straight defeat, Philadelphia was in eighth place with a 19–80 record, thirty games behind seventh-place Washington and thirty-eight and one-half games in back of first-place Chicago. During the streak, Philadelphia averaged 1.9 runs and 7.8 hits to 6.1 runs and 9.6 hits for the opposition. Four of the losses were shutouts, and the A's scored two runs or less in fifteen of the twenty games. They lost three games by one run, four by two runs, three by three runs, one by four runs, four by five runs, one each by six and seven runs, and three by nine runs.

Seven different pitchers lost games during the streak and, although Mack employed twenty pitchers that season, seven did all the pitching during the streak. Right-hander Elmer Myers lost five games, Bush and right-hander Jack Nabors lost four each, left-hander Les Lanning, right-handers Tom Sheehan and Jing Johnson lost two apiece, and right-hander Marsh Williams lost one. Bush and Myers each lost one game in relief.

Philadelphia led in only five games during the streak, once after the fourth inning and, with the final nineteen games being played on the road, the winning team batted only once in the final inning.

The A's best chance to win was in Game 5 (July 27) at St. Louis. After the home team scored in the third, the A's tied in the sixth when Strunk doubled, took third on an infield out, and scored on a sacrifice fly by McInnis, then took a 2–1 lead in the eighth when Strunk walked, stole second, and came home on Lajoie's double down the left-field line. St. Louis came back in the home eighth to win, 3–2, on a walk, a two-base error, and a two-run single to left by outfielder Ward Miller.

Philadelphia's only extra-inning loss was in Game 11 (July 31) at Chicago. Trailing 3–0 after seven innings, the A's tied in the eighth on two walks around a pinch single by catcher Val Picinich, a two-run single by Walsh, and a run-scoring single by Strunk. Chicago won in the eleventh after outfielder Happy Felsch, who had hit a two-run homer in the fourth, singled for his fourth hit. He reached third on an error but was out at home on a bunt before first baseman Jack Fournier batted for right-hander Red Faber and hit a two-out single to win the game, 4–3.

The other one-run loss was in Game 13 (August 1) at Chicago. Lajoie's double, an error, and Witt's single gave the A's a 1–0 lead in the fourth. Chicago put together a walk and singles by Felsch, catcher Jack Lapp, and third baseman Fred McMullin for two runs in the fifth, and second baseman Eddie Collins scored the final Chicago run in the sixth. The A's scored in the seventh when third baseman Charlie Pick singled, stole second, and scored on a single by Myers before left-hander Dave Danforth, who had relieved in the fourth, retired the side to preserve the 3–2 victory.

In desperation Mack decided to use his three best pitchers for three innings each in Game 18 (August 6) at Cleveland, but that failed to end the streak. Nabors pitched three scoreless innings at the start, but Myers gave up three runs in the middle three innings, and Bush yielded single runs in the seventh and eighth in the 5–2 loss.

Not much improved after the losing streak, and the A's finished last with a 36–117 record, setting a league record for defeats that still stands, and put them forty games behind seventh-place Washington and fifty-four and one-half games in back of first-place Boston.

Philadelphia finished last in batting (.242), last in fielding (.951), and last in pitching (3.84). Although Bush led the league with twenty-four defeats, he won fifteen games and was second in shutouts with eight, including a no-hitter against Cleveland on August 26. Myers won fourteen and lost twenty-three, and no other pitcher won more than two games. Strunk batted .316 to lead the hitters.

1943 Philadelphia Athletics

20 Consecutive Losses

In the American League's first thirty-one years, the Philadelphia Athletics won nine pennants, including three in a row from 1929 through 1931. Four years after the last championship, the A's finished last and were in the second division from 1934 through 1947, with nine eighth-place finishes in that span of fourteen seasons.

Philadelphia finished last for the third straight year in 1942, and there was no reason for optimism in 1943 after the team's best pitcher, right-hander Phil Marchildon, entered the Canadian Air Force. Young outfielder Elmer Valo also went into the service in midseason of 1943, but all the clubs were losing players to service calls.

The A's lost its season opener in Washington but, helped by right-hander Don Black's one-hit shutout of St. Louis, held third place at the end of May with a 19–17 record, only two games behind first-place New York.

A loss June 30 at St. Louis dropped the A's into the cellar, one-half game from seventh and seven and one-half games behind New York. An eight-game losing streak that ended July 24 dropped them lower, and they were nineteen games back at the end of July and nine and one-half games behind seventh-place St. Louis.

The second game the A's won in August was a 4–0 shutout over New York at home on August 6 as right-hander Roger Wolff pitched an eight-hitter and was especially effective over the final five innings. Three singles, a stolen base and a passed ball helped the A's score twice in the first inning off left-hander Marius Russo. Philadelphia added a run in the third, and second baseman Pete Suder homered for the fourth run in the sixth.

The victory gave the last-place A's a 40–58 record that left them four games from seventh place and nineteen and one-half games from first place. The twenty-game losing streak began the next afternoon at Philadelphia's Shibe Park.

1. Saturday, August 7

New York	010 002 000	3	8	1
Philadelphia	000 100 000	1	5	3

WP **Wensloff**; LP **Black**

2. Sunday, August 8[1]

New York	001 111 102	7	8	2
Philadelphia	100 000 000	1	5	0

WP **Chandler**; LP **Harris**, Fagan (9)

3. Sunday, August 8[2]

New York	000 010 030 4	8	9	1
Philadelphia	100 020 010 0	4	10	0

WP Bonham, **Murphy** (8), Zuber (10); LP Flores, Black (8), **Wolff** (8) (10 innings)

4. Wednesday, August 11[1]

Philadelphia	000 031 100	5	10	1
Cleveland	051 010 03x	10	13	1

WP **Reynolds**, Heving (7); LP **Ciola**

5. Wednesday, August 11[2]

Philadelphia	000 100 000	1	2	2
Cleveland	010 000 01x	2	3	0

WP **Smith**; LP Wolff, **Flores** (8)

6. Thursday, August 12

Philadelphia	000 100 002	3	10	0
Cleveland	100 001 02x	4	10	3

WP **Bagby**, Heving (9); LP **Arntzen**

7. Friday, August 13

Philadelphia	100 020 100	4	8	1
Cleveland	000 300 30x	6	10	2

WP **Harder**, Reynolds (9); LP **Black**

8. Saturday, August 14

Philadelphia	001 042 011	9	12	2
Cleveland	021 600 30x	12	17	0

WP **Dean**, Naymick (5), Salveson (6), Heving (6); LP **Fagan**, Ciola (4)

9. Sunday, August 15[1]

Philadelphia	020 020 000 00	4	10	3
Detroit	200 100 010 01	5	9	2

WP Trucks, **Trout** (8); LP **Harris** (11 innings)

10. Sunday, August 15[2]

Philadelphia	000 001 010	2	6	0
Detroit	010 101 00x	3	8	2

WP **Bridges**; LP **Wolff**, Arntzen (8)

11. Tuesday, August 17

Philadelphia	000 000 003	3	6	1
Detroit	010 110 10x	4	13	0

WP **Trout**, Gorsica (9); LP **Flores**

12. Wednesday, August 18

Philadelphia	000 000 000	0	5	0
St. Louis	010 012 00x	4	10	0

WP **Muncrief**; LP **Arntzen**

13. Thursday, August 19

Philadelphia	000 000 000	0	4	2
St. Louis	010 020 00x	3	5	1

WP **Galehouse**; LP **Black**

14. Saturday, August 21[1]

Philadelphia	201 000 000	3	9	0
St. Louis	012 010 10x	5	10	2

WP **Sundra**; LP **Harris**

[1]*First game of a doubleheader.* [2]*Second game of a doubleheader.*

15. Saturday, August 21[2]

Philadelphia	010 000 000	1	9	0
St. Louis	010 100 20x	4	10	0

WP **Newsom**, Caster (9); LP **Wolff**, Ciola (8)

16. Sunday, August 22[1]

Philadelphia	000 100 010	2	6	0
Chicago	002 002 10x	5	9	2

WP **Smith**, Maltzberger (9); LP **Mains**

17. Sunday, August 22[2]

Philadelphia	100 000 100	2	9	1
Chicago	200 000 001	3	6	1

WP **Humphries**; LP **Flores**

18. Monday, August 23[1]

Philadelphia	100 120 002	6	11	3
Chicago	001 300 003	7	7	1

WP Lee, **Maltzberger** (6); LP **Ciola**, Christopher (9)

19. Monday, August 23[2]

Philadelphia	000 000 000	0	6	2
Chicago	000 020 50x	7	8	0

WP **Grove**; LP **Black**

20. Tuesday, August 24[1]

Philadelphia	102 020 000	5	11	1
Chicago	103 000 002	6	11	1

WP **Ross**; LP **Harris**

The losing streak ended in the night game of the twilight-night doubleheader, the seventh twin bill played by the Athletics during the streak, at Chicago's Comiskey Park.

Tuesday, August 24[2]

Philadelphia	008 000 000	8	9	1
Chicago	000 000 010	1	8	4

WP **Wolff**; LP **Dietrich**, Haynes (4)

Unusual play figured in Philadelphia's eight-run second-inning rally. After third baseman Eddie Mayo singled, Wolff bunted poorly to first baseman Joe Kuhel, whose throw to second to start what might have been a double play hit Umpire Cal Hubbard, and both men were safe. Right-hander Bill Dietrich then cracked wide open in an inning in which right fielder Jimmy Ripple hit three-run double and Wolff singled in a run. Wolff, the last A's pitcher to win a game, allowed only an unearned run in posting his ninth victory.

Philadelphia was in eighth place with a 40–78 record after its twentieth straight loss, thirteen and one-half games behind seventh-place St. Louis and thirty-two and one-half in back of league-leading New York.

During the losing streak, Philadelphia averaged 2.8 runs and 7.7 hits to 5.4 runs and 9.2 hits for the opposition. Cleveland and Chicago won five games apiece from the A's, St. Louis won four, and New York

[1]First game of a doubleheader. [2]Second game of a doubleheader.

and Detroit three each, both winning an extra-inning game. Eight of the losses were in one-run games, three were lost by two runs, four by three runs, two by four runs, and one each by five, six, and seven runs. The A's were shut out three times, and seventeen of their twenty losses were on the road.

Strangely enough, nineteen different pitchers beat Philadelphia during the losing streak, with Detroit right-hander Dizzy Trout, who won Game 9 (August 15) in relief and Game 11 (August 17) as a starter, the only double winner. Eight different pitchers lost games for the A's. Black lost four complete games, and right-hander Lum Harris, who had three complete games, also lost four. Wolff and right-hander Jesse Flores lost three apiece, right-handers Louis Ciola and Arnie Arntzen each lost two, and right-handers Everett Fagan and Jim Mains lost the other two games.

Philadelphia lost two games in extra innings and three in the last of the ninth.

The first overtime win was in Game 3 (August 8) when New York snapped a 4–4 tie with four runs in the tenth to win, 8–4. Pinch-hitter Ken Sears and shortstop Frankie Crosetti hit run-scoring singles, and first baseman Nick Etten hit a two-run double in the extra inning.

One week later in Game 9 (August 15), the A's had a 4–3 lead until shortstop Joe Hoover homered in the Detroit eighth to tie the score. With two out in the eleventh, first baseman Rudy York hit his ninth homer in the last nine games to give the Tigers a 5–4 victory.

Third baseman Tony Cuccinello led off the last of the ninth inning with a home run, to give Chicago a 3–2 win over the A's in Game 17 (August 22), and in Game 18 (August 23) right-hander Russ Christopher walked right-hander Gordon Maltzberger with the bases loaded and two out to cap a three-run rally and give Chicago a 7–6 win after White Sox outfielder Guy Cutright had hit a two-run homer to tie the score.

The next night in Game 20 (August 24), outfielder Ralph Hodgin doubled to right center to bat in the tying run with two out in the ninth, and Cutright followed with a single to center to win the game for Chicago, 6–5.

Philadelphia won only nine of its last thirty-six games and finished eighth with a 49–105 record, forty-nine games in back of pennant-winning New York, for their poorest record since 1920. The A's were last in batting, in runs scored, and in pitching. No regular hit as high as .260, and Flores, who had a 12–14 record, was the lone pitcher to win more than ten games. Harris led the league in losses with twenty-one.

1969 Montreal Expos

20 Consecutive Losses

The National League, which expanded from eight to ten teams before the 1962 season, expanded again before the 1969 season, adding the San Diego Padres and the Montreal Expos, and splitting the league into Eastern and Western Divisions of six teams each.

In the expansion draft, Montreal selected a mixture of veterans and youngsters from the other ten teams to play under Manager Gene Mauch, who had managed the Philadelphia Phillies from 1960 until June of 1968.

Montreal won the first game in its history, taking an 11–10 decision on April 8, 1969, at New York from the eventual champion Mets. But the Expos finished April with a 7–13 record that put them in last place in the East.

In May Montreal broke even in its first eight games, posting the fourth win by beating visiting Cincinnati, 7–6, on May 10 when second baseman Gary Sutherland hit a two-run single in the three-run eighth to give the Expos a one-run lead and then eventually scored the winning run on a wild pitch. Left-hander Dan McGinn was the winning pitcher, hurling two hitless innings in relief before being lifted for a pinch-hitter in the winning rally in the eighth.

After a rainout and an open date, Montreal began the second longest losing streak in National League history at Montreal's Jarry Park on May 13, resting in sixth place in the Eastern Division with an 11–17 record, eight games behind first-place Chicago.

1. Tuesday, May 13

Houston	015 000 040	10	8	2
Montreal	110 100 000	3	9	3

WP Griffin, Quinn (2), Womack (2), Coombs (4), **Billingham** (5); LP Wegener, Face (1), **McGinn** (3), Robertson (4), Jaster (6), Shaw (9)

2. Wednesday, May 14

Houston	001 000 020	3	7	0
Montreal	010 000 000	1	5	2

WP **Lemaster**; LP **Grant**

3. Friday, May 16

Atlanta	000 014 000 002	7	12	1
Montreal	000 210 020 000	5	10	2

WP Pappas, Johnson (6), **Raymond** (11); LP Stoneman, McGinn (7), **Face** (12) (12 innings)

4. Sunday, May 18

Atlanta	103 000 40	8	9	1
Montreal	001 020 0x	3	8	2

WP **Reed**; LP **Wegener**, Shea (3), Robertson (7), Face (7), Sembera (8) (Rain ended game with one out in top of eighth inning.)

5. Tuesday, May 20

Montreal	000 000 000	0	4	3
Houston	202 010 00x	5	8	0

WP **Dierker**; LP **Grant**, Wegener (5), Shea (5), Sembera (8)

6. Wednesday, May 21

Montreal	000 100 010	2	9	0
Houston	011 001 00x	3	7	1

WP **Lemaster**, Gladding (9); LP **Stoneman**, McGinn (6), Shaw (8)

7. Thursday, May 22

Montreal	000 300 001	4	8	1
Houston	230 000 20x	7	8	3

WP **Wilson**; LP **Jaster**, Shea (2), Sembera (3), Shaw (5), Face (7)

8. Friday, May 23

Montreal	010 200 000	3	4	2
Cincinnati	010 000 12x	4	9	1

WP Maloney, Granger (5), **Carroll** (8); LP Robertson, **McGinn** (7), Sembera (8)

9. Saturday, May 24

Montreal	000 000 200	2	8	2
Cincinnati	420 014 00x	11	15	0

WP **Cloninger**; LP **Grant**, Shea (1), Shaw (3), Jaster (4), Face (7)

10. Sunday, May 25

Montreal	010 000 010	2	10	1
Cincinnati	103 011 10x	7	8	1

WP **Merritt**, Carroll (9); LP **Stoneman**, Sembera (7)

11. Tuesday, May 27

Los Angeles	100 022 000	5	7	1
Montreal	000 030 000	3	4	1

WP **Singer**; LP Jaster, **McGinn** (6), Shaw (8)

12. Wednesday, May 28

Los Angeles	201 010 101	6	12	1
Montreal	000 000 000	0	5	2

WP **Sutton**; LP **Robertson**, Shaw (4), Sembera (6), Shea (9)

13. Thursday, May 29

Los Angeles	301 010 000	5	5	1
Montreal	000 010 002	3	6	3

WP **Osteen**; LP **Stoneman**, Face (6), Shaw (9)

14. Friday, May 30

San Diego	001 000 010 1	3	5	1
Montreal	000 010 010 0	2	11	3

WP Kelley, Ross (7), McCool (8), Sisk (8), **Baldschun** (9); LP Wegener, **McGinn** (10), Face (10) (10 innings)

15. Saturday, May 31

San Diego	100	202	100	6	11	1
Montreal	000	000	200	2	5	0

WP **Niekro**; LP **Jaster**, Sembera (4), Shea (7), Grant (9)

16. Sunday, June 1

San Diego	010	011	020	5	8	1
Montreal	010	000	010	2	7	1

WP **Podres**, Sisk (8); LP **Robertson**, Face (6), McGinn (8)

17. Tuesday, June 3

San Francisco	005	301	000	9	10	3
Montreal	100	110	000	3	10	2

WP **Sadecki**, Linzy (8); LP **Stoneman**, Shaw (4), Sembera (5), McGinn (7), Face (9)

18. Wednesday, June 4

San Francisco	000	500	003	8	12	0
Montreal	021	000	000	3	8	2

WP **McCormick**, Linzy (9); LP **Wegener**, McGinn (5), Face (8), Shaw (9)

19. Friday, June 6

Montreal	000	020	000	2	7	1
Los Angeles	100	002	10x	4	6	0

WP **Sutton**, Brewer (9); LP **McGinn**, Waslewski (7), Shaw (7)

20. Saturday, June 7

Montreal	030	000	011	5	11	3
Los Angeles	241	001	10x	9	14	2

WP **Osteen**; LP Martentette, **Stoneman** (3), Reed (5), Shaw (6), Jaster (7)

The losing streak ended the next afternoon against Los Angeles in Dodger Stadium.

Sunday, June 8

Montreal	000	301	000	4	6	1
Los Angeles	000	010	002	3	5	0

WP **Robertson**, Face (9); LP **Singer**, Foster (8)

Montreal scored three runs in the third inning when outfielder Rusty Staub homered with shortstop Maury Wills on base and outfielder Mack Jones came home on an out by Sutherland, and added what proved to be the winning run in the sixth when Jones hit his tenth homer of the season. Montreal right-hander Jerry Robertson gave up a run in the fifth, but was working on a two-hitter until the ninth when two hits with none out brought on right-hander Roy Face in relief. He walked second baseman Jim Lefebvre and gave up a run-scoring single to outfielder Ron Fairly, then balked home the game's final run before retiring pinch-hitter Ken Boyer and outfielder Willie Crawford to end the game and the losing streak.

After the twentieth straight defeat, Montreal was in last place in the

Eastern Division with an 11–37 record, seven games behind fifth-place Philadelphia and twenty-three games in back of first-place Chicago.

During the streak, Montreal averaged 2.5 runs and 7.5 hits to 6.3 runs and 9.1 hits for the opposition, which hit thirty homers to twelve for the Expos. Three of the twenty defeats were by one run, five by two runs, two by three runs and by four runs, four by five runs, two by six runs, one by seven runs, and one by nine runs. Two of the losses were shutouts.

McGinn and right-hander Bill Stoneman each lost five games, right-hander Mudcat Grant lost three, right-hander Mike Wegener, Robertson, and left-hander Larry Jaster lost two apiece, and Face lost one. Grant pitched the only complete game, while four of McGinn's losses, one of Stoneman's, and the one by Face were lost in relief. Mauch employed a total of thirteen pitchers and made fifty-four pitching changes in the twenty games, all of which were lost to Western Division teams, Houston and Los Angeles each winning five.

Montreal led in eight of the games, three of them past midgame, and was beaten three times in the winning team's last time at bat, including once in the twelfth inning and once in the tenth.

In Game 3 (May 16) at Montreal, Atlanta took a 5–3 lead in the four-run sixth inning when outfielder Rico Carty batted for right-hander Milt Pappas and hit a three-run homer off Stoneman. Two Montreal runs scored on third baseman Coco Laboy's homer and the Expos scored twice in the eighth to tie. The Braves won, 7–5, in the twelfth, when outfielder Tito Francona hit a two-out, two-run homer off Face, his first of the season.

Montreal's best chance for a victory was in Game 8 (May 23) at Cincinnati. Jones homered in the second and scored along with Staub in the fourth when the Expos took a 3–1 lead. Catcher Johnny Bench homered for one Cincinnati run, shortstop Chico Ruiz hit a sacrifice fly to drive in another, and second baseman Tommy Helms doubled off McGinn with the bases loaded in the eighth to drive in the tying and winning runs in the 4–3 win.

Montreal's other extra-inning defeat was in Game 14 (May 30) at home against San Diego. Errors helped the Padres score an unearned run in both the third and eighth off Wegener, while Sutherland scored one Montreal run and catcher John Boccabella's only homer of the season produced the other. In the tenth inning, second baseman John Sipin hit the first homer of his major league career off McGinn to win the game, 3–2.

In the twentieth loss (June 7) at Los Angeles, the Dodgers scored twice in the first, and the Expos parlayed two errors, three singles, and catcher Ron Brand's sacrifice fly into a 3–2 lead in the second. But outfielder Andy Kosco's three-run homer highlighted a four-run Dodger second and Los Angeles went on to win, 9–5.

That loss made Mauch the only man in major league history to manage two teams that lost twenty or more games in succession. In 1961 his Philadelphia team lost twenty-three in a row.

Later in 1969 Montreal had two seven-game losing streaks and finished with a 52–110 record in sixth place, eleven games behind fifth-place Philadelphia and forty-eight games in back of first-place Chicago. Montreal finished eleventh in the league in batting (.240), last in pitching (4.33), and last in fielding (.971). Staub's .302 average and twenty-nine homers led the club, as did Laboy's eighty-three runs batted in. Stoneman was the only pitcher to win more than seven games. He won eleven, with five shutouts, including an April 17 no-hitter at Philadelphia. It was 1979 before Montreal won more games than it lost.

1906 Boston Braves

19 Consecutive Losses

From 1876 through 1898, the Boston Braves were baseball's most successful franchise, winning eight National League pennants and finishing in the first division seventeen times in twenty-three seasons. From then until they moved to Milwaukee in the spring of 1953, however, the Braves finished in first place only in 1914 and 1948, and in thirty-nine of those fifty-four years they finished in the second division.

Boston finished seventh in 1904, and again in 1905, when first baseman Fred Tenney became manager of the club, then hit bottom in 1906 when four of its pitchers were twenty-game losers for the second straight season.

In 1906 Boston posted a 7–8 record in April and lost eight of its first twelve games in May. Then, on May 16, the Braves, then also known as the Beaneaters, edged the Cincinnati Reds, 6–5. Right-hander Gus Dorner, sold to Boston by Cincinnati three days before, was the winning pitcher despite issuing eight walks. Catcher Tom Needham's only home run of the season, a drive that bounced into the center-field bleachers, accounted for the winning run in the sixth inning.

That win was Boston's twelfth victory against sixteen defeats, a record that had the Braves in sixth place, eight and one-half games behind first-place Chicago.

The long losing streak began the next afternoon at Cincinnati's Redland Field, exactly one week before the other Boston team, the American League Red Sox, completed a then-modern-record twenty-game losing streak.

1. Thursday, May 17

Boston	000 000 000	0	3	0
Cincinnati	001 100 00x	2	6	2

WP **Weimer**; LP **Lindaman**

2. Friday, May 18

Boston	110 000 130	6	9	3
Cincinnati	000 300 40x	7	9	2

WP **Overall**, Chech (9); LP **Pfeffer**

3. Saturday, May 19

Boston	000 000 000	0	8	3
Cincinnati	015 400 50x	15	19	2

WP **Fraser**; LP **Young**, Witherup (4)

4. Monday, May 21

Boston	000 000 000	0	7	1
Pittsburgh	012 000 14x	8	14	0

WP **Willis**; LP **Young**

5. Tuesday, May 22

Boston	000 000 000	0	9	1
Pittsburgh	010 000 00x	1	4	0

WP **Leever**; LP **Dorner**

6. Wednesday, May 23

Boston	000 000 000	0	8	1
Pittsburgh	000 000 50x	5	8	0

WP **Leifield**; LP **Lindaman**

7. Thursday, May 24

Boston	010 120 100	5	10	2
Pittsburgh	000 020 40x	6	8	2

WP Phillippe, **Karger** (6); LP **Pfeffer**, Dorner (7)

8. Friday, May 25

Boston	000 000 010	1	4	1
Chicago	000 002 00x	2	7	1

WP **Pfeister**; LP **Young**

9. Saturday, May 26

Boston	000 130 000	4	8	5
Chicago	210 003 30x	9	9	2

WP **Beebe**; LP **Dorner**

10. Monday, May 28

Boston	020 000 000	2	8	2
Chicago	101 000 02x	4	9	2

WP **Brown**; LP **Lindaman**

11. Wednesday, May 30

Boston	000 020 000	2	4	4
Philadelphia	010 100 50x	7	13	0

WP **Sparks**; LP **Pfeffer** (morning game)

12. Wednesday, May 30

Boston	000 000 000	0	1	1
Philadelphia	000 120 00x	3	9	1

WP **Lush**; LP **Young** (afternoon game)

13. Thursday, May 31

Boston	000 000 000	0	3	2
Brooklyn	000 001 00x	1	3	1

WP **Eason**; LP **Dorner**

14. Friday, June 1

Boston	000 000 000	0	4	4
Brooklyn	103 100 00x	5	10	0

WP **Stricklett**; LP **Lindaman**, Witherup (4)

15. Saturday, June 2

Boston	100 000 000	1	6	2
Brooklyn	000 001 001	2	5	2

WP **Pastorius**; LP **Young**

16. Sunday, June 3

Boston	001 000 000	1	5	1
Brooklyn	200 000 01x	3	6	0

WP McIntire, **Scanlan** (4); LP **Pfeffer**

17. Tuesday, June 5						**18. Wednesday, June 6**				
Pittsburgh	212 030 001	9	12	4		Pittsburgh	024 000 200	8	6	0
Boston	100 200 000	3	7	5		Boston	000 000 000	0	2	4

WP **Leever**; LP **Dorner**, Lindaman (6)   WP **Leifield**; LP **Young**

19. Friday, June 8

Pittsburgh	331 300 000	10	19	1
Boston	001 020 100	4	15	3

WP **Phillippe**; LP **Pfeffer**, Witherup (3)

The losing streak ended the next afternoon at Boston's South End Grounds.

Saturday, June 9

St. Louis	000 101 010	3	8	4
Boston	010 203 00x	6	9	1

WP **Dorner**; LP **Karger**, Brown (7)

Outfielder Cozy Dolan singled and scored for Boston in the second inning on an infield out and a wild throw, but St. Louis tied in the fourth. Outfielder Homer Smoot doubled and was thrown out at the plate on a single by first baseman Jake Beckley, who scored on a single by third baseman Art Hoelskoetter. A walk, a hit batsman, a sacrifice, and singles by catcher Sam Brown and shortstop Allie Strobel gave Boston a 3–1 lead in the fourth. Three more runs scored in the sixth on singles by Dolan and Dorner around Strobel's triple, an error, a hit batsman, and third baseman Dave Brain's single. For St. Louis, Smoot singled home a sixth-inning run and doubled across the game's final run in the eighth, but Dorner, the last Boston pitcher to win a game, went the route for the victory.

After the nineteenth consecutive loss, at the time the longest National League losing streak after 1900, Boston was in eighth place with a 12–35 record, six games behind seventh-place Cincinnati and twenty and one-half games in back of first-place Chicago. During the losing streak, Boston's opponents averaged 5.6 runs and 9.3 hits to 1.5 runs and 6.4 hits for the Braves. Shut out nine times during the streak, Boston lost six games by one run, three by two runs, one by three runs, four by five runs, two by six runs, two by eight runs, and one by fifteen runs.

Boston employed only five pitchers during the losing streak, and just four had decisions. Left-hander Irv Young lost six games, and Boston scored a total of just two runs in those six losses. Right-hander Big Jeff Pfeffer lost five, and Dorner and right-hander Vive Lindaman each lost four. Dorner and Lindaman were employed once each in relief, and right-hander Roy Witherup relieved three times. Seven of the losses were to Pittsburgh, four to Brooklyn, three each to Cincinnati and Chicago, and two to Philadelphia.

Four of the nine shutouts were to Pittsburgh, five of the shutouts came in the streak's first six games, and four of the nine were to left-handed pitchers, including two to Pittsburgh's Lefty Leifield. Philadelphia left-hander Johnny Lush, who had pitched a no-hit game at Brooklyn on May 1, narrowly missed another in Game 12 (May 30). A double to left by Brain in the fifth inning was Boston's lone hit in a 3–0 defeat.

Boston led in only five of the nineteen losses, but in only one after the fifth inning. In the first sixteen games, all of which were on the road, only once did the winning team bat in the ninth inning.

That was in Game 15 (June 2) at Brooklyn. Boston ended a scoreless streak of thirty-one straight innings by scoring once in the first on two hits. They were a single by shortstop Al Bridwell, a force, and a single by outfielder Johnny Bates. Then, outfielder Del Howard grounded to shortstop for the second out, and, after taking the throw, first baseman Tim Jordan threw to third, trapping Dolan off the bag. In the rundown, catcher Lew Ritter threw the ball away for an error. Brooklyn tied in the sixth on a fumble by Bridwell and outfielder Harry Lumley's triple to center. In the ninth Brooklyn won, 3–2, when outfielder Emil Batch bunted safely, took second on a sacrifice, and scored on Jordan's drive over the right-field wall. Under the rules at that time, Jordan was credited with only a double.

The biggest lead Boston enjoyed in the streak was in Game 7 (May 24) at Pittsburgh when the Braves had a 4–0 edge until the home fifth. In the second inning, Brain homered into the left-field bleachers to snap a Boston streak of thirty-eight straight scoreless innings, then a major league record. Howard tripled and Bates singled for a run in the fourth, and singles by catcher Jack O'Neill, Bridwell, and Dolan around two outs and an error gave Boston two more runs and a 4–0 lead in the fifth. Three singles and Brain's error gave Pittsburgh two runs in the fifth, and the Pirates won the game with four runs in the seventh after Tenney's bunt single, his steal of second, an error, and a squeeze bunt had given the Braves a 5–2 advantage in the top of that inning. Three singles by Pittsburgh, a walk, and a hit batsman produced three runs and finished Pfeffer. First baseman Jim Nealon then grounded to second and Strobel's wild throw allowed outfielder Dutch Meier to score with the run that won the game, 6–5.

Boston finished the season in eighth place with a 49–102 record, three and one-half games behind seventh-place St. Louis and sixty-six and one-half games in back of first-place Chicago, a modern major league record for games behind, which still stands. Only four pitchers won a game for Boston during the season, and all four ended up with more than twenty defeats. Boston was last in batting (.226), last in fielding (.947) and last in pitching (3.17). Manager Tenney was the team's leading hitter with a .283 average, and no other regular batted over .261.

Boston finished last four of the next seven years and did not have a winning record until 1914, when it jumped from fifth to first, coming from last place on July 4 to the league lead, and went on to win the world championship, earning the tag of "Miracle Braves."

1914 Cincinnati Reds

19 Consecutive Losses

The Cincinnati Reds became charter members of the National League in 1876 and, after finishing last in 1880, dropped out. They returned to stay in 1890, but it wasn't until their thirty-fifth season that they won a pennant. In the twentieth century, Cincinnati finished as high as third only once before 1918.

In 1913 Cincinnati finished seventh under Manager Joe Tinker, the Hall of Fame shortstop who had been traded by the Chicago Cubs after the 1912 season. The 1914 season brought a host of changes. One was another trade of Tinker, this time to Brooklyn, but Joe jumped to the Federal League. Another was with the New York Giants, which brought Buck Herzog to Cincinnati as the shortstop and manager of the Reds.

The changes didn't help the club's fortunes. On September 4 Cincinnati beat Chicago, 4–2, as right-hander Phil Douglas outpitched right-hander Larry Cheney and won when Cincinnati overcame Chicago's 2–1 lead with three runs in the home seventh, the tying and winning runs scoring on Cheney's wild throw on a bunt by Douglas. That win gave Cincinnati a record of fifty-six wins, sixty-five losses, and had the club in sixth place, twelve games behind first-place New York.

The longest losing streak in the long history of the Reds started the next afternoon at Cincinnati's Redland Field.

1. Saturday, September 5					
St. Louis	300 102 510	12	19	0
Cincinnati	002 000 000	2	8	3
WP **Perdue**; LP **Ames**, Fittery (8)					

2. Sunday, September 6					
St. Louis	003 000 121	7	13	1
Cincinnati	110 000 000	2	6	4
WP **Griner**; LP **Yingling**, Fahrer (9)					

94

3. Monday, September 7[1]

Cincinnati	000 020 000	2	9	1
Chicago	100 001 01x	3	8	1

WP **Pearce**; LP **Schneider**

4. Monday, September 7[2]

Cincinnati	000 000 010	1	5	0
Chicago	100 000 20x	3	6	2

WP **Humphries**; LP **Fittery**

5. Tuesday, September 8

Cincinnati	001 200 000 0	3	6	2
Chicago	102 000 000 1	4	11	2

WP Lavender, **Zabel** (5); LP Douglas,
Ames (4) (10 innings)

6. Thursday, September 10

St. Louis	000 000 300	3	1	3
Cincinnati	101 000 000	2	4	1

WP **Perritt**; LP **Benton**, Douglas (7)

7. Saturday, September 12

St. Louis	110 001 000	3	9	2
Cincinnati	001 000 000	1	8	2

WP **Griner**; LP **Fittery**

8. Sunday, September 13[1]

St. Louis	010 200 100	4	10	3
Cincinnati	000 020 010	3	9	1

WP **Doak**; LP **Douglas**

9. Sunday, September 13[2]

St. Louis	000 200 001	3	6	1
Cincinnati	020 000 000	2	7	2

WP Perdue, **Sallee** (2); LP **Schneider**

10. Tuesday, September 15

Cincinnati	000 000 000	0	6	4
Pittsburgh	004 001 40x	9	11	0

WP **Adams**; LP **Benton**, Lear (7)

11. Wednesday, September 16

Cincinnati	000 000 010	1	5	3
New York	500 021 00x	8	6	3

WP **Demaree**; LP **Ames**, Fittery (4)

12. Thursday, September 17

Cincinnati	010 000 000	1	6	3
New York	000 302 41x	10	9	0

WP **Mathewson**; LP **Douglas**, Yingling (8)

13. Friday, September 18

Cincinnati	011 000 000	2	4	2
New York	002 000 001	3	6	2

WP O'Toole, **Fromme** (2); LP **Schneider**

14. Saturday, September 19[1]

Cincinnati	000 000 000	0	1	2
Brooklyn	005 000 10x	6	9	2

WP **Pfeffer**; LP **Ames**, Yingling (6)

15. Saturday, September 19[2]

Cincinnati	300 210 000	6	11	1
Brooklyn	100 111 22x	8	14	2

WP Ragan, Schmutz (2), Steele (6), **Allen**
(8); LP Lear, **Douglas** (7)

16. Monday, September 21[1]

Cincinnati	102 002 001	6	10	1
Brooklyn	100 007 01x	9	11	1

WP Reulbach, **Steele** (6); LP Fittery,
Schneider (6), Ames (8)

17. Monday, September 21[2]

Cincinnati	000 000 110	2	12	1
Brooklyn	302 001 11x	8	10	1

WP **Allen**; LP **Benton**

18. Tuesday, September 22

Cincinnati	000 300 001 0	4	6	1
Brooklyn	200 000 200 1	5	8	1

WP **Aitchison**; LP Yingling, **Douglas** (8)
(10 innings)

[1]*First game of a doubleheader.* [2]*Second game of a doubleheader.*

19. Wednesday, September 23[1]

| Cincinnati | 010 000 001 | 2 | 8 | 2 |
| Boston | 000 200 110 | 3 | 8 | 3 |

WP **James**; LP **Ames**

The losing streak ended in second game of that doubleheader at Boston's South End Grounds.

Wednesday, September 23[2]

| Cincinnati | 000 000 003 | 3 | 5 | 0 |
| Boston | 000 000 000 | 0 | 4 | 0 |

WP **Lear**; LP **Davis**

Cincinnati won a pitching duel between former Princeton University right-hander King Lear, a rookie who posted his only victory of the season and the lone shutout of his brief major league career, and former Williams College right-hander George Davis, who had pitched a no-hit game two weeks before against Philadelphia.

Boston led off the fourth through the seventh innings with a hit, twice with doubles, but could not score, while Cincinnati, held to two hits for eight innings, won with three runs in the ninth. The rally began with a walk to Lear, followed by Herzog's one-out single, a force-out, and successive doubles down the right-field line by pinch-hitter Doc Miller and third baseman Bert Niehoff.

After the nineteenth loss in a row, Cincinnati was in eighth place with a 56–84 record, twenty-six and one-half games behind first-place Boston.

During the losing streak, the Reds lost eight games by one run, including two in the tenth inning. Three of the defeats were by two runs, one by three runs, one by five runs, two by six runs, one by seven runs, two by nine runs, and one by ten runs. Thirteen of the nineteen losses were suffered on the road, and the opposition averaged 5.8 runs and 9.2 hits during the streak to 2.2 runs and 6.9 hits for Cincinnati.

Six different pitchers lost games, with right-hander Red Ames dropping five, Douglas, and right-hander Pete Schneider losing four apiece, left-hander Rube Benton three, left-hander Paul Fittery two, and left-hander Earl Yingling one. Eight of the losses were complete games, three pitched by Schneider and two by Fittery.

Cincinnati scored two runs or less in fourteen of the nineteen

---

[1]*First game of a doubleheader.* [2]*Second game of a doubleheader.*

Infielder Buck Herzog managed the Cincinnati Reds for the first time in 1914 when the club lost nineteen straight games and finished last. (Courtesy of National Baseball Library, Cooperstown, New York.)

games and was shut out twice. Right-hander Babe Adams of Pittsburgh shut out the Reds, 9–0, with a six-hitter in Game 10 (September 15), and Brooklyn right-hander Jeff Pfeffer pitched a 6–0 one-hitter in Game 14 (September 19). The only hit Pfeffer allowed was a single to right with two out in the eighth inning by Yingling, who had relieved Ames in the sixth inning.

In Game 6 (September 10), St. Louis won despite getting only one hit in a 3–2 win. With Cincinnati ahead, 2–0, in the seventh, Benton issued three walks and Douglas relieved. One run scored on a force-out, one on a sacrifice fly by outfielder Owen Wilson, tying the score, and the winning run came in on a steal of second, a single to shortstop by pinch-hitter Ivy Wingo for the lone St. Louis hit, and walks to outfielder Walton Cruise and third baseman Zinn Beck to force in the third and winning run.

Cincinnati led at some point in ten games, and five of the nineteen losses came in the final inning.

Chicago won, 4–3, in the tenth inning of Game 5 (September 8), when outfielder Wilbur Good singled and eventually scored on a one-out single to right by outfielder Wildfire Schulte.

St. Louis won, 6–5, in the ninth inning of Game 9 (September 13) as catcher Wingo singled with two out and scored when Miller misjudged a high fly to right by Cruise and let it fall for a hit.

New York won, 3–2, in Game 13 (September 18) in the ninth on a single by right-hander Art Fromme, an error, a walk, and a single to left by shortstop Art Fletcher.

Brooklyn won Game 18 (September 22) in the tenth inning, 5–4, when shortstop Dick Egan doubled and scored on a one-out single to left by first baseman Jake Daubert, and Boston won Game 19 (September 23) in the ninth, 3–2, when third baseman Red Smith bounced a one-out homer into the center-field stands.

After the nineteenth loss in a row, Cincinnati had a 56–84 record, twenty-seven games behind first-place Boston. The Reds went on to finish the 1914 season in the National League cellar for the first time since 1901 with a 60–94 record, nine games behind seventh-place Pittsburgh and thirty-four and a half games in back of pennant-winning Boston. Since 1914 Cincinnati has never lost more than fourteen games in succession.

1975 Detroit Tigers

19 Consecutive Losses

In the first seventy-three years the Detroit Tigers were in the American League, they finished in the first division forty-two times. They won seven pennants before divisional play began in 1969, including three in a row from 1907 through 1909.

The Tigers have had a host of great players, led by outfielder Ty Cobb, a superstar for two decades. Other prominent Hall of Famers included catcher Mickey Cochrane, first baseman Hank Greenberg, second baseman Charlie Gehringer, and outfielders Harry Heilmann and Al Kaline.

Those greats helped account for the fact that Detroit finished last in only one of its first sixty-eight seasons. After divisional play began in 1969, the Tigers won the Eastern title in 1972, then finished sixth in 1974, a last-place landing for the second time in club history.

There were some changes in the unpredictable 1975 Tigers, but no improvement at season's end. They had a winning record in April, and Ralph Houk, serving the second of his five seasons as Detroit's manager, was optimistic. The club fell back in May, lost eleven of its last twelve games in June to fall into the cellar, then won twelve of its first fourteen games in July, including nine in a row, to move within three games of fourth place at the All-Star Game break.

On July 28 Detroit right-hander Vern Ruhle shut out New York on six hits, winning 3–0, helped by designated hitter Willie Horton's second-inning homer off left-hander Larry Gura. It was Ruhle's ninth win and third and last shutout of 1975.

That win gave Detroit a 46–54 record, fifth place and a virtual tie with sixth-place Cleveland, fifteen games behind first-place Boston and four in back of fourth-place New York. The longest losing streak in Detroit's history began the next night at Yankee Stadium.

1. Tuesday, July 29

Detroit	000 002 000	2	8	1
New York	100 030 00x	4	5	0

WP **Medich**, Martinez (9); LP **Coleman**, Pentz (6)

2. Wednesday, July 30

Detroit	000 010 000	1	3	0
New York	000 002 00x	2	5	2

WP **May**; LP **Lolich**

3. Thursday, July 31[1]

Detroit	110 000 000 0	2	11	1
Boston	100 000 100 1	3	8	1

WP **Lee**; LP Bare, **Reynolds** (8) (10 innings)

4. Thursday, July 31[2]

Detroit	000 010 000	1	9	1
Boston	001 103 10x	6	6	1

WP **Moret**; LP **Lemanczyk**, Walker (6)

5. Friday, August 1

Detroit	011 000 104	7	14	2
Boston	010 140 002	8	15	0

WP Tiant, **Willoughby** (9); LP LaGrow, Arroyo (5), **Pentz** (9)

6. Saturday, August 2

Detroit	011 000 000	2	8	1
Boston	100 500 10x	7	13	0

WP **Wise**, Drago (8); LP **Ruhle**, Arroyo (4)

7. Sunday, August 3

Detroit	000 200 020	4	9	0
Boston	201 000 12x	6	13	0

WP **Cleveland**, Willoughby (9); LP Coleman, **Walker** (7)

8. Monday, August 4

Detroit	000 030 001	4	9	0
Cleveland	020 030 01x	6	12	0

WP **Eckersley**, Bibby (6), Brown (9); LP **Lolich**

9. Tuesday, August 5

Detroit	001 102 000	4	12	1
Cleveland	320 001 02x	8	12	0

WP **Raich**, Brown (6), Waits (8); LP **Bare**, Arroyo (2), Pentz (6)

10. Wednesday, August 6[1]

Baltimore	012 100 000	4	9	2
Detroit	000 001 100	2	7	1

WP **Torrez**, Garland (7); LP **LaGrow**

11. Wednesday, August 6[2]

Baltimore	000 215 000	8	12	1
Detroit	000 002 000	2	10	2

WP **Grimsley**, Miller (6); LP **Lemanczyk**, Walker (6), Reynolds (6)

12. Thursday, August 7

Baltimore	000 006 000 1	7	12	2
Detroit	300 001 002 0	6	14	0

WP Cuellar, Garland (6), Jackson (9), **Miller** (9); LP Ruhle, Pentz (6), **Reynolds** (10) (10 innings)

13. Friday, August 8

Minnesota	110 000 001	3	12	1
Detroit	000 000 100	1	7	1

WP **Hughes**; LP **Coleman**, Arroyo (9)

14. Saturday, August 9

Minnesota	000 100 000	1	6	1
Detroit	000 000 000	0	5	1

WP **Goltz**; LP **Lolich**

[1]*First game of a doubleheader.* [2]*Second game of a doubleheader.*

15. Sunday, August 10

Minnesota	000 000 202	4	9	0
Detroit	000 000 000	0	4	2

WP **Blyleven**; LP **Bare**, Reynolds (8)

16. Monday, August 11

Texas	021 120 010	7	14	0
Detroit	000 000 000	0	5	2

WP **Perry**; LP **LaGrow**, Arroyo (4), Walker (5)

17. Tuesday, August 12

Texas	400 000 000	4	5	0
Detroit	001 000 200	3	8	0

WP **Perzanowski**, Thomas (7), Foucault (7); LP **Ruhle**

18. Wednesday, August 13

Texas	001 000 040 01	6	12	1
Detroit	010 001 300 00	5	16	2

WP **Jenkins**, Umbarger (7), Thomas (8), **Foucault** (8); LP **Coleman**, Reynolds (8), **Pentz** (9) (11 innings)

19. Friday, August 15

Detroit	000 000 000	0	4	1
California	000 001 16x	8	14	2

WP **Tanana**; LP **Lolich**

The losing streak ended the next night at Anaheim Stadium.

Saturday, August 16

Detroit	200 000 231	8	16	2
California	000 000 000	0	2	2

WP **Bare**; LP **Hockenbery**, Kirkwood (7), Brewer (8), Lange (9)

Right-hander Ray Bare, who lost six of his next seven, got his first big-league shutout and had a no-hitter until the seventh, when he walked his second batter, outfielder Mickey Rivers, then walked first baseman Bruce Bochte two outs later, and gave up a single to left to third baseman Dave Chalk to load the bases before striking out Ellie Rodriguez to end the inning. Shortstop Mike Miley, who drew Bare's first walk earlier, led off the eighth with a single for the only other hit off Bare.

Detroit scored twice in the first when first baseman Dan Meyer doubled with two out, Horton walked, catcher Bill Freehan bounced a run-scoring single to right, and second baseman Jerry Remy erred on outfielder Ben Oglivie's grounder, allowing Horton to score. Freehan led Detroit's sixteen-hit attack with a triple, double, two singles, and three runs batted in, while shortstop Tom Veryzer, who had two singles, also batted in three runs.

After the nineteenth straight defeat, Detroit was last in the East with a 46–74 record, twenty-six games behind first-place Boston and eight in back of fifth-place Cleveland.

During the streak Detroit averaged 2.4 runs and 8.6 hits to 5.4 runs and 10.2 hits for the opposition, which was outhit in six of the nineteen games. Seven of the nineteen losses were by one run, five by two runs, two by four runs and five runs, and one each by six, seven, and eight runs. The Tigers were shut out four times, including three times in a row in a streak in which they went scoreless for thirty-one consecutive innings.

Houk used ten pitchers in the streak, and nine of them lost at least one game. Left-hander Mickey Lolich lost four games and all were complete games, including the nineteenth game, in which he gave up eight California runs.

Right-handers Joe Coleman, Dave Lemanczyk, Ruhle, Bare, and Lerrin LaGrow each lost two games as starters, while in relief, right-handers Bob Reynolds and Gene Pentz lost two apiece and Tom Walker lost one. The other pitcher used was right-hander Fernando Arroyo, who relieved in five games without a decision.

Detroit, which played ten of the nineteen games on the road, led in seven games but only twice after the fifth inning, and lost four games in the other team's last at bat, three in extra innings.

In Game 2 (July 30), Detroit took a 1–0 lead in the fifth when third baseman Aurelio Rodriguez doubled, advanced on a long fly, and scored on shortstop Gene Michael's sacrifice fly. New York won, 2–1, with two runs in the sixth on doubles by outfielders Bobby Bonds and Roy White and a single by catcher Thurman Munson.

In Game 3 (July 31), a sacrifice fly by outfielder Leon Roberts and a home run by Oglivie produced Detroit runs in the first and second. Boston first baseman Carl Yastrzemski drove home designated hitter Juan Beniquez in the first and shortstop Rich Burleson with the tying run in the seventh. Boston won in the tenth when second baseman Denny Doyle singled, outfielder Fred Lynn was walked one out later, and outfielder Jim Rice singled.

Detroit enjoyed its biggest inning of the losing streak in Game 5 (August 1), scoring four runs in the ninth inning to take the lead, but still lost. Boston snapped a 2–2 tie in the four-run fifth when outfielder Bernie Carbo homered, Yastrzemski singled, and Lynn and Rice hit consecutive homers. Detroit came back with a run in the seventh and went ahead, 7–6, in the ninth on Horton's three-run homer and Freehan's solo homer. Each had homered earlier in the game.

Boston came back to win in the home ninth. Doyle beat out a grounder to shortstop and continued to second on Michael's wild throw, then scored the tying run on a single by Yastrzemski. After Lynn was intentionally walked, Rice bunted safely for his fourth hit and Pentz, with no play at first, threw late and wildly past third, allowing Yastrzemski to score the winning run.

Another Boston win in its last at bat came in Game 7 (August 3). Boston had a 3–0 lead until Rodriguez hit a two-run homer in the fourth and, after Burleson homered in the Boston seventh, Detroit tied in the eighth on Oglivie's two-run single. But in the home eighth designated hitter Cecil Cooper homered to snap the tie, and another run scored on a walk, an infield out, and a single by Doyle, whose two-run homer in the first had extended his batting streak to twenty-one straight games.

Detroit's second extra-inning loss came in Game 12 (August 17), when Baltimore overcame a 3–0 Detroit lead with six runs in the sixth inning. The Tigers tied the score in the ninth when Gates Brown hit his sixteenth career homer as a pinch-hitter to set an American League record followed by singles by outfielder Ron LeFlore, Meyer, and Freehan for the tying run. In the Baltimore tenth, second baseman Bobby Grich and designated hitter Tommy Davis singled, first baseman Tony Muser struck out, outfielder Paul Blair hit a grounder on which Grich was nailed at the plate, but outfielder Don Baylor doubled home the winning run.

Lolich pitched superbly in Game 14 (August 9) but lost, 1–0, when third baseman Eric Soderholm doubled, outfielder John Briggs walked and catcher Glenn Borgmann singled. The loss broke the club record of thirteen losses, set in 1920 and tied in 1953.

The third extra-inning loss was in Game 18 (August 13) after Detroit built a 5–1 lead after seven innings, helped by a homer and a run-scoring single by Freehan. First baseman Jim Spencer doubled home a run before designated hitter Tom Grieve hit a three-run homer to tie the score in the eighth. Texas won in the eleventh, 6–5, on singles by catcher Jim Sundberg and outfielder Dave Moates and a force-play grounder by second baseman Lenny Randle on which Michael relayed the ball past first, allowing pinch-runner Cesar Tovar to score the winning run.

After its nineteenth straight loss, Detroit won four games in a row but lost forty-seven of its last fifty-eight games to finish sixth with a 57–102 record, eight and one-half games behind fifth-place Milwaukee and thirty-seven and one-half games in back of first-place Boston.

With twenty-five homers and ninety-two runs batted in, Horton was Detroit's most productive 1975 batter. Lolich won twelve games, Ruhle eleven, and Coleman ten, but Arroyo, with a 2–1 record, was the only Tiger pitcher with more wins than losses.

WINNING STREAKS
BY PITCHERS

19 Games • Rube Marquard, 1912

17 Games • Roy Face, 1959

16 Games • Walter Johnson, 1912

16 Games • Joe Wood, 1912

16 Games • Lefty Grove, 1931

16 Games • Schoolboy Rowe, 1934

16 Games • Carl Hubbell, 1936

16 Games • Ewell Blackwell, 1947

16 Games • Jack Sanford, 1962

Winning Streaks by Pitchers

Pitcher	Team	Year	Games Won	Games Pitched	Games Started	Complete Games	Shutout Games	Starts with No Decision	Games Pitched in Relief	Games Won in Relief	Team Yielded Two Runs or Less	Games Won by One Run Margin	Games Won in Final Inning
Rube Marquard	Giants	1912	19	21	18	16	1	0	3	1	9	5	2
Elroy Face	Pirates	1959	17	47	0	0	0	0	47	17	0	8	14
Walter Johnson	Senators	1912	16	19	12	10	2	0	7	4	7	5	3
Joe Wood	Red Sox	1912	16	19	16	14	6	0	3	0	10	7	3
Lefty Grove	Athletics	1931	16	18	14	13	1	0	4	2	4	3	0
Schoolboy Rowe	Tigers	1934	16	23	15	10	1	3	8	4	5	3	4
Carl Hubbell	Giants	1936	16	19	15	14	1	1	4	2	12	8	3
Ewell Blackwell	Reds	1947	16	17	17	16	5	1	0	0	10	4	2
Jack Sanford	Giants	1962	16	20	20	6	1	4	0	0	6	4	2

Rube Marquard
1912 New York Giants

19 Consecutive Wins

Richard ("Rube") Marquard was an outstanding teenage pitcher in Cleveland, Ohio, where he was born on October 9, 1889, and the six-foot three-inch, 180-pound left-hander was an immediate sensation in organized baseball.

At the age of fifteen, Marquard pitched against professional players in a postseason barnstorming tour, and three years later Rube gave up a job with an ice cream company and signed his first professional baseball contract for $200 a month.

In that season of 1907, Marquard won twenty-three games for the Canton, Ohio, club and led the Central League in victories. Indianapolis, which had signed him the year before and optioned him to Canton, promoted him to the American Association club in 1908, and he had a 28–19 record, struck out 250 batters in 367 innings, and led that league in victories, innings, strikeouts, and games.

Late that season a number of major league scouts showed up in Columbus to see Marquard pitch. He hurled a no-hitter on September 3 and the New York Giants outbid several other clubs for him, paying a then record price of $11,000 for his contract.

With New York, Marquard struggled at the start. He lost the only game he pitched for the Giants in 1908, had a 5–13 record in 1909 and a 4–4 log in 1910, and was quickly tabbed the "$11,000 Lemon."

In 1911 Marquard suddenly blossomed into a star, employing his outstanding curve ball effectively. The handsome southpaw, an intelligent and polished gentleman despite his nickname, won twenty-four games and lost only seven to help the Giants win the National League pennant.

In 1912, Marquard put together the longest winning streak in modern major league history. He won his first nineteen decisions, and under modern scoring rules would have been credited with twenty, with the streak beginning on opening day at Brooklyn's Washington Park.

1. Thursday, April 11

New York	032 454	18	21	2
Brooklyn	003 000	3	7	3

WP **Marquard**; LP **Rucker**, Barger (4), Dent (6) (6 innings, darkness)

2. Tuesday, April 16

New York	010 034 000	8	12	2
Boston	000 002 000	2	6	3

WP **Marquard**; LP **Tyler**, Dent (7)

3. Wednesday, April 24

New York	110 141 3	11	11	2
Philadelphia	001 210 0	4	7	6

WP **Marquard**; LP **Alexander**, Shultz (6) (7 innings, darkness)

4. Wednesday, May 1

Philadelphia	000 000 031	4	10	2
New York	100 550 00x	11	11	2

WP **Marquard**, Drucke (8); LP **Seaton**, Shultz (6)

5. Tuesday, May 7

New York	200 100 003	6	9	1
St. Louis	000 000 002	2	6	1

WP **Marquard**; LP **Steele**, Dell (9)

6. Saturday, May 11

New York	100 210 060	10	13	3
Chicago	000 000 021	3	8	3

WP **Marquard**; LP **Richie**, Cole (6), Moroney (9)

7. Thursday, May 16

New York	000 001 021	4	8	2
Pittsburgh	000 000 001	1	4	0

WP **Marquard**; LP **O'Toole**, Leifield (9)

8. Monday, May 20

New York	000 110 100	3	10	1
Cincinnati	000 000 000	0	6	0

WP **Marquard**; LP **Fromme**, Smith (9)

9. Friday, May 24

New York	003 021 000	6	7	1
Brooklyn	000 102 000	3	8	2

WP **Marquard**; LP **Ragan**, Knetzer (7)

10. Thursday, May 30

New York	011 001 301	7	10	1
Philadelphia	100 000 000	1	9	5

WP **Marquard**; LP **Seaton** (morning game)

11. Monday, June 3

St. Louis	000 201 000	3	9	3
New York	007 010 00x	8	9	1

WP **Marquard**; LP **Sallee**, Dale (4)

12. Saturday, June 8

Cincinnati	000 001 010	2	4	1
New York	100 000 41x	6	5	2

WP **Marquard**; LP **Benton**, Fromme (8)

13. Wednesday, June 12

Chicago	020 000 000	2	9	4
New York	000 100 02x	3	9	1

WP **Marquard**, Crandall (9); LP Richie, **Brown** (8)

14. Monday, June 17

Pittsburgh	100 020 000 01	4	12	1
New York	100 010 010 02	5	8	1

WP **Marquard**; LP **O'Toole** (11 innings)

15. Wednesday, June 19

New York	010 020 200 1	6	12	1
Boston	000 002 210 0	5	10	1

WP Ames, **Marquard** (8); LP **Hess** (10 innings)

16. Friday, June 21

New York	020 020 100	5	9	2
Boston	011 000 000	2	10	2

WP **Marquard**; LP **Perdue**

17. Tuesday, June 25

Philadelphia	000 001 000	1	6	0
New York	002 000 00x	2	5	1

WP **Marquard**; LP **Alexander**

18. Saturday, June 29

Boston	000 030 021	6	11	2
New York	132 101 00x	8	10	3

WP **Marquard**; LP **Brown**

19. Wednesday, July 3[1]

Brooklyn	001 000 000	1	9	2
New York	000 100 10x	2	4	3

WP **Marquard**; LP **Rucker**

The streak ended five days later at Chicago's West Side Grounds before a capacity crowd of 25,000.

Monday, July 8

New York	001 010 000	2	5	3
Chicago	020 202 01x	7	10	0

WP **Lavender**; LP **Marquard**, Tesreau (7)

Marquard never really had a chance to win this game, for he didn't pitch well and the Giants did not play well. Chicago took a 2–0 lead in the second. Third baseman Heine Zimmerman and outfielder Tommy Leach singled, the former scoring when second baseman Heinie Groh, subbing for injured regular Larry Doyle, messed up first baseman Vic Saier's potential double-play ball. After second baseman Johnny Evers bunted safely to load the bases, Marquard struck out catcher Jimmy Archer and right-hander Jimmy Lavender, but then made a wild pitch

[1]*First game of a doubleheader.*

Left-hander Rube Marquard, ridiculed as the "$11,000 lemon" in his early days with the New York Giants, was his team's best pitcher in 1912, winning a career high twenty-six games. In the longest winning streak in major league history, the curveballing southpaw captured his first nineteen decisions that year and did not suffer defeat until July 8. (Courtesy of National Baseball Library, Cooperstown, New York.)

on which Leach scored before outfielder Jimmy Sheckard struck out. Chicago added two runs in the fourth on one of Marquard's seven walks, two errors by outfielder Fred Snodgrass in left field, a sacrifice, and Archer's sacrifice fly. Saier doubled and scored the final run on a single in the eighth.

Lavender, a twenty-eight-year-old rookie who entered the game with a 5–4 record and a streak of more than thirty straight scoreless innings, gave up a run in the third. Snodgrass was hit by a pitch, took third on a single by outfielder Beals Becker, and then was thrown out at the plate on first baseman Fred Merkle's smash to the mound before outfielder Red Murray singled to score Becker, with Merkle out at the plate trying to follow Becker home. New York's other run scored in the fifth on singles by Snodgrass, Becker and Merkle.

Marquard was not upset after his winning streak ended. In fact, he seemed to be relieved. "Of course, I am sorry I did not win my twentieth game," he said. "I would be a fool to deny it. I was confident I was going to do so, too, for I have never had more on the ball in my life and felt strong and good. I would like to have had our strongest team behind me [Doyle was injured], but I have been pretty lucky so far in having the good support I have had in both batting and fielding, and have no fault to find. . . . I am not worrying over my first defeat a little bit. In fact, I feel easier in my mind now that the strain is off. I did worry nights before every game, and now that I have done it in nineteen straight wins I am perfectly satisfied. . . . Did you ever work at a given task until you felt that it was 'getting' you, that you couldn't think of anything else when you were awake and that your sleep was troubled with dreams of it? Of course, I want to win every game I pitch, just as every pitcher who had the good of his team at heart, but to be candid I'm glad that streak is over. It was getting on my nerves. Why, several nights I went to bed and the moment I closed my eyes the air became full of baseballs, gloves and bats. I could see players running at me as though they were going to annihilate me. When I could finally get to sleep, I was pitching ball all night. When I awoke in the morning, I felt as if I hadn't been rested a bit. I want to tell you the strain of such a performance is awful. It isn't so bad when you're out there pitching. It's after the games and at nights when it gets you. When you are on the mound your mind is taken up with your work, and you don't worry. Why, when I had won my eighteenth straight game I wanted to go back the next day and try it again. I couldn't get away from the feeling that I ought to pitch at once for fear something might happen to me."

After Marquard's nineteenth straight victory, New York was in first place with a 56–14 record and a fourteen-game lead over second-place Chicago.

During his streak Marquard beat Boston and Philadelphia four times each, Brooklyn three times and the other four clubs twice apiece. In the nineteen wins New York averaged 7.9 runs and 9.6 hits to 2.6 runs and 7.9 hits for its rivals.

In eleven of the games, including the fourth game when he was lifted because the Giants had an 11–0 lead after seven innings, Marquard gave up two runs or less, and gave up forty of the forty-nine runs the opposition scored in the nineteen games. In the streak Rube appeared in twenty-one games, made eighteen starts, pitched sixteen complete games, went seven and eight innings in his other two starts, pitched one shutout, and won one game in three relief appearances.

Marquard won five games by a one-run margin, including both his extra-inning games, won one by two runs, four by three runs, eight by between four and seven runs, and one by fifteen runs.

New York had to come from behind in only four of the nineteen games, two after the fourth inning, and won just twice in the final inning. The closest Marquard came to defeat was in Game 14 (June 17). A double by outfielder Josh Devore and Murray's single in the seventh gave New York a 3–3 tie. In the top of the eleventh, Pittsburgh scored when shortstop Honus Wagner tripled and came home on outfielder Owen Wilson's sacrifice fly, but New York came back to win, 5–4, with two runs on Murray's one-out single, Becker's triple to the left-field corner, and third baseman Buck Herzog's single.

The other extra-inning win was in Game 15 (June 19) at Boston. New York had a 5–2 lead after scoring twice in the seventh, but the Braves tallied two runs in the seventh on a hit batsman, a safe fielder's choice, and a triple by left-hander Otto Hess, and tied the score in the eighth on outfielder Jay Kirke's double, a fielder's choice, and a single by first baseman Ben Houser.

Marquard, relieving right-hander Red Ames at that point, blanked the Braves the rest of the way, and was credited with the win when New York scored in the tenth. Becker singled and Herzog tripled for the 6–5 victory, giving Marquard his only relief win in his streak.

There were three other one-run decisions. In Game 13 (June 12), New York trailed Chicago, 2–1, until the eighth. Then Tillie Shafer batted for Marquard and walked before Doyle doubled home the tying run and Snodgrass doubled in the run that won the game, 3–2.

In Game 17 (June 25), New York scored twice in the third inning on Marquard's single, a double by Snodgrass, Doyle's sacrifice fly, and Merkle's single. Philadelphia scored its only run in the sixth when catcher Bill Killefer hit his only home run of the season, a drive into the left-field bleachers. The Phillies wasted three singles in the seventh.

In the final game in the streak (July 3), Brooklyn, which left fourteen men on base in the game, eight in the first three innings, scored in the third on third baseman Red Smith's single, a walk to first baseman Jake Daubert, a safe bunt by outfielder Zack Wheat, and shortstop Bert Tooley's sacrifice fly. New York tied with two out in the fourth, when Murray grounded to third and was safe on Smith's low throw, stole second, and scored with two out when Tooley dropped Becker's high fly. In the seventh Murray doubled, Becker beat out a bunt, and catcher Chief Myers hit a long sacrifice fly to left to bring home Murray with the winning run.

Brooklyn, which loaded the bases with none out in both the second and third innings and scored just once, threatened in the ninth when outfielder Hub Northen and Daubert singled with one out. Marquard then ended the game by striking out Wheat and retiring second baseman John Hummel on a pop fly to first to clinch Marquard's nineteenth victory.

Marquard always maintained his streak should have been twenty games, and under modern scoring rules it would have been. On April 20 New York right-hander Jeff Tesreau had a 2–0 lead after eight innings against Brooklyn at the Polo Grounds. In the ninth, two walks and a single scored one run and brought Marquard on in relief.

After a sacrifice Daubert bounced to the mound, and the runner on third was caught in a rundown until catcher Art Wilson threw the ball past third, allowing two more runs to score and giving Brooklyn a 3–2 lead. In New York's ninth Groh singled to left with one out and Wilson homered into the upper right-field stands near the foul line to win the game.

The official scorer gave the victory to Tesreau because he "had done the bulk of the work." Under modern rules, the scorer would not have that option.

In his first outing after his first loss, Marquard lost in relief at St. Louis, 3–2, in the opener of a July 14 doubleheader, then started and lost the second game that day, 4–2. In his next start Marquard posted his twentieth victory in the first game of a doubleheader at Pittsburgh, winning 5–4. He finished the season with a 26–11 record and an earned run average of 2.57, tying for the National League lead in victories, only one of which was a shutout. He pitched two complete game victories in the World Series, but New York lost in seven games to the Boston Red Sox.

Marquard won twenty-three games in 1913, his last twenty-win season. He went to Brooklyn on waivers on August 31, 1915, and helped the Dodgers win pennants in 1916 and 1920. He was traded to Cincinnati after the 1920 season and dealt to the Boston Braves before the 1922 season. He pitched for them through 1925, finishing his major league career with 201 wins, 177 losses, and a 3.08 earned run average, and one of his thirty shutouts was a no-hitter for the Giants against Brooklyn on April 15, 1915.

Marquard went to the minors in 1926, serving as occasional pitcher, manager and coach through 1932, in the 1931 season as an umpire in the Eastern League and as coach and scout for Atlanta of the Southern Association in 1932, his final year in baseball. He was elected to the Hall of Fame in 1971 and died on June 1, 1980, in Pikesville, Maryland.

Roy Face
1959 Pittsburgh Pirates

17 Consecutive Wins

Even forty years ago, Roy Face was small for a major league pitcher. The slightly built right-hander was only five feet eight inches tall and weighed just 155 pounds. Born February 20, 1928, in Stephentown, New York, he was originally signed by the Philadelphia Phillies before the 1949 season and pitched in the Philadelphia and Brooklyn minor league systems until he was drafted by the Pittsburgh Pirates after the 1952 season.

Face made his major league debut with Pittsburgh in 1953, spent the 1954 season with New Orleans of the Southern Association, and was back with Pittsburgh in 1955. By 1956 Face had developed a fork ball, and that pitch helped him become a star relief pitcher. He started only one game while relieving in fifty-eight in 1957. He pitched only in relief for the remainder of his outstanding sixteen-year major league career.

In 1958 Face appeared in fifty-eight games, losing his first two decisions and then winning his last five. His second defeat that year was in the opener of a May 30 doubleheader, when Milwaukee scored four runs off him in the ninth inning to win, 7–4. It was more than fifteen months before he lost again.

Face relieved in three of Pittsburgh's first five 1959 games without a decision as the Pirates lost all five. Face began his seventeen-game one-season and twenty-two-game two-season winning streak on April 22 at Pittsburgh's Forbes Field with the Pirates in last place in the National League with a 1–5 record, four games behind first-place Milwaukee.

1. Wednesday, April 22

| Cincinnati | 006 010 010 | 8 | 11 | 3 |
| Pittsburgh | 000 000 702 | 9 | 8 | 0 |

WP Friend, Blackburn (3), Daniels (7), **Face** (8); LP Nuxhall, **Pena** (7), Jeffcoat (9)

2. Friday, April 24

| Pittsburgh | 202 000 004 | 8 | 12 | 0 |
| Philadelphia | 000 003 020 | 5 | 11 | 2 |

WP Kline, Porterfield (6), Smith (6), **Face** (7); LP Owens, **Schroll** (7), Farrell (9), Meyer (9)

3. Sunday, May 3[1]

| St. Louis | 000 020 100 0 | 3 | 9 | 1 |
| Pittsburgh | 000 020 100 1 | 4 | 12 | 3 |

WP Law, **Face** (8); LP Jackson, **Brosnan** (7), Kellner (10), Nunn (10) (10 innings)

4. Thursday, May 7

| Philadelphia | 020 020 000 0 | 4 | 10 | 1 |
| Pittsburgh | 000 400 000 1 | 5 | 7 | 0 |

WP Law, **Face** (10); LP **Owens** (10 innings)

5. Wednesday, May 13

| Pittsburgh | 000 030 030 | 6 | 9 | 2 |
| Los Angeles | 000 301 000 | 4 | 6 | 0 |

WP Kline, **Face** (7); LP **Drysdale**, Labine (8)

6. Thursday, May 14

| Pittsburgh | 002 400 001 | 7 | 12 | 1 |
| Los Angeles | 100 000 140 | 6 | 12 | 1 |

WP Friend, **Face** (8); LP Podres, Klippstein (4), Fowler (8), **Labine** (9)

7. Sunday, May 31[2]

| Pittsburgh | 004 223 300 | 14 | 17 | 1 |
| Cincinnati | 022 430 000 | 11 | 15 | 0 |

WP Jackson, Blackburn (4), Williams (4), Smith (5), **Face** (7); LP Newcombe, Jeffcoat (4), Pena (5), **Mabe** (6), Acker (7), Schmidt (8)

8. Monday, June 8

| San Francisco | 200 200 230 00 | 9 | 18 | 1 |
| Pittsburgh | 011 100 150 03 | 12 | 18 | 0 |

WP Kline, Daniels (4), Blackburn (8), **Face** (9); LP Miller, Jones (4), Zanni (8), Worthington (8), **McCormick** (8) (11 innings)

9. Thursday, June 11

| San Francisco | 140 000 031 | 9 | 9 | 5 |
| Pittsburgh | 020 003 25x | 12 | 13 | 7 |

WP Friend, **Face** (8), Law (9); LP Sanford, Worthington (2), Shipley (2), G. Jones (6), **Miller** (8), Zanni (8)

10. Sunday, June 14[1]

| Los Angeles | 002 001 000 | 3 | 8 | 1 |
| Pittsburgh | 000 030 03x | 6 | 11 | 1 |

WP Witt, Porterfield (3), Jackson (6), **Face** (8); LP Williams, **Labine** (5)

11. Thursday, June 18

| Pittsburgh | 000 000 200 000 2 | 4 | 9 | 0 |
| Chicago | 000 010 010 000 0 | 2 | 5 | 3 |

WP Kline, **Face** (9); LP Drabowsky, Elston (7), **Henry** (9), Hobbie (13) (13 innings)

12. Thursday, June 25

| Pittsburgh | 000 000 100 002 | 3 | 7 | 0 |
| San Francisco | 001 000 000 000 | 1 | 6 | 0 |

WP Haddix, **Face** (10); LP Miller, **Fisher** (12) (12 innings)

---

[1]*First game of a doubleheader.* [2]*Second game of a doubleheader.*

13. Thursday, July 9

Chicago	000 000 102 0	3	11	2
Pittsburgh	000 000 300 1	4	9	0

WP Law, **Face** (9); LP Anderson, Elston (7), **Henry** (9) (10 innings)

14. Sunday, July 12[1]

St. Louis	000 010 031 0	5	13	3
Pittsburgh	200 300 000 1	6	15	2

WP Haddix, **Face** (8); LP Broglio, Urban (5), Blaylock (7), **McDaniel** (8) (10 innings)

15. Sunday, August 9

Pittsburgh	000 001 002 2	5	9	1
Chicago	010 001 010 0	3	11	1

WP Law, **Face** (8); LP Hillman, Henry (9), **Elston** (9), Hobbie (10), Ceccarelli (10) (10 innings)

16. Sunday, August 23[2]

Los Angeles	000 010 020 0	3	10	0
Pittsburgh	000 010 011 1	4	15	0

WP Law, **Face** (9); LP Sherry, Podres (8), **Drysdale** (8) (10 innings)

17. Sunday, August 30[2]

Philadelphia	500 000 000 1	6	9	1
Pittsburgh	000 000 122 2	7	12	1

WP Daniels, Porterfield (1), Kline (3), Green (6), Gross (8), **Face** (10); LP Semproch, **Farrell** (8) (10 innings)

The winning streak ended twelve days later in first game of twilight-night doubleheader at the Los Angeles Coliseum.

Friday, September 11[1]

Pittsburgh	000 001 120	4	7	1
Los Angeles	000 011 012	5	11	0

WP Koufax, **Churn** (8); LP Friend, **Face** (8)

Home runs by first baseman Dick Stuart and catcher Smoky Burgess helped Pittsburgh take a 4–2 lead before outfielder Wally Moon hit his second homer of the game to lead off the Los Angeles eighth. One out later, first baseman Norm Larker singled and Face relieved right-hander Bob Friend and retired the side. In the home ninth, shortstop Maury Wills singled, pinch-hitter Ron Fairly sacrificed, and third baseman Jim Gilliam tripled to the right-field corner to tie the score before second baseman Charlie Neal singled to left to win the game, 5–4. The loss was Face's first after he had pitched in ninety-eight games without losing over most of two seasons during which he won twenty-two straight games, a streak that was two short of the two-season major

---

[1]*First game of a doubleheader.* [2]*Second game of a doubleheader.*

league record set by left-hander Carl Hubbell of the New York Giants in 1936 and 1937.

After Face won his seventeenth straight game, Pittsburgh was in fourth place with a 70–62 record, one game behind third-place Milwaukee and four games in back of first-place San Francisco, which eventually finished third behind Los Angeles and Milwaukee. The Pirates wound up fourth, five games from third and nine games from first.

During his 1959 streak Face pitched in forty-seven games, was scored on in twelve, including six that he won. In addition to his seventeen wins, ten of which came in extra-inning games, the last seven of them in succession, Face saved nine games, and his earned run average for the forty-seven games was 2.24 for 76.2 innings in which he yielded seventy-two hits. In his seventeen successive wins, he was scored on in seven and gave up thirty-seven hits in forty innings. He finished sixteen of the seventeen wins, and his longest stint was five innings in Game 11 (June 18), which lasted thirteen innings, but he pitched three innings in six other games. His shortest stint was one inning.

Face beat every team in the league except Milwaukee during his streak, and he posted four wins over Los Angeles, three over Philadelphia, San Francisco and Chicago; and two each over Cincinnati and St. Louis. He beat fourteen rival pitchers, including three of them twice. Ten of the wins were in Pittsburgh.

Fifteen of Face's seventeen straight victories came in Pittsburgh's last time at bat, and five of the wins were on home runs. In seven of his seventeen wins, he gave up the tying or lead run before Pittsburgh came back to win.

In Game 4 (May 7) at home, first baseman Ted Kluszewski homered in the tenth to give Pittsburgh and Face a 4–3 win, and Stuart homered in the eighth for the winning run in Game 5 (May 13) at Los Angeles, won by Pittsburgh, 6–4. Stuart also homered to snap a tie in the ninth inning to give Pittsburgh and Face a 7–6 win in Game 6 (May 14) at Los Angeles.

In Game 7 (May 31) at Cincinnati, pinch-hitter Burgess hit a three-run homer to break an 11–11 tie, and Face, although not the pitcher of record since the homer was hit in the seventh and he did not enter the game until the bottom of that inning, was given the win after pitching three scoreless innings in the 14–11 victory.

Face also pitched three scoreless innings in Game 8 (June 8) at home against San Francisco and won, 12–9, when pinch-hitter Harry Bright hit a three-run homer with two out in the eleventh inning.

Elroy Face developed a fork ball and became a star major league relief pitcher. In 1959, the five-foot eight-inch, 155-pounder relieved in fifty-seven games and won his first seventeen decisions, ten of them in extra-inning games. He finished with an 18–1 record. (Courtesy of National Baseball Library, Cooperstown, New York.)

At San Francisco in Game 12 (June 25), Face again pitched three scoreless innings and won, 3–1, when outfielder Ramon Mejias hit a two-run homer in the twelfth.

Face won his seventeenth straight game (August 30) at home despite giving up a solo homer to first baseman Ed Bouchee in the tenth inning for a 6–5 Philadelphia lead. Pittsburgh came back to win, 7–6, on a single by third baseman Don Hoak, a walk and a two-run double to center by Stuart off right-hander Dick Farrell with one out.

Face finished the 1959 season with an 18–1 record and his .947 winning percentage established a big-league record for at least sixteen decisions. He also had ten saves and an earned run average of 2.71 for fifty-seven games.

Face helped Pittsburgh win the 1960 pennant and World Series with ten wins and twenty-four saves. He never led the league again in relief wins, but led in saves three times, with a career high of twenty-eight in 1962. He pitched for Pittsburgh until Detroit bought his contract on August 31, 1968. Released from Detroit, he was signed by Montreal on April 28, 1969, and posted a 4–2 record with five saves in his final big league season.

Face finished his major league career with a 104–95 record, 193 saves, and a 3.48 earned run average for 848 games over sixteen years.

Walter Johnson
1912 Washington Senators
16 Consecutive Wins

For more than three-quarters of a century, Walter Johnson has been the man against whom fastball pitchers have been measured. The six-foot one-inch, 200-pound sidearming right-hander, nicknamed the Big Train, seldom threw anything but his blazing fastball.

Born November 6, 1887, in Humboldt, Kansas, Johnson was signed at age nineteen out of the semipro ranks in Idaho in 1907 and joined the Washington Senators that August without minor league experience. He didn't become a winning pitcher until his third full season with Washington, which finished seventh or eighth in the American League every year from 1903 through 1911.

A twenty-five game loser in 1909, Johnson won twenty-five games in both 1910 and 1911. In 1912 Johnson got away to a fast start, and on June 12 at Detroit he posted his twelfth victory against four defeats. Tonsillitis then sidelined him for two weeks and on his return he lost three games in a row, the third by a 2–1 score on June 29 to Philadelphia. The winning run that day scored when catcher Eddie Ainsmith dropped a two-out pop fly in front of the plate for his second error of the inning.

Four days later on July 3, Washington played a home doubleheader at National Park, beating New York, 3–2, in the first game. Johnson then went to the mound with a 12–7 record in the second game and began his sixteen-game winning streak.

After the win in the opener that day, Washington, which had won seventeen straight games in a streak that ended in mid–June, was in

121

fourth place with a 40–31 record, half a game behind third-place Chicago and eight games in back of first-place Boston.

1. Wednesday, July 3[2]

New York	010 000 100	2	6	2
Washington	040 131 01x	10	15	1

WP **Johnson**, Musser (7); LP **Fisher**

2. Friday, July 5

New York	200 300 000 000 000 0	5	6	1
Washington	020 003 000 000 000 1	6	16	5

WP Engel, **Johnson** (4); LP Fisher, **Warhop** (2) (16 innings)

3. Tuesday, July 9[2]

Cleveland	010 020 000	3	8	2
Washington	200 100 10x	4	7	2

WP **Johnson**; LP Kahler, **Mitchell** (5)

4. Saturday, July 13

Chicago	000 100 100	2	7	3
Washington	111 010 00x	4	6	1

WP **Johnson**; LP **Cicotte**

5. Tuesday, July 16

Chicago	000 020 00	2	7	3
Washington	210 002 02	7	9	2

WP **Johnson**; LP **Peters**, Bell (2), Benz (6), Lange (8) (8 innings, time limit)

6. Monday, July 22

Detroit	000 000 201	3	7	1
Washington	020 300 00x	5	14	3

WP **Johnson**; LP **Works**

7. Thursday, July 25[2]

Detroit	101 100 020	5	8	5
Washington	200 020 21x	7	6	2

WP **Johnson**; LP Mullin, **Works** (6)

8. Sunday, July 28[1]

Washington	101 001 010	4	10	0
Cleveland	000 000 010	1	8	1

WP **Johnson**; LP **Gregg**

9. Friday, August 2

Washington	001 002 001	4	8	1
Detroit	000 000 000	0	7	0

WP **Johnson**; LP **Willett**

10. Monday, August 5

Washington	001 002 130 1	8	16	3
Chicago	106 000 000 0	7	9	0

WP Groom, Cashion (3), **Johnson** (8); LP Cicotte, Benz (8), **White** (8) (10 innings)

11. Wednesday, August 7

Washington	021 031 300	10	13	1
Chicago	000 000 001	1	6	3

WP **Johnson**, Engel (7); LP **Lange**, Peters (7)

12. Sunday, August 11

Washington	000 110 010	3	6	2
St. Louis	000 010 010	2	4	1

WP **Johnson**; LP **Hamilton**

13. Thursday, August 15

Chicago	000 200 001 0	3	8	4
Washington	100 002 000 1	4	7	2

WP Cashion, **Johnson** (9); LP White, **Walsh** (9) (10 innings)

14. Friday, August 16

Chicago	000 000 000	0	1	3
Washington	201 001 00x	4	7	2

WP **Johnson**; LP **Benz**

[1]*First game of a doubleheader.* [2]*Second game of a doubleheader.*

15. Tuesday, August 20[1]

Cleveland	000 000 200	2	10	2
Washington	000 012 10x	4	7	0

WP Schegg, **Johnson** (1); LP Gregg, **Steen** (1), Mitchell (8)

16. Friday, August 23[1]

Detroit	000 100 000	1	7	4
Washington	013 003 01x	8	7	1

WP **Johnson**; LP **Dubuc**, Works (4)

Johnson's American League record streak ended three days later at Washington's National Park.

Monday, August 26[2]

St. Louis	000 020 200	4	8	4
Washington	011 000 100	3	5	3

WP **Hamilton**; LP Hughes, **Johnson** (7)

With the score tied, 2–2, one out in the seventh inning, and St. Louis catcher Paul Kritchell on first base and shortstop Bobby Wallace on second, Johnson replaced right-hander Long Tom Hughes. A short passed ball allowed the runners to move to second and third, and both scored when outfielder Pete Compton singled for a 4–3 St. Louis win as left-hander Earl Hamilton, helped by a sensational catch in center field by outfielder Burt Shotton, held the Senators to five hits.

The official scorer charged Johnson with the loss, although Hughes put the tying and winning runs on base in the seventh and under modern rules would have suffered the defeat. American League President Ban Johnson, who often overruled scoring decisions in those days, upheld the scorer's ruling, and the point became moot two days later when Johnson went the route and lost to St. Louis, 3–2, despite striking out twelve.

Washington had a 74–45 record after Johnson's sixteenth straight win and had climbed into second place, eight games behind Boston.

During his streak Johnson pitched in nineteen games, had ten complete games in twelve starts and won four games in his seven relief appearances. One of his other three relief stints ended in an eleven-inning 3–3 tie with St. Louis before darkness ended it, with Johnson pitching the last two and one-third innings without allowing a hit or a walk on July 20. Another ended in a 3–2 Washington win at Chicago on August 4 as Johnson earned a save with a hitless ninth inning after a run had scored off Hughes, and the third saw Washington lose, 2–1, at

---

[1]*First game of a doubleheader.* [2]*Second game of a doubleheader.*

WALTER JOHNSON, PIT(
WASHINGTON
                     PI

In twenty-one years with the Washington Senators, Walter Johnson won 416 games with a great fast ball and an easy motion. He won thirty-two games in 1912, and set an American League record with sixteen victories in succession. (Courtesy of National Baseball Library, Cooperstown, New York.)

St. Louis on August 10 in the second game of a doubleheader, Johnson pitching a scoreless eighth in which he allowed one hit.

In the nineteen games during the streak, Johnson pitched 130⅔ innings, gave up twenty-two runs and ninety hits while averaging just over one walk and more than seven strikeouts per nine innings. He faced only five teams, not pitching against either Boston or Philadelphia. He beat Chicago six times, Detroit four times, Cleveland three times, New York twice, and St. Louis once. The streak consumed only fifty-two days, the fewest of any streak of sixteen or more games in modern major league history.

Five of Johnson's victories were by a one-run margin, four were by two runs, one by three runs, two by four runs, one each by five runs, seven, eight and nine runs.

The first of the two shutouts Johnson pitched during the streak was in Game 9 (August 2) at Detroit. He allowed seven hits and one walk while striking out eight. The Tigers threatened to score only in the seventh when two singles put runners on first and second with one out. Then, third baseman Charlie Deal bunted to the mound for a force at third, catcher Oscar Stanage was thrown out at first on a tap in front of the plate by Ainsmith, and right-hander Ed Willett popped out to first.

Johnson's second shutout was the best game he pitched that season in Game 14 (August 16), beating Chicago, 4–0, with a one-hitter in which he issued no walks, struck out seven, and did not allow a runner to reach third. After an error put a Chicago runner on first in the third inning, second baseman Morrie Rath hit a sharp grounder that shortstop George McBride knocked down for a single and the lone hit. Outfielder Wally Mattick then grounded into a double play. A sensational catch by outfielder Howard Shanks robbed third baseman Rollie Zeider of a possible home run in the Chicago eighth. Two singles and first baseman Chick Gandil's two-run double in the first inning gave Johnson all the runs he needed.

In the only two games Johnson started and failed to complete during the streak, Washington piled up big leads and Manager Clark Griffith wanted to rest his ace, who often pitched with minimum time between starts. In Game 1 (July 3), Johnson was taken out after six innings with the Senators ahead, 9–1, and they won, 10–2. In Game 11 (August 7) Washington scored three times in the seventh inning to take a 10–0 lead, and right-hander Joe Engel pitched the last three innings of the 10–1 victory at Chicago.

Three of the five one-run victories were in extra innings, including a sixteen-inning 6–5 win over New York in Game 2 (July 5). Johnson replaced Engel in New York's three-run fourth inning as the visitors took a 5–2 lead. Washington tied with three runs in the sixth on a walk, McBride's single, an error, a single by Ainsmith, and a triple by Johnson. Neither team scored again until the bottom of the sixteenth, when outfielder Danny Moeller led off with a single, took second on third baseman Eddie Foster's single, was forced at third on outfielder Clyde Milan's bunt, and, after Gandil grounded out, second baseman Ray Morgan singled to drive in the winning run.

Johnson relieved in Game 10 (August 5) at Chicago after Washington had overcome a 7–1 White Sox lead with two runs in the sixth, one in the seventh, and three in the eighth. The Senators won, 8–7, in the tenth when McBride doubled and scored on a single by Johnson, who didn't give up a hit in the two and one-third innings he pitched. That hit was one of fifteen Johnson had during the streak, in which he batted .319.

Johnson also relieved in Game 13 (August 15) after Chicago scored a run in the ninth inning off right-handed starter Carl Cashion on two errors by Foster to tie the score, 3–3. Johnson gave up two hits in the one and two-thirds innings he pitched and became the winning pitcher in the tenth, when Foster redeemed himself with a double to right, took third on a passed ball, and scored on a wild pickoff throw past third by Chicago catcher Walt Kuhn to give Washington the 4–3 victory.

Johnson broke the American League record for consecutive victories set at fourteen in 1904 by New York right-hander Jack Chesbro in Game 15 (August 20) that began with both managers starting left-handed pitchers, then switching to right-handers after one batter. McBride singled home a run in the fifth and Washington went ahead, 3–0, with two runs in the sixth on a walk, Moeller's double and Gandil's single. After Cleveland scored twice on three hits in the seventh, McBride's single, a passed ball and Johnson's single in the home half gave the Nats their final run in the 4–2 win.

Three days later, Johnson won his sixteenth game in a row handily, 8–1, for his twenty-eighth win of the season against seven losses. He then slumped, losing five games in a row from August 26 through September 11 before winning, 6–3, at Detroit on September 15. One of the losses was at Boston, where right-hander Joe Wood won, 1–0, for the fourteenth victory in the Red Sox pitcher's sixteen-game winning streak.

Johnson finished the 1912 season with a 32–12 record, thirty-four complete games in thirty-seven shutouts. However, he led the league only in earned run average with 1.39 and in strikeouts with 303.

Johnson pitched twenty-one seasons in his major league career, all with Washington. He won more than thirty games twice, and won twenty or more games twelve times, finishing with an American League record 416 victories while losing 279, with 110 shutouts, still the major league record. He retired with 3,508 strikeouts, a major league record that has since been broken. He also won thirty-eight of sixty-four games that ended 1–0.

After pitching his final game in 1927, Johnson managed Newark of the International League in 1928, Washington from 1929 through 1932, and then Cleveland from June 1933 until August 1935. Elected to the Hall of Fame in 1936, he died on December 10, 1946, in Washington, D.C., five weeks after his fifty-ninth birthday.

Joe Wood
1912 Boston Red Sox

16 Consecutive Wins

Right-hander Joe Wood had a relatively short major league pitching career because of arm trouble, but at his peak he was as good as any pitcher of his time. In his prime, the five-foot eleven-inch 180-pounder reputedly threw as hard as anyone in the history of baseball.

Born October 25, 1889, in Kansas City, Wood pitched as a teen-ager for the Bloomer Girls. In 1907 he won eighteen games as a seven-teen-year-old for Hutchinson of the Western Association. He moved up to Kansas City of the American Association in 1908 and, despite a 7–12 record, he was purchased on August 12 by the Boston Red Sox for $3,200.

Wood appeared in six games with the Red Sox that season and made two starts. He lost his first, 6–4, then, on October 3, he pitched a 5–0 shutout at Philadelphia. In 1909 he became a regular starter for the Red Sox and compiled an 11–7 record, followed by a 12–13 log in 1910. By 1911 Wood was the Boston ace, winning twenty-three games and losing seventeen, and pitching a no-hitter against St. Louis on July 29, some three weeks after racking up fifteen strikeouts in a nine-inning game.

In 1912 Wood had one of the great seasons in big league history, winning sixteen games before the end of June. In the July 4 morning game, Wood lost, 4–3, at Philadelphia, the winning run scoring in the seventh inning on catcher Jack Lapp's single, a force-out, outfielder Bris Lord's double and outfielder Rube Oldring's sacrifice fly.

That was Wood's fourth defeat in twenty decisions. Four days

128

later at Boston's new Fenway Park, Wood began his sixteen-game winning streak for first-place Boston, which had a six and one-half game lead over second-place Washington, having won fifty-one games and lost twenty-four.

1. Monday, July 8

St. Louis	100 000 000	1	7	4
Boston	300 001 01x	5	11	1

WP **Wood**; LP **Allison**, C. Brown (8)

2. Friday, July 12[1]

Detroit	000 000 000 00	0	5	2
Boston	000 000 000 01	1	7	0

WP **Wood**; LP **Willett** (11 innings)

3. Wednesday, July 17

Chicago	100 002 000	3	5	2
Boston	000 210 04x	7	15	3

WP **Wood**; LP **Peters**

4. Tuesday, July 23

Cleveland	100 000 101	3	8	2
Boston	011 002 20x	6	9	3

WP **Wood**; LP **Blanding**, Kahler (7)

5. Sunday, July 28

Boston	201 020 000	5	13	2
Chicago	000 040 000	4	8	3

WP **Wood**, Bedient (5); LP **Cicotte**

6. Friday, August 2

Boston	000 610 110	9	12	2
St. Louis	000 000 000	0	3	1

WP **Wood**; LP **Hamilton**, Powell (6)

7. Tuesday, August 6

Boston	000 201 000 02	5	11	3
Cleveland	000 003 000 01	4	13	3

WP **Wood**; LP **Blanding** (11 innings)

8. Saturday, August 10

Boston	000 002 110	4	9	0
Detroit	100 000 000	1	7	3

WP **Wood**; LP **Willett**

9. Wednesday, August 14[1]

St. Louis	000 000 00	0	4	3
Boston	005 200 1x	8	9	0

WP **Wood**; LP **Allison**, Adams (4) (8 innings, darkness)

10. Tuesday, August 20

Detroit	000 100 001	2	6	3
Boston	002 002 20x	6	8	4

WP **Wood**; LP **Dubuc**

11. Saturday, August 24

Cleveland	000 101 011	4	7	3
Boston	300 401 00x	8	9	5

WP **Wood**; LP **Gregg**, Kahler (5)

12. Wednesday, August 28[1]

Chicago	000 000 000	0	6	0
Boston	000 300 00x	3	7	0

WP **Wood**; LP **Taylor**, White (8)

13. Monday, September 2[1]

Boston	100 000 000	1	7	0
New York	000 000 000	0	8	2

WP **Wood**; LP **McConnell**

14. Friday, September 6

Washington	000 000 000	0	6	0
Boston	000 001 00x	1	5	0

WP **Wood**; LP **Johnson**

[1]*Second game of a doubleheader*

15. Tuesday, September 10

| Boston | 030 010 100 | 5 | 9 | 3 |
| Chicago | 000 001 021 | 4 | 12 | 1 |

WP **Wood**, Hall (9); LP **Benz**, White (2)

16. Sunday, September 15[1]

| Boston | 000 010 01 | 2 | 5 | 0 |
| St. Louis | 000 000 10 | 1 | 7 | 0 |

WP **Wood**; LP **Hamilton** (8 innings, darkness)

Five days later at Detroit's Navin Field, Wood's record-tying streak came to an end.

Friday, September 20

| Boston | 000 130 000 | 4 | 4 | 2 |
| Detroit | 003 020 01x | 6 | 7 | 3 |

WP Covington, **Lake**, (5); LP **Wood**

Boston, which had clinched the American League pennant two days earlier, gave some of its regulars a day off, and that proved costly for Wood. Sub-shortstop Marty Krug dropped a pop fly for a damaging error. However, Wood paved the way for his defeat by walking four batters in a row in Detroit's three-run third. With none out in Boston's fifth, Detroit right-hander Bill Covington got into an argument with Umpire Silk O'Loughlin over a decision and was ejected. He was replaced by right-hander Joe Lake, who blanked Boston on three hits for the rest of the game.

After the sixteenth win, Boston had a 97–39 record and led Philadelphia by sixteen and one-half games.

During his streak Wood appeared in nineteen games, made sixteen starts and completed fourteen, pitched six shutouts, and appeared three times in relief, being credited with one save. In 140⅓ innings, he gave up only twenty-seven runs and 112 hits. In addition to his six shutouts, he allowed one run in three games, two runs in one game, three runs in two games, and four runs in four games. He won four games from both St. Louis and Chicago, three from Detroit and Cleveland, and one each from New York and Washington. He did not face Philadelphia during that streak.

Boston trailed in only four of the sixteen games in the streak, all in the first eight games and was behind only once as late as the fifth inning. The first extra-inning win was by 1–0 in eleven innings in Game 2 (July 12), as Wood won a duel with Detroit right-hander Ed Willett

[1]*Second game of a doubleheader*

Smokey Joe Wood helped pitch the 1912 Boston Red Sox to the world championship by winning thirty-four games, including a league record of sixteen in a row. (Courtesy of National Baseball Library, Cooperstown, New York.)

at home. With two out, Boston outfielder Tris Speaker lined a hit to left center that was misplayed into three bases by outfielder Jim Delahanty, and outfielder Duffy Lewis singled to center on the next pitch to win the game.

The other overtime win was in Cleveland, where the Indians scored three runs in the sixth inning to tie the score at 3–3 in Game 7

(August 6). In the eleventh, Boston scored twice on first baseman Jake Stahl's single, a walk, a passed ball, an intentional walk to outfielder Harry Hooper that loaded the bases, and a two-run single to center by second baseman Steve Yerkes.

Cleveland came back in its half of the eleventh to score once when second baseman Larry Lajoie singled, first baseman Art Griggs singled and the ball went through Lewis in left field, and outfielder Joe Birmingham hit a sacrifice fly to right. Griggs took second on Hooper's futile throw to the plate, but Wood bore down to strike out pinch-hitters Ted Easterly and Bill Hunter to end the 5–4 Boston victory.

Wood pitched shutouts in his last start in August and in his first two starts in September. His last four victories were all by a one-run margin. Boston scored the only run in the first inning of Game 13 (September 2) when Hooper singled, took second on New York right-hander George McConnell's wild pickoff throw, went to third on a sacrifice by Yerkes, and scored on Speaker's sacrifice fly.

The only run of Game 14 (September 6) was scored in Boston's sixth inning when Speaker doubled down the third-base line into the crowd that overflowed the Fenway Park outfield and scored with two out when Lewis doubled to right on a high fly that Washington outfielder Danny Moeller was barely able to touch near the foul line after first losing it in the sun. This game was a spectacular and highly publicized duel between Wood and Washington's great right-hander, Walter Johnson, whose own sixteen-game winning streak had ended less than two weeks before.

In Game 16 (September 15), the final win in the streak, Boston scored in the top of the fifth inning on a walk, shortstop Heinie Wagner's single, and catcher Hick Cady's sacrifice fly to center. St. Louis tied in the home seventh to end Wood's thirty-four-inning scoreless streak against the Browns when shortstop Del Pratt doubled, took third on an outfield fly, and scored on pinch-hitter Pete Compton's single. Wood scored the winning run in the eighth after he walked with one out, and advanced on a single by Hooper, who was forced by Yerkes. Speaker was walked intentionally to load the bases, and right-hander Earl Hamilton then made a wild pitch, allowing Wood to score. Wood then retired St. Louis in order in the home eighth, and the game was called because of darkness.

Wood, who batted .290 that season, hit .333 during his winning streak, getting a triple, five doubles, and ten singles in forty-eight official times at bat.

After his streak-ending loss, Wood beat New York, 6–0, on September 25 and on October 3 beat Philadelphia, 17–5, to make his final record thirty-four victories, five defeats, and an earned run average of 1.91. He completed thirty-five of his thirty-eight starts and pitched ten shutouts, leading the American League in wins, winning percentage, shutouts, and complete games.

In the World Series victory over the New York Giants, Wood posted three of Boston's four victories.

Wood pitched three more seasons with Boston with only modest success, sat out the 1916 season with arm trouble, and then was sold to Cleveland on February 24, 1917. He switched to the outfield in 1918 when his arm problems persisted. He retired after the 1922 season, the only one in which he was an outfield regular.

Wood, whose son, Joe, pitched briefly for the Boston Red Sox in 1944, served as Yale University's baseball coach from 1923 through 1942. He died on July 27, 1985, three months before his ninety-sixth birthday.

Lefty Grove
1931 Philadelphia Athletics
16 Consecutive Wins

Lefty Grove worked in a coal mine, a glass works, and a railroad shop after leaving school in the eighth grade, and didn't enjoy any job until he entered professional baseball. He went on to become one of the greatest left-handed pitchers in baseball history.

Born March 6, 1900, at Lonaconing, Maryland, Robert Moses Grove began playing organized sandlot baseball at the age of seventeen. A first baseman in the beginning, he was moved to the pitching mound because he could throw harder than anyone in his area. By the time the six-foot three-inch, 190-pounder reached the major leagues, he was rated a fastball pitcher second to none.

Grove made his professional debut with Martinsburg of the Blue Ridge League in 1920, and later that season he was purchased for $2,000 by the Baltimore Orioles of the International League. He pitched for Baltimore through 1924 with outstanding success, but wildness and the high price Baltimore demanded for his contract delayed his entry to the major leagues.

After Grove had won twenty-seven games for the second year in a row with Baltimore in 1924, the Philadelphia Athletics paid $100,600 for him. The $600 was added because Baltimore owner Jack Dunn wanted the price to be higher than what the New York Yankees paid the Boston Red Sox for Babe Ruth after the 1919 season. Grove was worth every penny.

Wildness hampered him with the Athletics in 1925 and 1926, but he enjoyed the first of his eight twenty-win seasons in 1927. He posted

20-12, 24-8, 20-6 and 28-5 records from 1927 through 1930, leading the American League in strikeouts every year.

Grove helped the A's win world championships in 1929 and 1930, when he won seven games in a row and fifteen of his last sixteen decisions. A workhorse, Grove often relieved between starts.

In 1931 Grove won the season opener in relief at Washington, lost his first start, 2-1, four days later at Washington, started and beat Washington, 5-1, at home on April 22 to begin an eight-game winning streak. A severe cold kept Grove inactive for the next two weeks, probably costing him three starts, and he didn't start again until May 12 when he won, 5-2, at Chicago. That winning streak, along with a twenty-five scoreless-inning string, ended June 5 when the Chicago White Sox beat the left-hander, 7-5, by scoring two runs in the twelfth inning after the A's star had relieved in the seventh.

That defeat was Grove's second of the season against nine victories, and three days later, with the A's leading the American League with a 33-11 record, five games ahead of second-place Washington, the left-hander began his league-record-tying sixteen-game winning streak at Philadelphia's Shibe Park.

1. Monday, June 8

Detroit	200 000 001	3	7	0
Philadelphia	000 014 02x	7	8	3

WP **Grove**; LP **Whitehill**

2. Saturday, June 13

St. Louis	000 101 001	3	7	1
Philadelphia	000 301 42x	10	9	1

WP **Grove**; LP **Stewart**, Stiles (8)

3. Friday, June 19

Philadelphia	201 113 020	10	14	0
Chicago	003 000 100	4	12	1

WP **Grove**; LP **Caraway**, Moore (5), Faber (7), Frasier (8)

4. Tuesday, June 23

Philadelphia	010 000 002	3	12	0
St. Louis	000 000 000	0	2	1

WP **Grove**; LP **Collins**, Stiles (9)

5. Saturday, June 27

Philadelphia	301 020 003	9	13	1
Detroit	220 010 000	5	12	0

WP **Grove**; LP **Herring**, Sullivan (9), Hoyt (9)

6. Wednesday, July 1

Philadelphia	000 102 010	4	11	1
Cleveland	000 100 200	3	11	1

WP **Grove**; LP **Ferrell**

7. Saturday, July 4

Boston	040 020 010	7	10	0
Philadelphia	700 010 10x	9	14	0

WP Mahaffey, Rommel (2), **Grove** (3); LP **Morris**, Durham (1), Lisenbee (2), Russell (8) (morning game)

8. Wednesday, July 8

Philadelphia	410 001 000	6	11	2
Washington	000 003 000	3	11	0

WP **Grove**; LP **Brown**, Burke (3), Fischer (7), Hadley (9)

9. Monday, July 13[1]

Washington	032 000 020	7	13	0
Philadelphia	301 000 17x	12	11	4

WP **Grove**, Earnshaw (9); LP Marberry, **Hadley** (8), Burke (8)

10. Friday, July 17

Detroit	000 001 002	3	9	0
Philadelphia	040 000 11x	6	10	1

WP **Grove**; LP **Uhle**

11. Saturday, July 25

Cleveland	001 002 000	3	8	0
Philadelphia	000 200 31x	6	11	1

WP **Grove**; LP **Ferrell**

12. Tuesday, July 28

St. Louis	000 000 120	3	9	3
Philadelphia	100 010 13x	6	9	1

WP Earnshaw, **Grove** (8); LP **Hebert**, Kimsey (9)

13. Monday, August 3[1]

Washington	000 000 020	2	11	0
Philadelphia	003 000 00x	3	8	1

WP **Grove**; LP **Jones**, Hadley (3)

14. Tuesday, August 11

Philadelphia	240 000 020	8	14	0
Detroit	001 000 000	1	8	1

WP **Grove**; LP **Sorrell**, Sullivan (2)

15. Saturday, August 15

Philadelphia	300 000 100	4	6	1
Cleveland	000 002 010	3	8	1

WP **Grove**; LP **Ferrell**

16. Wednesday, August 19

Philadelphia	021 000 010	4	12	1
Chicago	000 000 002	2	7	3

WP **Grove**; LP **Faber**, Moore (9)

Grove's streak ended four days later at Sportsman's Park, St. Louis.

Sunday, August 23[1]

Philadelphia	000 000 000	0	3	0
St. Louis	001 000 00x	1	7	0

WP **Coffman**; LP **Grove**

Right-hander Dick Coffman, who won a one-hit, 1–0 game from Chicago two weeks before, posted his fourth straight victory by outpitching Grove, whose streak ended on a tainted run in the third inning. With two out in that inning, outfielder Fred Schulte singled to center field and second baseman Oscar Melillo followed with a line drive to left field. Jim Moore misjudged the ball, came in, and the ball carried over his head for a run-scoring double. Moore was subbing for star slugger Al Simmons, who was sidelined for the sixth straight game because of an infected toe.

Philadelphia's only hits were a bunt single by first baseman Jimmie Foxx with one out in the second, a single by Moore with two out in the

---

[1]First game of a doubleheader.

fourth, and a leadoff single by catcher Mickey Cochrane to right field in the seventh. Cochrane became the only player to reach second against Coffman on Moore's sacrifice. But Foxx then looked at a third strike and, after outfielder Bing Miller drew Coffman's only walk, third baseman Eric McNair ended the A's only scoring threat with a short fly to right. That ended the only shutout game Philadelphia lost in 1931. The Athletics bats came alive in the second game that day in a 10–0 victory, but that was small solace for the hot-tempered Grove.

After Grove won his sixteenth straight game, Philadelphia had an 82–31 record and a thirteen-game lead over second-place Washington.

During the streak, Grove appeared in eighteen games, relieving four times. He won twice in relief while he failed to complete only one of his fourteen starts. He beat every team in the league in the streak except New York—a team he faced only once, and that was in a two-inning scoreless relief stint. He beat Detroit four times; St. Louis, Cleveland and Washington three times apiece; Chicago twice; and Boston once. Philadelphia trailed in five of the sixteen games, three after the fifth inning.

Detroit scored twice in the first inning of Game 1 (June 8), but two home runs by Foxx around a four-run outburst in the sixth inning gave Grove and the A's a 7–3 win.

Grove's worst outing in the streak was in Game 9 (July 13). He gave up five runs in the first three innings, and Washington scored twice more in the eighth to forge a 7–5 lead. In the home eighth, Foxx tripled and right-hander Bump Hadley walked three batters in a row to force in a run. Left-hander Bobby Burke relieved, and shortstop Dib Williams batted for Grove and hit a grand-slam homer. Later in the inning Simmons hit a two-run homer for a 12–7 victory.

Cleveland right-hander Wes Ferrell held a 3–2 lead over Philadelphia until Williams hit a two-run single in the three-run seventh as Grove won, 6–3, in Game 11 (July 25). In Game 6 (July 1) Williams had knocked in the winning run off Ferrell in the eighth inning to snap a 3–3 tie and give Grove a 4–3 victory.

Grove's first relief win was Game 7 (July 4), when he came on in the third inning, Philadelphia leading, 7–4. He struck out ten but Boston scored three runs before the game ended with the A's winning, 9–7.

In his other relief victory, Grove replaced right-hander George Earnshaw in Game 12 (July 28) after St. Louis outfielder Goose Goslin had tied the score, 3–3, with a two-run homer and third baseman Red Kress had followed with a triple. Grove retired the next three batters without Kress scoring, and Simmons then homered in the home eighth to start a three-run rally in the 6–3 victory.

The best game Grove pitched in the streak was a two-hit, 3–0 win in Game 4 (June 23) for the third of his four 1931 shutouts. A double by Goslin and a single by outfielder Larry Bettencourt were the only St. Louis hits. Miller singled home the first Philadelphia run in the second inning. Second baseman Max Bishop hit a two-run single in the ninth.

In Game 16 (August 19) Grove shut out Chicago until the ninth when an error helped the home team score twice, while two errors by forty-two-year-old right-hander Red Faber and run-scoring singles by McNair and outfielder Roger Cramer helped the A's win, 4–2.

Grove won his next six starts after his winning streak ended, beating Boston, 9–4, on September 24 for his thirty-first victory of the season. Three days later in New York, the left-hander left after three innings with the A's trailing, 5–1, and was charged with his fourth loss of the season as New York went on to win, 13–1, in the final game of the season.

Grove's great season helped Philadelphia win its third straight pennant, the A's finishing with a 107–45 record, thirteen and one-half games in front of second-place New York. Grove led the league in wins, in winning percentage with a mark of .886, with a 2.06 earned run average, with twenty-seven complete games, and with 175 strikeouts. He was named the American League's most valuable player.

In the 1931 World Series, Grove won the first and sixth games and lost the third to St. Louis, which beat the A's in seven games. In the 1929 World Series, Grove did not start a game but saved two, and in 1930 he had a 2–1 record, one of the wins coming in relief.

Grove won twenty-five games in 1932 and twenty-four in 1933, then was traded to the Boston Red Sox on December 12, 1933. Arm trouble then hit the left-hander, and he was never again the overpowering pitcher he had been. He had an 8–8 record in 1934, recovered to win twenty games in 1935, and was a productive pitcher through 1939. He won seven games in each of the next two seasons, winning his three-hundredth and final game on July 25, 1941, beating Cleveland, 10–6.

Grove lost only 141 games in his seventeen-year major league career for a sparkling winning percentage of .680. In his career, he relieved 160 times, winning thirty-three and saving fifty-five. He pitched in a total of 616 games and hurled thirty-five shutouts.

Grove, voted into the Hall of Fame in 1947, died in Norwalk, Ohio, on May 23, 1975.

Schoolboy Rowe
1934 Detroit Tigers

16 Consecutive Wins

Lynwood ("Schoolboy") Rowe was one of America's great all-around athletes in the 1930s. Born January 11, 1910, in Waco, Texas, the six-foot four-and-one-half-inch, 210-pound Rowe grew up in El Dorado, Arkansas, where in high school he was an all-state selection three years in football and two years in basketball, was high-point man in eleven track meets, won the state interscholastic golf championship, was an outstanding boxer, and was a star pitcher and hitter in baseball.

The right-hander made his professional debut in 1932 and helped Beaumont win the Texas League pennant, winning nineteen games and losing only seven, leading the league with a 2.34 earned run average while batting .295 with ten home runs.

Rowe won a job with the Detroit Tigers the next spring, but came up with arm trouble in midseason and pitched in only nineteen games, winning seven and losing four. In his major league debut, he shut out the Chicago White Sox, 3–0, on six hits.

His arm was fine in 1934, but Rowe lost three of his first four decisions before winning three in a row. In his next start on June 10, at home against Chicago, Rowe gave up two runs in the seventh inning on two walks, an infield out, and a single by third baseman Jimmy Dykes, the White Sox manager, to lose, 3–1, to forty-one-year-old right-hander Sad Sam Jones. That defeat evened the twenty-four-year-old Rowe's record at 4–4.

Five days later at Boston's Fenway Park, Rowe began his American League record-tying winning streak. Going into that game, Detroit

had a 30–21 record and was in second place behind New York, which
had a 29–20 log.

1. Friday, June 15

| Detroit | 103 004 210 | 11 | 12 | 1 |
| Boston | 010 200 100 | 4 | 9 | 1 |

WP **Rowe**; LP **Ostermueller**, Johnson (6),
Welch (7)

2. Sunday, June 24

| Detroit | 101 050 001 | 8 | 12 | 2 |
| Philadelphia | 000 100 300 | 4 | 12 | 2 |

WP **Rowe**; LP **Wilshere**, Mahaffey (5),
Cascarella (6), Benton (9)

3. Sunday, July 1[2]

| Detroit | 214 030 002 | 12 | 15 | 0 |
| St. Louis | 003 000 000 | 3 | 13 | 1 |

WP **Rowe**; LP **Newsom**, Coffman (3),
Mills (5)

4. Wednesday, July 4[2]

| Cleveland | 100 000 10 | 2 | 9 | 1 |
| Detroit | 200 020 1x | 5 | 6 | 0 |

WP Fischer, **Rowe** (3); LP **Hudlin** (7½
innings, darkness)

5. Sunday, July 8

| St. Louis | 000 021 010 | 4 | 6 | 3 |
| Detroit | 000 000 113 | 5 | 10 | 1 |

WP Marberry, **Rowe** (7); LP Blaeholder,
Newsom (9), Wells (9)

6. Thursday, July 12

| New York | 100 001 000 | 2 | 6 | 0 |
| Detroit | 201 000 01x | 4 | 8 | 0 |

WP **Rowe**; LP **Broaca**

7. Sunday, July 15

| New York | 000 011 100 | 3 | 10 | 2 |
| Detroit | 010 004 21x | 8 | 12 | 0 |

WP **Rowe**, Marberry (7); LP **Murphy**,
MacFayden (8)

8. Sunday, July 22[2]

| Philadelphia | 033 000 200 | 8 | 13 | 4 |
| Detroit | 033 004 34x | 17 | 14 | 1 |

WP Marberry, **Rowe** (3); LP Benton,
Marcum (4), Mahaffey (7)

9. Saturday, July 28

| Detroit | 502 110 002 | 11 | 14 | 0 |
| Chicago | 000 010 000 | 1 | 3 | 4 |

WP **Rowe**; LP **Lyons**

10. Sunday, July 29[1]

| Detroit | 300 204 232 | 16 | 18 | 1 |
| Chicago | 000 060 720 | 15 | 19 | 2 |

WP Bridges, Phillips (5), Auker (7), **Rowe**
(8); LP Earnshaw, Gallivan (6), **Heving**
(8), Jones (9)

11. Friday, August 3

| Chicago | 000 000 000 | 0 | 1 | 3 |
| Detroit | 420 160 10x | 14 | 16 | 2 |

WP **Rowe**, Gaston (8); LP **Gaston**, Kinzy
(5)

12. Friday, August 10

| Cleveland | 000 100 400 00 | 5 | 13 | 1 |
| Detroit | 100 000 130 01 | 6 | 19 | 2 |

WP **Rowe**; LP Hildebrand, **Harder** (7) (11
innings)

13. Tuesday, August 14[2]

| Detroit | 201 000 022 | 7 | 12 | 1 |
| New York | 000 012 000 | 3 | 4 | 0 |

WP **Rowe**; LP **Ruffing**

14. Friday, August 17[2]

| Detroit | 020 000 000 | 2 | 5 | 0 |
| New York | 000 000 000 | 0 | 3 | 1 |

WP **Rowe** LP **DeShong**

---

[1]*First game of a doubleheader.* [2]*Second game of a doubleheader.*

15. Tuesday, August 21

Detroit	010 303 001	8	10	1
Boston	020 020 000	4	9	2

WP **Rowe**; LP **Ostermueller**, Rhodes (6), Johnson (8)

16. Saturday, August 25

Detroit	000 001 003	4	12	3
Washington	001 000 100	2	9	1

WP **Rowe**; LP **Weaver**, Russell (9)

Four days later, Rowe's sixteen-game winning streak ended at Philadelphia's Shibe Park.

Wednesday, August 29[1]

Detroit	200 000 120	5	11	0
Philadelphia	000 251 50x	13	16	3

WP **Marcum**; LP **Rowe**, Sorrell (7)

Singles by outfielder Jo-Jo White and catcher Mickey Cochrane, Detroit's manager, and a run-scoring force-out and a two-out single by shortstop Billy Rogell staked Rowe to 2–0 lead in the first inning. Philadelphia tied in the fourth on second baseman Rabbit Warstler's single, outfielder Bing Miller's double, a run-scoring infield out by first baseman Jimmie Foxx, and a safe fielder's choice by third baseman Pinky Higgins, and broke the game open in the five-run fifth when Miller hit a three-run double and Higgins hit a two-run homer. Rowe gave up twelve hits and ten runs before being lifted in the five-run seventh, while Philadelphia right-hander Johnny Marcum, who had three singles and batted in two runs, won his tenth game of the season and his sixth in a row.

During his streak, Rowe pitched in twenty-three games, making fifteen starts and completing ten, pitching one shutout and one game in which he was replaced after seven innings with Detroit ahead, 14–0. He had no decision in three of his starts, one of which Detroit lost, and in relief he won four games and saved one. He beat every team in the league, winning four from New York, three from Chicago, one from Washington, and two from each of the other four clubs.

Rowe had some close shaves during his streak, his first coming in his second start on June 20 when he was chased in a six-run sixth as Washington took a 9–6 lead. Detroit rallied for four runs in the seventh and scored three runs in the eleventh to win, 13–10.

On August 7, after third baseman Harlond Clift opened the game

---

[1]*Second game of a doubleheader.*

with a single, Rowe was replaced because of a muscle spasm in his back. St. Louis scored in that inning, and Detroit tied in the last of the first, then overcame a 4–1 deficit with an eight-run seventh to win, 12–8.

In Game 12 (August 10) Cleveland built a 5–1 lead against Rowe, but Detroit scored once in the seventh and three times in the eighth when Rowe singled home one of the runs. In the eleventh, with first baseman Hank Greenberg on third, Rowe's high fly to left scored him with the run that won the game, 6–5.

In Game 16 (August 25) second baseman Buddy Myer singled in the run that gave Washington a 2–1 lead in the home seventh. In the ninth Detroit rallied for three runs to win, 4–2, Greenberg's homer tying the score and singles by third baseman Marv Owen, outfielder Pete Fox, and Rowe producing the winning run, with another run scoring on an error.

Rowe, who batted .303 that season, really helped himself with his bat during his streak. In his sixteen straight wins, he hit .389 with twenty-one hits, including six doubles, one triple, and a homer, and batted in thirteen runs.

In Game 5 (July 8) Detroit trailed St. Louis, 3–0, when Rowe relieved in the seventh, He singled across a seventh-inning run, and Detroit matched the run St. Louis scored in the eighth. In the ninth, Detroit scored three runs to win, 5–4, on singles by Owen and Rowe, a fumble by second baseman Oscar Melillo, a bases-loaded walk to Cochrane, and outfielder Goose Goslin's grounder to second that Melillo threw past the plate, allowing Rowe and Fox to score and end the game.

In Game 9 (July 28) Rowe doubled twice, singled and drove in three runs as Detroit scored eight unearned runs in an 11–1 win over Chicago. In Game 10 (July 20) he relieved to pitch hitless ball over the last one and two-thirds innings and hit a two-run homer in the ninth inning to win the game, 16–15, at Chicago.

In Game 11 (August 3) Dykes singled over second for the only Chicago hit in the seventh. Rowe then was lifted as Detroit won, 14–0. In Game 14 (August 17) Rowe pitched a three-hitter at New York to win, 2–0, for his first shutout of the season.

Rowe's most spectacular relief effort was on August 1, when he entered the game with Detroit leading at Cleveland, 10–7, one out and the bases loaded. He struck out first baseman Hal Trosky, who had homered earlier in the game, and second baseman Odell Hale to end the game.

Rowe broke even in his last eight decisions after his sixteenth straight win to finish with a 24–8 record, then split even in two starts in the World Series that Detroit lost to the St. Louis Cardinals in seven games.

After Rowe's sixteenth straight win, Detroit had a 79–42 record and a five-game lead over New York. The Tigers finished with 101 wins, fifty-three losses, to finish seven games ahead of New York.

Rowe never again won twenty games, but he did win nineteen in 1935 and nineteen again in 1936 before a recurrence of arm trouble forced his return to the minors for part of the 1938 season. He won sixteen games in 1940 to help Detroit win its third pennant in seven years, but he was no longer the overpowering fastball pitcher he had been. He was sold to Brooklyn early in the 1942 season and sold to the Philadelphia Phillies before the 1943 season, then spent the 1944 and 1945 seasons in the service. He returned to pitch for the Phillies from 1946 through 1949, then pitched three seasons in the minor leagues before retiring.

Rowe finished his major league career with 158 wins, 101 defeats, and an earned run average of 3.87, with twenty-three shutouts. As a batter he ranks among the best hitting pitchers of all time. He had a .263 average, hit eighteen homers, and batted in 153 runs. As a pinch-hitter, he hit .277 in 101 times at bat. He died in El Dorado on January 8, 1961, three days before his fifty-first birthday.

Carl Hubbell
1936 New York Giants

16 Consecutive Wins

Tall, lean left-hander Carl Hubbell was born in Carthage, Missouri, on June 22, 1903, and grew up on an Oklahoma pecan farm. On graduation from high school, he worked for an oil company but that summer made his professional debut with Cushing of the Oklahoma State League. That was in 1923, and in 1924 he pitched for Cushing, Ardmore, and Oklahoma City without distinction.

While pitching for Oklahoma City of the Western League in 1925, Hubbell learned how to throw a screwball, the pitch that would eventually land him in the Hall of Fame. He compiled a 17–13 record that year and was sold to Detroit for $20,000. At spring training in Augusta, Georgia, in 1926, Tigers Manager Ty Cobb advised the six-foot, 170-pounder to give up the screwball because it might hurt his arm.

The left-hander pitched for Toronto in 1926 and, after training with Detroit again in 1927, he pitched for Decatur and Fort Worth in 1927. Released to Beaumont of the Texas League in 1928, Hubbell began throwing the screwball again, winning twelve games before being purchased by the New York Giants in midseason for $30,000.

Hubbell had a 10–6 record for the Giants the last half of that season, posting his first major league win at Chicago on July 31. His eighteen wins in 1929 included a no-hitter against Pittsburgh. He became a twenty-game winner for the first time in 1933 when he set a league record with forty-six straight scoreless innings. He also won the first of his two Most Valuable Player Awards as New York won the pennant and World Series that year. He won twenty-three games that year, twenty-one in 1934, and twenty-three in 1935.

On July 13, 1936, Hubbell lost at Chicago, 1–0, on a fourth-inning walk, a sacrifice, a wild throw, and catcher Ken O'Dea's single. That was his sixth defeat against ten victories for the season. After a brief relief stint two days later, Hubbell began his sixteen-game winning streak on July 17 at Pittsburgh's Forbes Field. At that time New York was in fifth place with a 42–41 record, ten and one-half games behind first-place Chicago. It was ten and one-half months before he lost another game.

1. Friday, July 17

New York	330 000 000	6	10	1
Pittsburgh	000 000 000	0	5	0

WP **Hubbell**; LP **Swift**, Weaver (1), Welch (2), Birkofer (9)

2. Sunday, July 19[1]

New York	100 000 201	4	14	2
Cincinnati	100 100 100	3	9	1

WP Fitzsimmons, Coffman (7), **Hubbell**(7); LP Hollingsworth, Derringer (7), Brennan (8), **Davis** (9)

3. Tuesday, July 21

St. Louis	000 001 000 0	1	9	0
New York	000 010 000 1	2	5	0

WP **Hubbell**; LP **J. Dean** (10 innings)

4. Thursday, July 30

Chicago	100 000 000	1	7	1
New York	000 003 00x	3	6	0

WP **Hubbell**; LP **Davis**, Henshaw (6), Warneke (7)

5. Sunday, August 2

Pittsburgh	000 000 002	2	4	1
New York	002 010 00x	3	9	0

WP **Hubbell**; LP **Swift**

6. Saturday, August 8

New York	200 000 100	3	10	0
Philadelphia	002 000 000	2	7	1

WP **Hubbell**; LP **Bowman**

7. Saturday, August 15

Philadelphia	010 000 000	1	9	2
New York	000 004 00x	4	7	0

WP **Hubbell**; LP **Walters**, Jorgens (6), Kowalik (8)

8. Wednesday, August 19

Brooklyn	010 000 001	2	5	1
New York	100 000 02x	3	7	0

WP **Hubbell**; LP **Butcher**

9. Wednesday, August 26

New York	400 000 020	6	10	1
Cincinnati	100 011 002	5	11	0

WP **Hubbell**; LP **Derringer**, Stine (6), Frey (7)

10. Sunday, August 30[1]

New York	020 001 012	6	12	2
Chicago	000 000 001	1	7	0

WP **Hubbell**; LP **Lee**, Bryant (9)

[1]*First game of a doubleheader.*

11. Thursday, September 3

New York	001 000 001	2	8	1
St. Louis	000 100 000	1	4	1

WP **Hubbell**; LP **J. Dean**

12. Monday, September 7[1]

New York	210 100 011	6	11	0
Philadelphia	010 100 000	2	7	2

WP **Hubbell**; LP **Bowman**, Benge (8), Jorgens (9)

13. Friday, September 11

Chicago	010 000 000	1	4	0
New York	100 003 10x	5	8	1

WP **Hubbell**; LP **Davis**, Root (6), Henshaw (7), Bryant (8)

14. Monday, September 14

St. Louis	200 201 000	5	13	0
New York	006 001 00x	7	8	0

WP Gabler, Coffman (4), **Hubbell** (5); LP **Walker**, Winford (3), McGee (3), Heusser (4), J. Dean (6)

15. Saturday, September 19

New York	001 052 010	9	10	2
Brooklyn	010 000 000	1	4	3

WP **Hubbell**; LP **Mungo**

16. Wednesday, September 23

New York	101 200 100	5	15	0
Philadelphia	000 000 031	4	8	2

WP **Hubbell**; LP **Sivess**, Jorgens (4), Benge (9)

After Hubbell's sixteenth straight victory, New York was in first place with a 90–59 record, having won forty-eight and lost eighteen during the ten weeks the streak lasted. They had a five-game lead over second-place Chicago and clinched the pennant the next day with a ten-inning, 2–1 win in the opener of a doubleheader at Boston.

During the streak, Hubbell pitched in nineteen games, had fourteen complete games, and won two of his four relief stints. The only start he failed to complete was against Cincinnati at home in the opener of a July 26 doubleheader. He gave up ten hits, and New York was behind, 4–2, when he left for a pinch-hitter in the seventh inning of a game the Giants won, 5–4, with three runs in the ninth. In the nineteen games, he pitched 145 innings and gave up thirty runs and 111 hits while walking only twenty-five.

Hubbell beat Philadelphia four times, St. Louis and Chicago three times, and Pittsburgh, Cincinnati and Brooklyn twice, facing every team except Boston. He won eight games by a one-run margin, two by two runs, one by three runs, two by four runs, and one each by five, six and eight runs. He allowed five runs once, four runs once, and two runs or less in the rest.

New York was behind in five of Hubbell's sixteen straight wins, only three after the fourth inning. The Giants won four of the games in their last at bat, one in the tenth.

The streak began with Hubbell's third and last shutout of the year as he allowed no walks and five singles in a 6–0 win at Pittsburgh in

[1]*First game of a doubleheader.*

Game 1 (July 17). His first relief win was in Game 2 (July 19) when he came on with the score tied, 3–3, bases loaded and one out in the seventh inning at Cincinnati. A double-play grounder ended that inning and New York won, 4–3, in the ninth when outfielder Hank Leiber doubled, advanced on an out, and scored on third baseman Eddie Mayo's looping single to center.

Another double play helped Hubbell win Game 3 (July 21) over St. Louis. With one out in the top of the ninth and the score tied, 1–1, Cardinal manager and second baseman Frankie Frisch bounced to the mound, and Hubbell threw to the plate to start a home-to-first double play. In the tenth, New York shortstop Dick Bartell homered to win the game, 2–1.

Hubbell helped himself with his bat several times in the streak. In Game 4 (July 30) he singled to tie the score in the three-run sixth, then scored the winning run on second baseman Burgess Whitehead's single in the 3–1 win over Chicago.

In Game 6 (August 8), with the score tied, 2–2, and two out in the seventh, Hubbell, outfielder Joe Moore, and Whitehead singled in succession for the run that won the game, 3–2, at Philadelphia.

Hubbell capped a four-run sixth with a two-run single in a 4–1 win over Philadelphia in Game 7 (August 15), after the lefty had pitched in two consecutive no-decision relief stints. The loss was the thirteenth in a row for the Phillies.

Successive eighth-inning home runs by outfielders Mel Ott and Jimmy Ripple gave Hubbell a 3–2 win over Brooklyn in Game 8 (August 19), and New York won Game 9 (August 26) at Cincinnati, 6–5, on two runs in the eighth on third baseman Travis Jackson's single, an infield out, an intentional walk, and run-scoring singles by Hubbell and Moore. This game was the fourteenth victory in a fifteen-game winning streak for New York, which took over the National League lead the day before.

With the score tied, 1–1, in the ninth inning of Game 11 (September 3) at St. Louis, New York catcher Gus Mancuso singled with one out, took third on Bartell's double, and scored in a close play at the plate on Hubbell's short fly to center field. The 2–1 New York win ended right-hander Dizzy Dean's seven-game winning streak.

Hubbell singled home what proved to be the winning run in the second inning and hit a run-scoring fly in the eighth as the left-hander won Game 12 (September 7) at Philadelphia, 6–2, before an overflow holiday crowd of 23,000.

In Game 14 (September 14) Hubbell came on at the start of the fifth after St. Louis had scored twice in the fourth to cut New York's lead to 6–4. The lefty gave up six hits in the last five innings, including a homer by right-hander Ed Heusser in the sixth, and won his second game in relief, 7–5.

Hubbell had a three-hit shutout and a 5–0 lead in Game 16 (September 23) until the eighth inning at Philadelphia, when three singles loaded the bases. Two runs scored on outs, and third baseman Pinky Whitney singled to cut the lead to 5–3. First baseman Dolf Camilli homered to lead off the Philadelphia ninth, and one out later Hubbell issued his only walk but then retired the next two batters to win, 5–4, and clinch a tie for the pennant that New York won the next day.

Hubbell did not pitch again in the regular season's last five games so that he could pitch the World Series opener. Both his 26–6 record and his 2.31 earned run average led the National League, and he won his second Most Valuable Player Award. In the six-game World Series the Giants lost to the New York Yankees, he won the opener, 6–1, and lost the fourth game, 5–2.

In 1937 Hubbell's winning streak continued through eight more games. He defeated Boston, 3–0, in the home opener on April 23; beat Brooklyn, 11–2, on April 30, and Cincinnati, 7–6, on May 4, when he failed to complete a regular-season start for the first time since last July 26. He then beat Chicago, 4–1, on May 9; Pittsburgh, 5–2, on May 13; won at St. Louis, 4–1, on May 19; at Pittsburgh, 4–3, on May 24, when he needed help to get the last out; and won in relief at Cincinnati, 3–2, on May 27. He pitched the last two innings and won in the ninth when Ott homered to snap a 2–2 tie.

The all-time-record two-season winning streak of twenty-four games ended in the opener of a May 31 Memorial Day doubleheader before a crowd of 60,747, the largest in the entire history of the Polo Grounds. Hubbell was chased in the fourth inning when the Brooklyn Dodgers scored on their sixth and seventh hits off the southpaw to take a 5–2 lead en route to a 10–3 victory behind right-hander Fred Frankhouse.

Hubbell won twenty-two games that year, the last season in which he won twenty or more games, although he pitched into 1943. He retired with 253 wins, 154 losses, a 2.97 earned run average and thirty-six shutouts in 535 games. In three World Series, he had a 4–2 record. He pitched in five All-Star Games without a win or a loss, but starred in the 1934 game when he struck out five future Hall of Fame sluggers in succession.

Elected to the Hall of Fame in 1947, Hubbell became Director of Player Development for the Giants in December, 1943, and was employed by the club through 1977. He died November 21, 1988, at Scottsdale, Arizona, two days after being injured in an automobile accident.

Ewell Blackwell
1947 Cincinnati Reds

16 Consecutive Wins

Physical problems ruined what might well have been a Hall of Fame career for Ewell Blackwell. At his best he was truly an awesome pitcher. Born in Fresno, California, on October 23, 1922, this six-foot six-inch, 195-pound right-hander spent only one season in the minor leagues. That was in 1942 when he won fifteen games for Syracuse of the International League before joining the Cincinnati Reds in September and pitching twice in relief without a decision.

Blackwell then went into the military service, returning to join Cincinnati after the Reds had already started spring training in 1946. He made the club that spring and, although he won only nine games while losing thirteen that season, he pitched six shutouts to lead the National League and establish himself as one of baseball's best young pitchers.

A long, gangling frame and a wicked sidearm motion, which earned him the nick-name the Whip, made Blackwell particularly difficult for right-handed batters to hit off. Left-handed hitters weren't overjoyed about facing him either.

In 1947 Blackwell won the season's opener, 3–1, on April 14, St. Louis spoiling his shutout bid in the last of the ninth inning on a walk and two of the three hits the Cards collected. In his next start, he beat Pittsburgh, then had a no-decision start, followed by 10–3 defeat at Boston and a 5–3 loss in the opener of a May 4 doubleheader at Philadelphia. Blackwell was leading in this game, 1–0, until the Phillies bunched five hits for their five runs in the sixth inning.

When Blackwell took the mound for his next start six days later at Cincinnati's Crosley Field, he had a 2–2 record and Cincinnati was in seventh place with an 8–12 record, five games behind Chicago and Boston, tied for the league lead.

1. Saturday, May 10

Chicago	100 000 000	1	5	2
Cincinnati	011 000 03x	5	8	1

WP **Blackwell**; LP **Lee**, Meyer (8), Erickson (8)

2. Wednesday, May 14

Brooklyn	000 000 000	0	6	1
Cincinnati	100 100 00x	2	4	1

WP **Blackwell**; LP **Hatten**, Taylor (8), Casey (8)

3. Sunday, May 18[1]

Boston	000 001 000	1	9	1
Cincinnati	000 000 011	2	10	0

WP **Blackwell**; LP **Cooper**

4. Tuesday, May 27

Pittsburgh	000 000 001	1	4	1
Cincinnati	001 050 00x	6	7	0

WP **Blackwell**; LP **Bahr**, Strincevich (5), Singleton (8)

5. Thursday, June 5[1]

Cincinnati	500 000 000	5	8	0
Philadelphia	000 000 000	0	6	4

WP **Blackwell**; LP **Raffensberger**, Hughes (1), Mauney (9)

6. Tuesday, June 10[1]

Cincinnati	000 002 010	3	4	0
Brooklyn	000 000 001	1	5	1

WP **Blackwell**; LP **Branca**, King (9)

7. Saturday, June 14

New York	000 100 200	3	8	0
Cincinnati	110 002 00x	4	8	2

WP **Blackwell**; LP **Koslo**, Trinkle (7)

8. Wednesday, June 18

Boston	000 000 000	0	0	2
Cincinnati	300 000 03x	6	12	0

WP **Blackwell**; LP **Wright**, Lanfranconi (2), Karl (8)

9. Sunday, June 22[1]

Brooklyn	000 000 000	0	2	0
Cincinnati	000 001 03x	4	4	0

WP **Blackwell**; LP **Hatten**, Behrman (6)

10. Thursday, June 26

Cincinnati	200 001 003	6	13	0
St. Louis	011 000 001	3	8	3

WP **Blackwell**; LP **Brecheen**, Burkhart (9)

11. Monday, June 30

Chicago	400 000 000	4	4	1
Cincinnati	001 202 10x	6	14	1

WP **Blackwell**; LP Erickson, **Schmitz** (4)

12. Friday, July 4[1]

Pittsburgh	000 000 000	0	6	2
Cincinnati	000 006 20x	8	8	0

WP **Blackwell**; LP **Roe**, Mabe (6), Singleton (7)

[1]*First game of a doubleheader.*

13. Friday, July 11

| Cincinnati | 300 002 302 | 10 | 12 | 2 |
| Boston | 101 100 210 | 6 | 11 | 6 |

WP **Blackwell**; LP **Sain**, Shoun (7), Lanfranconi (7), Karl (9)

14. Tuesday, July 15

| Cincinnati | 001 210 010 | 5 | 9 | 1 |
| Philadelphia | 202 000 000 | 4 | 10 | 1 |

WP **Blackwell**; LP **Jurisich**

15. Sunday, July 20[1]

| Cincinnati | 010 000 201 | 4 | 10 | 2 |
| New York | 000 000 001 | 1 | 7 | 1 |

WP **Blackwell**; LP **Koslo**, Beggs (9), Iott (9)

16. Friday, July 25

| Philadelphia | 001 100 011 | 4 | 13 | 0 |
| Cincinnati | 104 000 00x | 5 | 9 | 1 |

WP **Blackwell**; LP **Heintzelman**, Jurisich (3), Schanz (7)

Five days later Blackwell's streak ended in an extra-inning defeat.

Wednesday, July 30

| New York | 000 012 001 1 | 5 | 8 | 0 |
| Cincinnati | 002 002 000 0 | 4 | 7 | 0 |

WP Hartsung, Trinkle (6), **Kennedy** (7); LP **Blackwell** (10 innings)

Cincinnati scored twice in the third inning on a walk to outfielder Frankie Baumholtz, third baseman Grady Hatton's run-scoring double and first baseman Babe Young's single. Catcher Walker Cooper hit his twenty-third homer over the left-field wall for New York's first hit in the fifth. A single by right-hander Clint Hartung, a run-scoring double by shortstop Buddy Kerr, and a triple off the center-field wall by first-baseman Johnny Mize made it 3–2 in the New York sixth. Young's eleventh homer tied the score in the home sixth, and Cincinnati went ahead, 4–3, in that inning on a walk, a single by catcher Ray Lamanno, and, after right-hander Ken Trinkle relieved Hartung, shortstop Eddie Miller's single to center.

With one out in New York's ninth, outfielder Willard Marshall hit his twenty-seventh homer into the bleachers in right center to tie the score, 4–4. New York won in the tenth, when third baseman Buddy Blattner walked, was sacrificed to second by left-hander Monte Kennedy, and scored with two out when Kerr singled to center.

After Blackwell's sixteenth victory in a row, Cincinnati had a 43–49 record and was in sixth place, one game behind fifth-place Chicago and

[1]*First game of a doubleheader.*

In one of the greatest streaks of pitching in major league history, long, lean Ewell Blackwell won sixteen straight games for the 1947 Cincinnati Reds. During the streak, he pitched five shutouts, including a no-hit game, and allowed just one run in five other games. (Courtesy of National Baseball Library, Cooperstown, New York.)

thirteen games in back of first-place Brooklyn, which went on to win the pennant by five games.

During his streak, which may well be the most impressive one of sixteen or more games by any pitcher in modern major league history, Blackwell pitched five shutouts, including a no-hit game, and allowed one run in five other games. In three of those five, the lone run scored in the ninth inning. In his six other wins, he allowed three runs twice, four runs three times, and six runs once. In the sixteen games, he pitched 144 innings, gave up 104 hits, 29 runs and 46 walks while striking out 98 and hitting two batters. The opposition batted .202 in the 16 games, averaging 1.8 runs and 6.5 hits per game.

Blackwell appeared in seventeen games in his streak, had one no-decision start, and completed every one of his sixteen victories. The only other pitcher to complete sixteen games in a winning streak was New York Giants left-hander Rube Marquard, who also had sixteen in his nineteen-game streak in 1912. Blackwell beat every club in the league, downing Boston, Brooklyn, and Philadelphia three times; St. Louis once; and the other three teams twice.

The one no-decision start was at New York, the team that later ended Blackwell's streak. In the June 1 game, Cincinnati scored twice in the first inning and once in the fifth, but the Giants scored singles runs in the fourth, fifth and sixth to tie the score, 3–3.

Blackwell, bothered by a lame elbow, left the game for a pinch-hitter in the seventh, and right-hander Harry Gumbert was the winning pitcher when Miller homered after an error in the ninth for a 5–3 Cincinnati victory.

In the sixteen wins Blackwell won four games by a one-run margin, three by two runs, two by three runs, three by four runs, two by five runs, one by six runs, and one by eight runs. Cincinnati trailed in only four of the sixteen games, and the Reds scored the winning run in their last at bat only twice.

In Game 3 (May 18) Boston took a 1–0 lead in the top of the sixth, but Cincinnati first baseman Bert Haas drove home outfielder Tommy Tatum to tie the score in the eighth. Second baseman Benny Zientara and Miller hit successive doubles in the ninth to win the game, 2–1.

At St. Louis in Game 10 (June 26), Cincinnati took a 3–2 lead with a run in the sixth driven in by Haas, and then Haas, Miller, and Lamanno batted in runs in the three-run ninth to offset a St. Louis run in the ninth as Blackwell won, 6–3.

The biggest deficit Cincinnati overcame for Blackwell was in Game 11 (June 30), when Chicago bunched two singles and three walks and a force-play grounder on which Miller threw past first, trying for a double play, to take a 4–0 lead in the top of the first. The Reds scored once in the third, twice in the fourth, and went ahead in the sixth with two runs on Lamanno's infield hit, a force-out, a single by Baumholtz, a

wild throw on which the tying run scored and Hatton's scoring fly. Outfielder Eddie Lukon homered in the seventh to make the 6–4 win easier
for Blackwell, who struck out eleven, his high during the streak.

Blackwell gave up six runs in Game 13 (July 11), but the Reds led
all the way to win at Boston, 10–6. That was three days after the Cincinnati star started the All-Star Game and pitched three scoreless innings.

Blackwell was hit hard in the early innings of Game 14 (July 15) at
Philadelphia, and trailed, 4–1, after three innings, but then settled
down. The Reds tied by scoring two runs in the fourth and another
without a hit in the fifth, then won the game, 5–4, with an eighth-inning
run on singles by Young, outfielder Augie Galan, and Miller, whose
leaping catch of a line drive helped Blackwell survive the Philadelphia
eighth.

In the middle of his streak, Blackwell almost pitched two no-hit
games in a row. In Game 8 (June 18) he held visiting Boston hitless
while walking four, and the Reds scored the same way in both the first
and eighth innings to win, 6–0. Baumholtz singled, Hatton walked with
one out and Young homered into the right-field bleachers in both innings.

Four days later against Brooklyn in Game 9 (June 22), Blackwell
had faced only twenty-seven men and had one out in the top of top of
the ninth inning, when second baseman Eddie Stanky lined a single
through the pitcher's legs, ending the right-hander's streak of nineteen
consecutive hitless innings. With two out, first baseman Jackie Robinson looped a single to right before outfielder Carl Furillo hit a ground
ball to end the game.

Cincinnati had scored a run in the sixth when left-hander Joe Hatten walked three batters in a row with Hatton on base. Miller's double
in the eighth made the final score 4–0.

That was Blackwell's fourth shutout during the streak, and he
pitched his fifth three starts later. He went into the ninth inning in three
other games before giving up a run.

In Game 4 (May 27) Blackwell, who had missed a scheduled start
May 24 because of a bout with the flu, gave up only one hit until Pittsburgh outfielder Wally Westlake singled with two out in the ninth. Then
third baseman Frankie Gustine and outfielder Ralph Kiner singled, and
Blackwell had to settle for a 6–1 victory.

There were two out in the ninth inning at Brooklyn in Game 6
(June 10) when outfielder Gene Hermanski doubled and outfielder
Marv Rackley singled for the only Dodger run in a 3–1 victory.

Marshall, who homered ten days later in the streak-ending game, homered with one out in the ninth of Game 15 (July 20) for the only New York run in Cincinnati's 4–1 win. The only other homer Blackwell gave up during his streak was catcher Walker Cooper's two-run blast in Game 7 (June 14), as Cincinnati beat visiting New York, 4–3.

Cincinnati had lost six games in a row when Blackwell faced Philadelphia in Game 16 (July 25), but the Reds took a 5–1 lead in three innings and, although he gave up thirteen hits, Blackwell held on to win, 5–4. The Phillies loaded the bases with one out in the ninth but scored only one run on outfielder Harry Walker's fly ball before third baseman Jim Tabor flied to center to end the game. This was the only game in the streak in which the Cincinnati star didn't walk a batter.

After his sixteenth straight win gave him an 18–2 record for the season, Blackwell slumped. He lost six of his last ten decisions for a final record of 22–8, as Cincinnati finished fifth with seventy-three wins, eighty-one losses, twenty-one games from the top. He led the league in victories, complete games (23) and strikeouts (193), and was second in earned run average (2.47) and tied for second in shutouts (6).

Blackwell never again approached his 1947 form as he suffered with physical problems for the rest of his career. He won only seven games in 1948, and his seventeen wins in 1950 and sixteen in 1951 were his highs thereafter. He was traded to the New York Yankees late in the 1952 season, but won only six games after leaving Cincinnati. He pitched his final big league game for Kansas City in 1955 and finished his twelve-year career with eighty-two victories, seventy-eight defeats and sixteen shutouts in 236 games.

Jack Sanford
1962 San Francisco Giants

16 Consecutive Wins

Hard-throwing right-hander Jack Sanford spent seven years in the minor leagues and then had his career delayed by almost two years in the military service before he reached the major leagues.

Born in Wellesley Hills, Massachusetts, on May 18, 1929, the six-foot, 190-pounder pitched six no-hit games in high school. As a teenager he served as a driver for New England contractor Lou Perini, president and part owner of the Boston Braves. But the Braves showed no real interest in the youngster, and the Philadelphia Phillies signed him and he made his professional debut with Bradford of the Pony League in 1948.

Sanford pitched for seven teams in the Philadelphia minor league system, and four times won fourteen or more games. Still, he was never given a chance to pitch in the National League until after his Army service.

Sanford went into the service after the 1954 season and was awaiting his final discharge when he finally made his major league debut by pitching a four-hitter over seven innings to beat the Chicago Cubs, 4–1, on September 16, 1956.

In 1957 the twenty-eight-year-old Sanford won nineteen games and lost eight for the Phillies, led the league in strikeouts, and won the National League Rookie of the Year Award. He slumped to a 10–13 record in 1958 and in a one-sided deal was traded to San Francisco that December for pitcher Ruben Gomez and catcher Valmy Thomas.

In his first three years with the Giants, he won fifteen, twelve and

157

thirteen games, and then embarked on the best year of his career in 1962.

On June 13, 1962, at Cincinnati, Sanford lost, 5–0, to even his record at 6–6. Four days later, with the Giants in second place with a 42–34 record, one game behind Los Angeles, Sanford began his sixteen-game winning streak at San Francisco's Candlestick Park.

1. Sunday, June 17

St. Louis	000 100 020	3	5	0
San Francisco	120 000 003	6	7	1

WP **Sanford**; LP Broglio, McDaniel (2), Bauta (8), **Washburn** (9)

2. Tuesday, July 3

New York	001 000 000	1	9	1
San Francisco	140 020 03x	10	15	0

WP **Sanford**; LP **Jackson**, Moorhead (5), Mizell (8)

3. Saturday, July 7

Los Angeles	000 000 210	3	5	5
San Francisco	120 015 01x	10	11	0

WP **Sanford**, Miller (7); LP **Podres**, Sherry (6), Perranoski (6), Ortega (8)

4. Thursday, July 12

San Francisco	120 011 000	5	11	0
Philadelphia	000 000 120	3	9	1

WP **Sanford**, Miller (8); LP **Hamilton**, Brown (6), Owens (8)

5. Monday, July 16

San Francisco	100 000 101	3	8	0
New York	000 010 001	2	8	2

WP **Sanford**, Larsen (7), Miller (9), Garibaldi (9); LP **Craig**, R. L. Miller (8)

6. Friday, July 20

San Francisco	211 000 020	6	8	0
Pittsburgh	000 100 200	3	7	2

WP **Sanford**, Larsen (7); LP **Law**, Lamabe (4), Sturdivant (6), Olivo (8), Francis (8)

7. Tuesday, July 24

San Francisco	100 101 000	3	10	0
Houston	000 000 100	1	5	1

WP **Sanford**, Larsen (7); LP **Farrell**, McMahon (8)

8. Saturday, August 4

Pittsburgh	030 000 200	5	11	0
San Francisco	101 101 20x	6	10	0

WP **Sanford**, Bolin (8); LP Haddix, Sturdivant (6), Lamabe (7), **Olivo** (7), Face (7)

9. Thursday, August 9

New York	000 001 000	1	3	1
San Francisco	002 004 01x	7	13	1

WP **Sanford**; LP **R. L. Miller**, Moorhead (6), R. G. Miller (8)

10. Tuesday, August 14

San Francisco	023 100 300	9	12	0
Chicago	010 001 000	2	8	1

WP **Sanford**; LP **Hobbie**, Anderson (3), Gerard (6), Lary (8)

11. Saturday, August 18

San Francisco	000 301 002	6	15	2
Milwaukee	200 001 001	4	11	0

WP **Sanford**, Bolin (6); LP **Hendley**, Willey (4), Curtis (7), Burdette (9)

12. Sunday, August 26

San Francisco	212 100 010	7	7	0
Philadelphia	010 003 000	4	11	0

WP **Sanford**, McCormick (7), Bolin (8); LP **Mahaffey**, Owens (6), Baldschun (8)

13. Thursday, August 30

| Milwaukee | 000 000 200 | 2 | 8 | 0 |
| San Francisco | 200 001 00x | 3 | 6 | 1 |

WP **Sanford**, Bolin (7), O'Dell (7), Miller (7), McCormick (8), Larsen (9); LP **Spahn**

15. Friday, September 7

| Chicago | 200 100 020 | 5 | 8 | 2 |
| San Francisco | 002 120 10x | 6 | 9 | 1 |

WP **Sanford**, Miller (8); LP **Buhl**, Schultz (7)

14. Monday, September 3

| San Francisco | 013 210 000 | 7 | 8 | 0 |
| Los Angeles | 010 000 002 | 3 | 8 | 0 |

WP **Sanford**; LP **Williams**, Roebuck (4), Ortega (6), Perranoski (9)

16. Tuesday, September 11

| Pittsburgh | 000 000 000 | 0 | 8 | 1 |
| San Francisco | 000 101 00x | 2 | 4 | 0 |

WP **Sanford**; LP **Sturdivant**, Friend (8)

Sanford's winning streak ended four days later at Pittsburgh's Forbes Field.

Saturday, September 15

| San Francisco | 000 100 000 | 1 | 5 | 1 |
| Pittsburgh | 000 100 04x | 5 | 6 | 1 |

WP **Friend**; LP **Sanford**

San Francisco scored in the fourth inning when outfielder Felipe Alou reached second on a wild throw by third baseman Bob Bailey, took third on outfielder Willie McCovey's fly, and scored on first baseman Orlando Cepeda's infield out.

Pittsburgh tied the score in the home fourth when catcher Smoky Burgess walked, outfielder Roberto Clemente singled, first baseman Donn Clendenon walked, and Bailey grounded into a force-out at second. The Pirates won the game with four runs in the eighth on a two-out single by Burgess, a run-scoring double by Clemente, an intentional walk, Bailey's two-run triple to right, another intentional walk, and a looping single by right-hander Bob Friend, who posted his seventeenth win. This was Sanford's seventh and final loss of the season.

After Sanford's sixteenth straight victory, San Francisco had a 94–51 record in second place, one-half game behind Los Angeles in the exciting pennant race that had to be decided by a three-game playoff at the end of the season.

During his streak Sanford pitched in twenty games, all starts, and completed only six, the fewest by any pitcher in a streak of sixteen or more games except for Roy Face, who pitched only in relief. Sanford worked 141 innings in the twenty games, gave up 134 hits and fifty-five runs, and walked thirty-seven.

Sanford defeated eight of the other nine teams in the league during his streak, failing only against Cincinnati. In his only start against the Reds on June 26, he left for a pinch-hitter in the home seventh after giving up four runs. But the Giants rallied for four runs in the seventh, tied the score for the second time with a run in the eighth, and won, 6-5, in the tenth.

Sanford's other three no-decision starts were on June 22 in a game the Giants lost to Milwaukee, 11-9; on July 28 in an 8-6 San Francisco loss at Los Angeles, and on August 22 when the Giants lost at New York, 5-4. Sanford went seven innings in the second and fourth no-decision starts. The right-hander beat New York and Pittsburgh three times, won twice from Los Angeles, Philadelphia, Chicago, and Milwaukee, and beat St. Louis and Houston once each.

San Francisco hit well behind Sanford during the streak, averaging six runs in the sixteen wins, and scoring six or more runs in all but five. The Giants hit twenty-three homers in the streak, seven by outfielder Willie Mays.

The Giants trailed in just three of the sixteen games, only one after the third inning, and won just two games in their last time at bat.

The first was in Game 1 (June 17), when St. Louis scored twice in the eighth inning on a walk and second baseman Red Schoendienst's home run to tie the score at 3-3. In the home ninth, a walk, shortstop Jose Pagan's single and catcher Tom Haller's homer to right with none out won the game, 6-3.

The other game the Giants won in their final time at bat was at Milwaukee on August 18 in Game 11. The Giants had a 4-3 lead going into the ninth and scored twice in that inning on doubles by right-hander Bob Bolin, who had relieved Sanford in the sixth, and outfielder Harvey Kuenn, and a single by second baseman Chuck Hiller over shortstop. Milwaukee scored in the home ninth, making the final runs by the visitors decisive.

Following his first victory in the streak, Sanford had two no-decision starts in a row before breezing to a 10-1 win over New York in Game 2 (July 3). Mays hit solo homers in the first and fourth innings of Game 7 (July 24) at Houston, then was hit by a pitch in the sixth and scored when Cepeda singled and Felipe Alou hit a sacrifice fly for a 3-1 victory.

A two-run homer by outfielder Bob Skinner gave Pittsburgh a 5-4 lead in the seventh inning of Game 8 (August 4), but San Francisco came back to win, 6-5, in the home seventh on Felipe Alou's single, a passed ball, sacrifice, a run-scoring bunt single by pinch-hitter John Orsino, an intentional walk to McCovey, who was batting for Sanford, and Kuenn's single.

Homers by Mays and Cepeda in the first inning and one by third baseman Jim Davenport in the sixth gave the Giants their runs in a 3-2 win in Game 13 (August 30). Sanford had a one-hitter until second baseman Frank Bolling and left-hander Warren Spahn homered in succession in the seventh, and it took five relief pitchers to protect the lead.

The second and final shutout Sanford pitched in 1962 was in Game 16 (September 11), when he beat Pittsburgh, 2-0, walking one and allowing eight hits. Felipe Alou, who grounded out to third to end a streak of nine consecutive hits in the first inning, singled and was driven home by McCovey in the fourth and then hit his twenty-fifth homer for an insurance run in the sixth.

After his streak ended, Sanford won two more games without a loss to finish the season with a 24-7 record, helping San Francisco come back to tie Los Angeles for first place in the close of the regular schedule. The Giants then won the first and third games of the three-game playoff to capture the pennant.

In the World Series, Sanford won the second game, 2-0, lost the fifth game, 5-3, and then was beaten, 1-0, in the seventh and deciding game by the New York Yankees.

Sanford slumped to sixteen victories in 1963, was traded during the 1965 season to the California Angels, and ended his career with Kansas City in 1967. He finished his career with a 137-101 record, a 3.69 earned run average, and fourteen shutouts in 388 games. He coached for the Cleveland Indians in 1968 and 1969 and then left baseball to serve as golf director for a country club in West Palm Beach, Florida.

LOSING STREAKS
BY PITCHERS

19 Games • Jack Nabors, 1916

18 Games • Cliff Curtis, 1910

18 Games • Roger Craig, 1963

16 Games • Craig Anderson, 1962

16 Games • Mike Parrott, 1980

15 Games • Bob Groom, 1909

Losing Streaks by Pitcher

Pitcher	Team	Year	Games Lost	Games Pitched	Games Started	Complete Games	Starts with No Decision	Games Pitched in Relief	Games Lost in Relief	Opponent Scored Two Runs or Less*	Games Lost by One Run Margin*	Games Lost in Final Inning*
Jack Nabors	Athletics	1916	19	35	25	10	6	10	0	2	6	2
Cliff Curtis	Braves	1910	18	26	22	5	5	4	1	1	4	2
Roger Craig	Mets	1963	18	24	19	9	2	5	1	6	7	3
Craig Anderson	Mets	1962	16	29	12	2	2	17	6	0	5	3
Mike Parrott	Mariners	1980	16	26	15	1	1	11	2	1	5	2
Bob Groom	Senators	1909	15	21	16	7	1	5	0	3	3	1

*Refer only to games lost by the pitcher.

Jack Nabors
1916 Philadelphia Athletics

19 Consecutive Losses

Jack Nabors, a long, lanky right-hander from Alabama, had a major league career notable for its negative aspects. In one full season and parts of two others in the American League, the six-foot three-inch 185-pounder won only one game and set a major league record for consecutive defeats, although his streak is still controversial.

Nabors, born November 19, 1887, at Montevallo, Alabama, first attracted attention when he pitched a thirteen-inning, 1–0 no-hit game on June 15, 1915, for Newnan of the Georgia-Alabama League against Talladega, the team with which he had started the season.

In a league that played fewer than sixty-five games per club, Nabors posted a 12–1 combined record for the two teams in 1915 and sparked the interest of Connie Mack, manager of the Philadelphia Athletics. The A's had won the pennant in 1914 but were on their way to a last-place finish when they purchased Nabors late in the 1915 season in time for him to pitch in ten games, posting a 0–5 record. He completed two of his seven starts and relieved in three games without a decision.

Philadelphia won only forty-three games in 1915, and the A's were an even worse team in 1916. Nabors began that season as a regular starter and pitched the season opener at Boston on April 12. He hurled four scoreless against left-hander Babe Ruth before being lifted in the fifth for a pinch-hitter in a game the A's lost, 2–1, right-hander Joe Bush taking the loss.

Nabors started and lost his next start, 4–2, at New York on April 18 before going the route at home to beat Boston, 6–2, on April 22 for the only victory of his major league career. Nabors had a 1–1 record and the A's had a 4–8 record when the right-hander went to the mound on Friday, April 28, at Washington's Griffith Stadium.

1. Friday, April 28

Philadelphia	000 060 000	6	9	5
Washington	000 120 004	7	6	2

WP Dumont, Boehling (5), **Gallia** (5); LP **Nabors**, Crowell (9)

2. Tuesday, May 9

Detroit	180 061 000	16	12	0
Philadelphia	001 000 010	2	3	6

WP Cunningham, **Boland** (3); LP **Nabors**, Weaver (2), Day (3)

3. Saturday, May 27

Philadelphia	000 000 001	1	6	1
Washington	000 300 00x	3	4	1

WP **Johnson**; LP **Nabors**, Wyckoff (8)

4. Friday, June 16

Philadelphia	101 010 000	3	8	5
Detroit	120 001 00x	4	9	2

WP **Dubuc**; LP **Nabors**, Sheehan (8)

5. Saturday, June 24[1]

Philadelphia	000 200 000	2	8	3
Boston	100 000 002	3	3	1

WP Leonard, **Mays** (9); LP **Nabors**

6. Thursday, June 29

New York	300 000 011	5	7	1
Philadelphia	000 000 000	0	4	2

WP **Shawkey**; LP **Nabors**, Sheehan (2), Hesselbacher (9)

7. Monday, July 3

Boston	100 210 002	6	11	1
Philadelphia	002 000 011	4	12	2

WP **Shore**, Mays (9); LP **Nabors**, Sheehan (9)

8. Saturday, July 8

Detroit	100 010 001	3	9	1
Philadelphia	000 100 001	2	6	2

WP **James**; LP **Nabors**

9. Thursday, July 13

St. Louis	002 003 101	7	9	3
Philadelphia	000 101 001	3	6	4

WP **Weilman**; LP **Nabors**, Sheehan (6), Hesselbacher (7)

10. Friday, July 21

Cleveland	042 000 010	7	12	0
Philadelphia	010 000 001	2	7	3

WP **Coumbe**; LP **Nabors**

11. Thursday, July 27

Philadelphia	000 001 010	2	5	1
St. Louis	001 000 02x	3	11	0

WP **Hamilton**, Groom (9); LP **Nabors**

12. Tuesday, August 1[1]

Philadelphia	000 000 000	0	6	1
Chicago	001 000 02x	3	9	1

WP **Russell**; LP **Nabors**

[1]*First game of a doubleheader.*

13. Tuesday, August 8

Philadelphia	000 000 000	0	6	2
Detroit	120 010 32x	9	17	0

WP **Boland**; LP **Nabors**

14. Monday, August 14

Philadelphia	010 011 000	3	9	4
New York	400 000 00x	4	5	1

WP **Cullop**, Fisher (6); LP **Nabors**

15. Friday, September 1[1]

Philadelphia	000 000 001	1	5	2
Washington	100 010 01x	3	11	0

WP **Johnson**; LP **Nabors**

16. Monday, September 4

Philadelphia	000 000 000	0	7	0
Washington	000 002 00x	2	6	0

WP **Shaw**; LP **Nabors** (morning game)

17. Thursday, September 7

Boston	000 200 000	2	4	2
Philadelphia	000 000 000	0	7	1

WP **Foster**; LP **Nabors**

18. Thursday, September 14

Philadelphia	000 000 010	1	8	2
Cleveland	060 010 11x	9	11	1

WP **Gould**; LP **Nabors**, Sheehan (8)

19. Thursday, September 28

Washington	000 001 102	4	8	3
Philadelphia	001 000 000	1	5	2

WP **Gallia**; LP **Nabors**, Bressler (9)

After the nineteenth straight loss by Nabors, Philadelphia was eighth and last with a 33–115 record and trailed first-place Boston by fifty-four and one-half games. The A's ended that season with a 36–117 log and trailed by the same margin. They finished forty games behind seventh-place Washington.

During his streak Nabors appeared in thirty-five games, made twenty-five starts, completed ten, and made ten relief appearances without a decision. He lost to every team in the league at least once, with Washington beating him five times. He lost four to Detroit; three to New York, St. Louis and Cleveland; and one to Chicago.

Nabors was unlucky during the streak. In five of the losses Philadelphia was shut out, and the A's scored more than three runs behind him only twice. In the nineteen losses, the opposition averaged 5.3 runs and 8.6 hits to 1.7 runs and 6.7 hits for the A's. Six of his defeats were by one run and five were by a two-run margin.

Wins and losses were not part of the American League's official records in 1916, and not all record books agree on the number of games lost by Nabors that year.

The defeat Nabors suffered in Game 1 (April 28) of the streak was

---

[1]*First game of a doubleheader.*

Jack Nabors, a lanky right-hander from Alabama, won only one game in his major league career. That was six days before he began an all-time big league record 19 game losing streak for the last-place Philadelphia Athletics in 1916. (Courtesy of National Baseball Library, Cooperstown, New York.)

a questionable one and would not have been charged to him under modern scoring rules. In the game Philadelphia scored six runs in the fifth inning, and Nabors had a 6–3 lead going into the bottom of the ninth. He hit the first Washington batter and walked the next two, then was replaced by right-hander Cap Crowell.

A run-scoring force-out and outfielder Danny Moeller's single cut the A's lead to 6–5. Third baseman Eddie Foster then hit a potential double-play grounder to second baseman Nap Lajoie, whose throw to second was dropped by shortstop Whitey Witt, allowing the tying run to score. Outfielder Clyde Milan then singled to center to score Moeller with the winning run.

The other defeat Nabors suffered in the last of the ninth inning was in Game 5 (June 24) in Boston. After retiring pinch-hitters Olaf Henriksen, Pinch Thomas and Ruth in the eighth, Nabors went into the ninth with a 3-1 lead.

Outfielder Harry Hooper singled to open the Boston ninth and reached third, when Nabors made a poor throw on shortstop Hal Janvrin's bunt single. Outfielder Duffy Lewis grounded out to shortshop as Hooper held third, then broke for the plate after outfielder Wally Schang caught first baseman Dick Hoblitzel's fly to left.

Schang made a good throw home, but Hooper knocked the ball out of catcher Mike Murphy's glove, scoring the tying run. Janvrin reached third on the play, then scored the winning run on a passed ball.

Another disheartening loss for Nabors was in Game 11 (July 27), when he had a 2-1 lead at St. Louis in the last of the eighth. He then walked outfielder Burt Shotton, and rookie second baseman Otis Lawry made a wild throw on third baseman Jimmy Austin's single to put runners on second and third. Outfielder Ward Miller singled to bring in two runs, and the Browns put down a Philadelphia threat in the ninth to win, 3-2.

Nine days before his nineteenth straight loss, Nabors had another unlucky day. On September 19 at Chicago, the A's scored three runs in the eighth inning when Nabors was lifted for a pinch-hitter to take a 4-2 lead. Right-hander Tom Sheehan retired the White Sox in the eighth, but Chicago won, 5-4, with three runs in the ninth, second baseman Eddie Collins driving in the tying and winning runs with a two-out double to left field.

After his nineteenth consecutive loss, Nabors pitched in two more games in relief without a decision. On September 30 at home against Washington, Nabors relieved right-hander Socks Seibold with one out in the four-run ninth inning, one run in, the bases loaded, and the A's ahead, 6-5. His first pitch was wild, allowing the tying run to score, and two more runs followed in the 8-6 Washington victory. On October 3 Nabors pitched the final four innings of a 7-5 Philadelphia win over Boston to earn the only save of his big-league career, having relieved right-hander Elmer Myers, who left with the A's ahead, 4-2.

Despite his 1-20 record, Nabors had a 3.47 earned run average, the second best on the 1916 A's. In 1917 Nabors's major league career ended after he had pitched a total of three innings in two relief appearances.

Nabors died in Wilton, Alabama, on November 20, 1923, one day after his thirty-sixth birthday.

Cliff Curtis
1910 Boston Braves

18 Consecutive Losses

Cliff Curtis was twenty-six years old when he reached the major leagues, and thirty when he left after playing for four National League teams without posting a winning record for any of them.

Born July 3, 1883, in Delaware, Ohio, the rangy six-foot two-inch, 180-pound right-hander attracted notice when he had a 15–19 record for sixth-place Milwaukee of the American Association in 1908. In 1909 he had a 7–11 record for Milwaukee when the Boston Braves obtained him late that season.

The last-place Braves, more often called the Doves or Pilgrims at that time, put Curtis right into the starting rotation. He pitched a three-hitter against Cincinnati on August 27, shut out Pittsburgh on September 2, and blanked Philadelphia nine days later.

In 1910 Curtis lost his first three decisions, then won five of the next eight, including a game at Boston in the opener of a June 8 doubleheader, when he pitched a two-hitter to beat Pittsburgh, 4–0. He also singled home the second Boston run in the two-run fifth inning of his second shutout of that season.

The second longest one-season losing streak by a pitcher in major league history and the longest ever over two years began in his next start, five days later at Boston's South End Grounds.

When that game began, Boston was in last place with a 16–29 record, a full thirteen games behind first-place Chicago.

1. Monday, June 13[1]

| Cincinnati | 000 310 000 | 4 | 10 | 0 |
| Boston | 100 001 000 | 2 | 9 | 2 |

WP **Burns**; LP **Curtis**, Ferguson (8)

2. Saturday, June 18[1]

| St. Louis | 011 100 031 | 7 | 10 | 2 |
| Boston | 000 000 200 | 2 | 7 | 4 |

WP **Willis**; LP **Curtis**, Mattern (9)

3. Wednesday, June 22

| Boston | 010 000 000 | 1 | 5 | 5 |
| Philadelphia | 010 000 11x | 3 | 5 | 1 |

WP **Stack**; LP **Curtis**

4. Monday, June 27

| Brooklyn | 012 000 000 | 3 | 8 | 0 |
| Boston | 020 000 000 | 2 | 6 | 1 |

WP Barger, **Scanlan** (4); LP **Curtis**, Brown (3)

5. Thursday, June 30[1]

| Philadelphia | 002 011 000 | 4 | 11 | 1 |
| Boston | 000 000 100 | 1 | 5 | 2 |

WP **McQuillan**; LP **Curtis**, Evans (6)

6. Friday, July 15

| Boston | 000 100 000 | 1 | 11 | 2 |
| Cincinnati | 220 001 00x | 5 | 8 | 0 |

WP **Suggs**; LP **Curtis**, Ferguson (3)

7. Tuesday, July 19

| Boston | 040 000 000 00 | 4 | 10 | 2 |
| Pittsburgh | 300 000 001 01 | 5 | 13 | 3 |

WP Leever, Phillippe (2), **Leifield** (10); LP Frock, **Curtis** (2) (11 innings)

8. Sunday, July 24[1]

| Boston | 000 000 003 | 3 | 9 | 2 |
| Chicago | 101 020 01x | 5 | 10 | 1 |

WP **Overall**; LP **Curtis**, Good (8)

9. Thursday, July 28

| Boston | 000 000 000 00 | 0 | 5 | 2 |
| Brooklyn | 000 000 000 01 | 1 | 7 | 2 |

WP **Barger**; LP **Curtis** (11 innings)

10. Monday, August 1

| Boston | 000 000 000 | 0 | 6 | 0 |
| New York | 301 000 00x | 4 | 9 | 0 |

WP **Crandall**; LP **Curtis**, Burke (2)

11. Saturday, August 6

| Pittsburgh | 004 010 311 | 10 | 16 | 0 |
| Boston | 100 000 010 | 2 | 12 | 3 |

WP **White**; LP **Curtis**, Frock (3), Burke (9)

12. Wednesday, August 10

| Pittsburgh | 001 011 000 | 3 | 11 | 0 |
| Boston | 200 000 000 | 2 | 6 | 3 |

WP **Camnitz**; LP **Curtis**, Brown (9)

13. Saturday, August 13[2]

| Chicago | 020 200 250 | 11 | 14 | 2 |
| Boston | 001 000 010 | 2 | 11 | 5 |

WP **Cole**; LP **Curtis**, Evans (8)

14. Friday, August 19

| Boston | 100 101 030 | 6 | 13 | 3 |
| Pittsburgh | 110 001 50x | 8 | 10 | 2 |

WP **Leifield**, Phillippe (8); LP **Curtis**, Frock (8)

15. Wednesday, August 24

| Boston | 000 010 000 | 1 | 4 | 2 |
| Chicago | 010 109 00x | 11 | 9 | 0 |

WP **Richie**; LP **Curtis**, Evans (6)

16. Monday, September 5

| Boston | 000 000 000 | 0 | 6 | 7 |
| Philadelphia | 061 200 13x | 13 | 16 | 1 |

WP **Moren**, Slaughter (8); LP **Curtis** (afternoon game)

[1]*First game of a doubleheader.* [2]*Second game of a doubleheader.*

17. Saturday, September 10[2]

| Boston | 100 000 000 | 1 | 6 | 2 |
| New York | 000 010 11x | 3 | 9 | 0 |

WP **Mathewson**; LP **Curtis**

18. Tuesday, September 20[1]

| Pittsburgh | 520 002 000 | 9 | 17 | 1 |
| Boston | 000 010 001 | 2 | 4 | 3 |

WP **Adams**; LP **Curtis**, Frock (1), Tyler (7)

After the eighteenth straight loss by Curtis and Boston's defeat in the second game that day, the Braves were in eighth place with a 47–90 record, a whopping forty-six and one-half games behind first-place Chicago.

During the streak Curtis appeared in twenty-six games, starting twenty-two and losing seventeen while pitching five complete games, one of which ended in a tie. He relieved in four games, losing one and being credited with two saves. In his eighteen defeats the Braves averaged only 1.8 runs and 7.5 hits to 6.1 runs and 10.7 hits for the opposition. They were shut out three times and scored two runs or less in fifteen of the games. In addition Boston committed fifty errors to sixteen by the opposition.

Every team in the league beat Curtis at least once, and only St. Louis beat him just once. Pittsburgh defeated him five times, Philadelphia and Chicago three times, Cincinnati, Brooklyn and New York twice each.

The best pitching Curtis did was in Game 9 (July 28) at Brooklyn. He and right-hander Cy Barger both pitched shutout ball until the last of the eleventh. Then first baseman Jake Daubert doubled, outfielder Zack Wheat walked, and second baseman John Hummel beat out a bunt toward third on which first baseman Bud Sharpe muffed Bill Sweeney's late throw, Daubert scoring from second on the scratch hit and error.

The other extra-inning loss came in Game 7 (July 19), when Curtis relieved in the second inning after Pittsburgh scored three runs in the first. Boston took a 4–3 lead in the second, and Curtis held that advantage until the ninth, when pinch-hitter Vin Campbell singled, advanced on an infield out, and scored when Sweeney muffed third baseman Bobby Byrne's pop to third. Pittsburgh won in the eleventh when Campbell doubled to left and scored from second with two out when Curtis made a wild pitch.

On August 29 at Cincinnati, Curtis had a great chance to end his

---

[1]*First game of a doubleheader.* [2]*Second game of a doubleheader.*

losing streak at fifteen. Boston scored twice in the top of the eighth to take a 3–1 lead, but Cincinnati tied in the bottom of the inning on two singles around a walk for one run and a two-out single over second by catcher Tommy Clarke. The 3–3 game was then called because of darkness.

Curtis pitched twice in losing games after his eighteenth straight loss, then made his final appearance of the season in the second game, October 8, at home against Philadelphia. In this finale Curtis pitched his second 3–3 tie of the year, when Philadelphia scored the game's final run in the sixth inning in a game that darkness ended after seven innings. As a result Curtis finished the season with a 6–24 record and a 3.55 earned run average.

Bad luck continued for Curtis in 1911. In his first start he wrenched his arm in Boston's fourth game of the season, and pitched only once in relief until April 29, when he started and lost at Philadelphia, 7–4. He lost to Cincinnati in a fifteen-inning game in relief, 8–7, on May 10, lost as a starter to Pittsburgh on May 13 and 17 by scores of 9–3 and 7–6 in twelve innings, and lost to St. Louis, 3–1, on May 22 to extend his losing streak over two seasons to an all-time-record twenty-three games.

Finally, on May 26, more than eleven months after his last victory, Curtis went the route to beat Brooklyn's Barger, 7–2, at Boston, the Braves pounding out ten hits, one being a home run by Sweeney.

Curtis lost on successive days, June 8 and 9, at St. Louis and was traded on June 10 to Chicago. In mid–August he was traded to Philadelphia, and on July 10, 1912, he was claimed on waivers by Brooklyn. He pitched for the Dodgers through 1913 and then retired. He had a career record of twenty-eight wins, sixty-one losses, when he retired to his native Ohio. He went into the automobile agency business and was deputy State Automobile License Registrar in Utica, Ohio, where he died on April 23, 1943.

Roger Craig
1963 New York Mets

18 Consecutive Losses

Roger Craig pitched professionally for almost two decades. Born in Durham, North Carolina, on February 17, 1931, he attended North Carolina State University before making his pro debut in 1950 with Newport News, Virginia, the Piedmont League farm team of the Brooklyn Dodgers. He also pitched for Brooklyn minor league clubs at Valdosta, Elmira, Pueblo, Newport News again, and Montreal before making his major league debut with Brooklyn in midseason of 1955.

The six-foot four-inch, 185-pound right-hander pitched on two pennant-winning teams in Brooklyn and one after the club was transferred to Los Angeles. In the expansion draft after the 1961 season, when the National League went from eight to ten clubs, Craig was selected by the New York Mets. In 1962 he led the league with twenty-four losses, while winning ten games for the last-place Mets.

In 1963 Craig lost his first two decisions, then won at Chicago, 3–2, on April 25. In his next start at home on April 29, he beat Los Angeles, 4–2, winning when New York overcame a 2–1 deficit with three runs in the seventh inning. The tying run scored on right-hander Bob Miller's wild pitch, the winning run scored on a balk by right-hander Ed Roebuck, and an insurance run scored on outfielder Jim Hickman's single.

That win evened Craig's record at 2–2, but five days later his eighteen-game losing streak began when he pitched against San Francisco at New York's Polo Grounds with New York in ninth place, one game behind eighth-place Cincinnati and six games in back of first-place Pittsburgh.

1. Saturday, May 4

San Francisco	200 435 003	17	15	0
New York	000 400 000	4	8	4

WP **O'Dell**, Perry (7); LP **Craig**, Rowe (5), Bearnarth (7)

2. Monday, May 13

New York	000 000 002	2	3	4
Houston	010 020 10x	4	8	1

WP **Bruce**, McMahon (9); LP **Craig**

3. Friday, May 17

New York	000 020 010 00	3	6	2
San Francisco	200 100 000 01	4	6	3

WP Pierce, Larsen (6), Bolin (7), **Perry**, (10); LP Cisco, **Craig** (10) (11 innings)

4. Sunday, May 19[1]

New York	000 000 000	0	2	1
Los Angeles	100 000 00x	1	7	0

WP **Koufax**; LP **Craig**

5. Friday, May 24

New York	030 000 010	4	4	1
St. Louis	021 230 02x	10	14	2

WP **Gibson**, Shantz (9); LP **Craig**, MacKenzie (4), Hook (6), Stallard (8)

6. Tuesday, May 28

Chicago	300 000 200	5	11	1
New York	100 000 010	2	10	2

WP **Ellsworth**, McDaniel (9); LP **Craig**, Rowe (9)

7. Saturday, June 8

St. Louis	110 010 100	4	9	0
New York	000 000 000	0	2	1

WP **Broglio**; LP **Craig**, Bearnarth (9)

8. Sunday, June 16[2]

New York	000 100 002	3	11	2
Cincinnati	202 420 00x	10	15	2

WP **O'Toole**; LP **Craig**, MacKenzie (4)

9. Saturday, June 22

Philadelphia	000 100 001	2	10	0
New York	000 000 000	0	5	0

WP **Culp**; LP **Craig**, Cisco (9)

10. Friday, June 28

New York	000 010 000	1	5	1
Pittsburgh	002 000 10x	3	6	3

WP **Gibbon**, McBean (7); LP **Craig**

11. Thursday, July 4[1]

New York	000 001 000	1	2	3
Chicago	100 000 001	2	4	0

WP **Hobbie**; LP **Craig**

12. Thursday, July 11

Los Angeles	010 300 000	4	7	2
New York	002 001 000	3	8	2

WP **Drysdale**, Perranoski (8); LP **Craig**

13. Monday, July 15[2]

Houston	500 120 000	8	13	1
New York	000 000 000	0	4	1

WP **Nottebart**, Woodeshick (9); LP **Craig**

14. Friday, July 19

New York	000 100 000	1	6	0
Philadelphia	000 000 002	2	5	0

WP McLish, **Baldschun** (9); LP **Craig**

[1]*First game of a doubleheader.* [2]*Second game of a doubleheader.*

15. Tuesday, July 23

| New York | 000 100 000 | 1 | 4 | 1 |
| San Francisco | 340 011 00x | 9 | 11 | 1 |

WP **Marichal**; LP **Craig**, Bearnarth (2), MacKenzie (6), Powell (7)

16. Saturday, July 27

| New York | 000 000 000 | 0 | 4 | 1 |
| Houston | 000 000 01x | 1 | 4 | 2 |

WP **Bruce**, Woodeshick (9); LP **Craig**

17. Wednesday, July 31

| New York | 010 001 010 | 3 | 7 | 1 |
| Los Angeles | 030 200 00x | 5 | 6 | 1 |

WP **Richert**, Rowe (6), Perranoski (8); LP **Craig**

18. Sunday, August 4

| New York | 000 000 010 | 1 | 9 | 2 |
| Milwaukee | 100 001 00x | 2 | 8 | 0 |

WP **Schneider**, Raymond (7), Shaw (8); LP **Craig**, Bearnarth (7)

The National League record-tying eighteen-game losing streak ended five nights later at New York.

Friday, August 9

| Chicago | 000 020 010 | 3 | 8 | 2 |
| New York | 000 120 004 | 7 | 9 | 1 |

WP **Craig**; LP **Toth**, McDaniel (9)

Outfielder Frank Thomas homered for New York in the fourth, but Chicago took a 2–1 lead in the fifth on homers by shortstop Andre Rodgers and outfielder Lou Brock. New York regained the lead with two unearned runs in the fifth on a wild throw by third baseman Ron Santo, a walk, and singles by outfielders Duke Snider and Duke Carmel. Chicago tied in the eighth on a triple by outfielder Billy Williams and a sacrifice fly by Santo. New York won in ninth with four runs. Outfielder Joe Hicks singled with one out, shortstop Al Moran doubled into the left-field corner, and, after right-hander Lindy McDaniel relieved, Tim Harkness batted for Craig and walked to load the bases. Hickman then hit a 3–2 pitch off the left-field scoreboard for a grand-slam homer to win the game, 7–4.

After Craig lost his eighteenth straight game, New York was tenth and last with a 34–76 record, seven and one-half games in back of ninth-place Houston and thirty-two and one-half games behind first-place Los Angeles.

During the streak, Craig appeared in twenty-four games, made nineteen starts, losing seventeen, pitched nine complete games, and made five appearances in relief, one of which resulted in a loss. In five of his defeats, New York did not score and in five others tallied just one

Right-hander Roger Craig, who became a successful major league manager in the 1980s, was the best pitcher on the New York Mets in 1962 when he won ten games and lost twenty-four. In 1963, he won only five games and lost twenty-two, with eighteen coming in succession. In five of the defeats, the Mets failed to score. (Courtesy of National Baseball Library, Cooperstown, New York.)

run. The opposition averaged 5.2 runs and 8.8 hits to 1.6 runs and 5.6 hits for the Mets.

Seven of Craig's losses were by one run; four were by two runs; one each by three, four, six and seven runs; two by eight runs; and one by thirteen runs. He lost to every team in the league in the streak, dropping three games to San Francisco, Houston, Los Angeles; two games to St. Louis, Chicago and Philadelphia; and one each to Cincinnati, Pittsburgh and Milwaukee.

Craig's loss in relief was in Game 3 (May 17) at San Francisco. Craig came on in the tenth inning after right-hander Galen Cisco was lifted for a pinch-hitter with the score tied, 3–3. He didn't allow a hit until there was one out in the eleventh, when third baseman Joey Amalfitano hit a home run down the left-field line that the Mets heatedly argued was foul.

In Game 4 (May 19) at Los Angeles, Craig lost to left-hander Sandy Koufax, 1–0, giving up the run in the first inning on a walk, first baseman Ron Fairly's single, and a sacrifice fly by outfielder Tommy Davis.

In Game 11 (July 4) at Chicago, Craig gave up an unearned run in the first, and Hickman homered in the sixth to tie the score. In the Chicago ninth, first baseman Ernie Banks was safe on a two-base error by shortstop Chico Fernandez. Then, on a 2–2 pitch to second baseman Ken Hubbs, Craig made a wild pitch, and, when catcher Norm Sherry recovered the ball, he threw it past third base, allowing Banks to score the run that won the game, 2–1.

The most difficult defeat Craig suffered was in Game 14 (July 19) at Philadelphia. New York took a 1–0 lead in the fourth on outfielder Joe Christopher's double off the left-field wall, a fly to right by second baseman Ron Hunt, and a wild pitch by right-hander Cal McLish. Craig allowed only three singles until outfielder Tony Gonzales tripled off the scoreboard in right field with one out in the ninth. On the next pitch, first baseman Roy Sievers hit the ball into the upper left-field stands for the three-hundredth homer of his big-league career, winning the game, 2–1.

Craig suffered another 1–0 defeat in Game 16 (July 27) at Houston. Catcher John Bateman, batting only .195 at the time, hit Craig's first pitch of the eighth inning over the left-field fence for a home run.

An error by Craig led to the loss in Game 18 (August 4) at Milwaukee. After giving up a homer to third baseman Eddie Mathews in the first inning, Craig blanked the Braves until the sixth, when first baseman Lou Klimchock and outfielder Gene Oliver singled to put runners on first and third. Craig threw to first three times to hold Oliver close, and the third was in the dirt. It bounced away, allowing Klimchock to score. New York scored only in the eighth in the 2–1 defeat.

When he lost his eighteenth straight game, Craig's record was 2–20, and he finished the season with five victories and twenty-two defeats, including a major league record-tying five 1–0 losses. He appeared in forty-six games, starting thirty-one and relieving in fifteen. In relief, he lost one game and saved two.

Craig pitched for St. Louis in 1964, for Cincinnati in 1965, and finished his big-league pitching career with Philadelphia in 1966, being released July 18. He pitched in 368 major league games, won 74, lost 98, and had a 3.83 earned run average and pitched seven shutouts. He finished the 1966 season with Seattle of the Pacific Coast League.

In 1967 Craig became a scout for the Los Angeles Dodgers and began his managerial career in 1968 with Albuquerque, the Dodger farm club in the Texas League. Subsequently he served as a major league coach and a minor league pitching instructor, then managing the San Diego Padres in 1978 and 1979. After four years as Detroit's pitching coach, Craig scouted for a season and then was hired to manage San Francisco for the final eighteen games in 1985. In 1987 he managed the Giants to the National League's Western Division title.

Craig Anderson
1962 New York Mets
16 Consecutive Losses

Not many pitchers win both ends of a doubleheader in modern major league baseball. It happened to Craig Anderson early in 1962, the first season the New York Mets spent in the National League. The big right-hander never won another big-league game.

Anderson, a six-foot two-inch, 210-pounder, was born July 1, 1938, in Washington, D.C., and graduated in 1960 from Lehigh University. He signed his first professional contract with the St. Louis Cardinals and finished the 1960 season with their Tulsa farm club of the Texas League.

Promoted to the Pacific Coast League farm club at Portland for 1961, Anderson was brought up to St. Louis during that season and posted a 4–3 record for the Cardinals in twenty-five games, all in relief. In the expansion draft at the end of that season, the twenty-three-year-old was selected by the New York Mets for the standard price of $75,000.

Employed primarily as a reliever by the Mets, Anderson had the biggest day in his major league career on May 12 in a home doubleheader against Milwaukee at New York's Polo Grounds. He pitched the last two innings of the opener and won, 3–2, when catcher Hobie Landrith homered with a man on base and two out in the ninth inning. He pitched the ninth inning of the second game and won when first baseman Gil Hodges homered with one out in the ninth inning to win the game, 8–7. Those victories gave him a 3–1 record for the season, but twelve days later at Dodger Stadium in Los Angeles his sixteen-game losing streak began with New York in ninth place, two games in front of Chicago and twelve games in back of first-place San Francisco.

1. Thursday, May 24

New York	002 000 000	2	4	1
Los Angeles	010 000 12x	4	7	1

WP Podres, **Sherry** (8); LP R. L. Miller, **Anderson** (7)

2. Sunday, May 27

New York	030 011 000	5	7	0
San Francisco	000 200 04x	6	10	2

WP McCormick, **Duffalo** (6), S. Miller (9); LP Jackson, **Anderson** (8), R. G. Miller (8)

3. Wednesday, May 30[1]

Los Angeles	300 000 201	6	5	1
New York	003 010 100	5	9	1

WP Podres, **Sherry** (7); LP R. L. Miller, **Anderson** (8)

4. Saturday, June 2[1]

San Francisco	031 000 020	6	8	2
New York	003 100 000	4	12	0

WP Duffalo, Larsen (3), **O'Dell** (7), S. Miller (9); LP Mizell, **Anderson** (3), Jackson (9)

5. Tuesday, June 12

New York	000 001 100	2	5	2
Houston	010 000 002	3	6	2

WP **Johnson**; LP R. L. Miller, **Anderson** (6)

6. Monday, June 25

New York	020 000 010	3	8	2
Pittsburgh	600 304 00x	13	15	2

WP **Law**; LP **Anderson**, Daviault (1), Mizell (7)

7. Saturday, July 7[1]

St. Louis	000 200 010	3	5	0
New York	010 000 100	2	5	2

WP **Washburn**, McDaniel (9); LP **Anderson**

8. Saturday, July 14

Los Angeles	181 106 000	17	16	1
New York	000 002 100	3	6	0

WP **Williams**; LP **Anderson**, Daviault (2), MacKenzie (2), Moorhead (6), Mizell (8)

9. Saturday, July 21

New York	010 110 000	3	11	2
Cincinnati	200 020 01x	5	7	0

WP **Purkey**; LP **Anderson**

10. Thursday, July 26

New York	000 000 010	1	8	3
Milwaukee	010 122 00x	6	8	1

WP **Spahn**; LP **Anderson**, MacKenzie (7)

11. Thursday, August 2

Philadelphia	114 200 010	9	13	0
New York	010 000 201	4	5	2

WP **Mahaffey**; LP **Anderson**, MacKenzie (4), Daviault (9)

12. Tuesday, August 7

New York	021 000 200	5	11	0
Los Angeles	000 402 01x	7	8	2

WP **Drysdale**; LP **Anderson**, MacKenzie (4), Daviault (7)

[1]*Second game of a doubleheader.*

13. Sunday, August 26

| Los Angeles | 101 307 013 | 16 | 13 | 2 |
| New York | 000 000 032 | 5 | 7 | 5 |

WP **Richert**, Ortega (9); LP **Anderson**, Moorhead (6), R. G. Miller (7), Daviault (8)

14. Friday, August 31

| New York | 011 000 000 | 2 | 8 | 1 |
| St. Louis | 000 020 02x | 4 | 11 | 0 |

WP **L. Jackson**, Shantz (9); LP **Anderson**, Moorhead (8), Hunter (8)

15. Tuesday, September 4

| New York | 000 000 100 | 1 | 8 | 2 |
| Pittsburgh | 001 010 30x | 5 | 8 | 1 |

WP **Haddix**; LP **Anderson**, Hunter (7), Daviault (8)

16. Saturday, September 8

| New York | 200 000 001 | 3 | 6 | 5 |
| Houston | 000 000 112 | 4 | 10 | 2 |

WP Brunet, **Kemmerer** (8); LP Hook, Daviault (7), Hunter (9), **Anderson** (9) (afternoon game)

After Anderson's sixteenth defeat in a row, and New York's loss in the night game that followed, the Mets had a 35–109 record in tenth place, seventeen and one-half games behind ninth-place Chicago, and fifty-seven and one-half games in back of first-place Los Angeles. Anderson's record after that decision was three wins and seventeen losses, and he didn't have another decision that season.

Manager Casey Stengel decided to bring Anderson back the next afternoon, and the youngster made his fourteenth and final start of the season in the Sunday afternoon game that didn't start until 4 P.M. because of the heat and was suspended after eight innings because of a time limit put in place to allow New York to catch its scheduled flight. In the game Anderson lasted for only five batters as Houston scored three runs in the first inning. The Mets came back to tie, 7–7, before the game was called.

During the losing streak, Anderson appeared in twenty-nine games, losing ten starts and six games in relief. In the streak the opposition averaged 7.1 runs and 9.4 hits to 3.1 runs and 7.5 hits for New York, which was never shut out in the streak. Five of the defeats were by one run, five by two runs, one by four runs, two by five runs, and one each by ten, eleven and fourteen runs. Anderson lost five times to Los Angeles; twice each to San Francisco, Houston, Pittsburgh and St. Louis; and once each to Cincinnati, Milwaukee and Philadelphia. The only team he failed to lose to was Chicago, and his loss before the streak started was to Cincinnati. In the sixteen losses New York scored in only eight games while Anderson was on the mound, for a total of seventeen runs in sixty-three and one-third innings.

Anderson's best chance for victory during the streak was in Game 5 (June 12), at Houston. Right-hander Bob Miller started for the Mets, gave up a run in the second, then tripled and scored the tying run on outfielder Richie Ashburn's sacrifice fly in the sixth. Anderson then replaced Miller in the home sixth, and New York took a 2–1 lead in the seventh when a throwing error by shortstop Bob Lillis allowed first baseman Marv Throneberry to score. Anderson allowed only one hit until pinch-hitter Billy Goodman beat out an infield hit with one out in the Houston ninth. Jim Busby ran for Goodman and scored on pinch-hitter Pidge Browne's triple to left center. After an intentional walk to outfielder Al Spangler, second baseman Joey Amalfitano singled to left to score pinch-runner Roman Mejias with the run that won the game, 3–2.

That was one of six games Anderson lost in the rival team's final time at bat. Four of those came in his first five losses, all in relief.

In Game 3 (May 30) at New York, Anderson came on in the eighth after New York had tied the score, 5–5, in the seventh. In the ninth Los Angeles outfielder Willie Davis homered for the winning run.

In Game 7 (July 7) at New York, outfielder Stan Musial homered in the eighth to snap a 2–2 tie and give St. Louis a 3–2 win in one of Anderson's complete games.

In Game 16 (September 8) at Houston, Anderson relieved with two men on base, none out, and New York leading, 3–2. After pinch-hitter Amalfitano grounded to third into a double play, first baseman Norm Larker was intentionally walked. Third baseman Bob Aspromonte then singled to left, where Frank Thomas made a futile dive for the ball as the tying run scored. Thomas then threw the ball over second base, and Larker slid home with the run that won the game, 4–3.

After his streak, Anderson was in seven more games that season without a decision. He finished with a 3–17 record and a 5.36 earned run average in fifty games, thirty-six of them in relief. In 1963 Anderson had an 0–2 record in three games with New York, and in 1964 an 0–1 record in four games. He spent most of those two seasons with Buffalo of the International League and pitched in the minors through 1966. His major league totals for eighty-two games were seven victories, twenty-three losses, five saves, and an ERA of 5.10.

Mike Parrott
1980 Seattle Mariners

16 Consecutive Losses

A two-sport star at Camarillo High School in California, six-foot four-inch, 205-pound right-hander Mike Parrott was born on December 6, 1954. An all-league selection in basketball, Parrott as a pitcher in his senior year of 1973 struck out 116 batters in seventy-one innings and compiled an earned run average of 0.75.

In June 1973 Parrott was a first-round draft pick of the Baltimore Orioles and made his pro debut with Bluefield, West Virginia, of the Appalachian League that summer. Despite injuries, he worked his way up through the Baltimore system. After posting a 15–7 record for Rochester and being the International League's most valuable player in 1977, he joined the Orioles to pitch three times in relief without a decision.

Traded to Seattle on December 7, 1977, Parrott had shoulder problems in 1978 but recovered to win fourteen games against twelve defeats for the Mariners in 1979. That year he set club records for wins, complete games, innings pitched, strikeouts, and earned run average.

In 1980 Parrott beat Toronto, 8–6, in the opening game of the season, but he didn't win another game for almost thirteen months. In his next outing, six days after his win in the opener, Parrott started his sixteen-game losing streak in a game against the Oakland Athletics at the Oakland Coliseum. At the time Seattle was in first place in the American League's Western Division with a 4–1 record, one-half game in front of Kansas City and Chicago.

1. Tuesday, April 15

| Seattle | 000 000 003 | 3 | 7 | 0 |
| Oakland | 000 153 03x | 12 | 12 | 1 |

WP **McCatty**, Jones (9); LP **Parrott**, Heaverlo (5), Dressler (6), McLaughlin (8)

2. Sunday, April 20

| Minnesota | 100 200 010 | 4 | 8 | 1 |
| Seattle | 200 000 010 | 3 | 8 | 1 |

WP **Redfern**, Verhoeven (6), Marshall (8); LP **Parrott**

3. Friday, April 25

| California | 010 002 100 | 4 | 10 | 2 |
| Seattle | 010 000 002 | 3 | 10 | 0 |

WP **Aase**, Montague (9); LP **Parrott**, Heaverlo (7)

4. Wednesday, April 30

| Seattle | 003 000 000 | 3 | 9 | 0 |
| Minnesota | 102 041 11x | 10 | 16 | 2 |

WP **Redfern**; LP **Parrott**, D. Roberts (5), Dressler (7)

5. Monday, May 26

| Seattle | 000 000 100 | 1 | 10 | 2 |
| Milwaukee | 205 013 00x | 11 | 18 | 0 |

WP **Caldwell**, Cleveland (7), McClure (8), Castro (9); LP **Parrott**, D. Roberts (3), Dressler (6)

6. Saturday, May 31

| Seattle | 000 100 001 | 2 | 8 | 1 |
| Cleveland | 003 020 00x | 5 | 11 | 0 |

WP **Spillner**; LP **Parrott**, D. Roberts (5), McLaughlin (7)

7. Thursday, June 19

| Seattle | 000 000 000 | 0 | 8 | 2 |
| Boston | 000 002 00x | 2 | 7 | 0 |

WP **Stanley**; LP **Parrott**, Rawley (6)

8. Wednesday, June 25

| Seattle | 000 001 000 | 1 | 9 | 0 |
| Texas | 200 002 02x | 6 | 10 | 0 |

WP **Jenkins**; LP **Parrott**, Heaverlo (6)

9. Monday, June 30

| Texas | 006 000 302 | 11 | 15 | 0 |
| Seattle | 001 001 300 | 5 | 14 | 1 |

WP **Jenkins**, Lyle (7), Darwin (7); LP **Parrott**, McLaughlin (3), Beattie (7), Rawley (9)

10. Saturday, July 5

| Seattle | 010 100 110 | 4 | 10 | 0 |
| Kansas City | 004 001 00x | 5 | 9 | 0 |

WP Martin, **Twitty** (5), Quisenberry (7); LP **Parrott**, McLaughlin (3), Rawley (6), Heaverlo (7)

11. Sunday, July 20

| Detroit | 401 000 000 | 5 | 9 | 0 |
| Seattle | 010 000 001 | 2 | 7 | 2 |

WP **Schatzeder**; LP **Parrott**, D. Roberts (2), Heaverlo (5), Dressler (9)

12. Monday, September 1

| Seattle | 000 100 003 | 4 | 13 | 0 |
| Baltimore | 200 021 00x | 5 | 8 | 0 |

WP **D. Martinez**, Stoddard (8), T. Martinez (9); LP **Parrott**, McLaughlin (8)

13. Saturday, September 6

| Seattle | 000 001 000 | 1 | 6 | 1 |
| Boston | 011 001 02x | 5 | 9 | 1 |

WP **Drago**, Burgmeier (8); LP **Parrott**, Heaverlo (8)

14. Saturday, September 13

| Milwaukee | 012 000 050 | 8 | 12 | 0 |
| Seattle | 000 000 000 | 0 | 3 | 1 |

WP **Caldwell**; LP **Parrott**, R. Anderson (8)

15. Tuesday, September 30

Seattle   100 200 001 000 01 5 12 2
Kansas City001 002 100 000 03 7 18 1
WP Leonard, **Quisenberry** (11); LP
Honeycutt, McLaughlin (3), D. Roberts
(6), **Parrott** (10) (14 innings)

16. Sunday, October 5

Seattle   010 100 000 2 8 2
Texas   000 101 001 3 8 2
WP Kainer, **Darwin** (7); LP R. Anderson,
Parrott (6)

Parrott's sixteenth straight loss was on the final day of the 1980 season as Seattle finished seventh and last in the West with a 59–103 record, thirty-eight games behind Kansas City, which went on to win the American League pennant.

The 1980 season was a difficult one for Parrott for more reasons than the losing streak. In Game 4 (April 30), with the score tied, 3–3, Minnesota shortstop Roy Smalley led off the fourth inning with a line drive to the mound that hit Parrott in the groin area. The right-hander had to be carried off the field, and Smalley went on to score the lead run in a 10–3 win for the Twins.

Parrott was not able to return to action until May 26. Then, on August 8, he was optioned to Seattle's Pacific Coast League farm club at Spokane and did not return to the Mariners until September 1.

In his losing streak Parrott lost to ten different teams, bowing to Texas three times; Minnesota, Boston, Milwaukee and Kansas City twice each; and to Oakland, California, Cleveland, Detroit and Baltimore once each. During the streak, he pitched in twenty-six games, made fifteen starts, completed only one, and had just one no-decision. His last two defeats were as a relief pitcher, a role he filled eleven times during his streak. In his fifteen starts, he pitched more than six innings only five times.

The most runs Seattle scored in Parrott's sixteen losses was five, and that happened only twice. The Mariners scored four runs twice, three runs four times, two runs three times, one run three times, and were shut out twice.

In his fourteen losses as a starting pitcher, Parrott was scored on in the first inning six times and held the opposition scoreless until the sixth inning only once. That was in Game 7 (June 19) at Boston. He lost that game, 2–0, when outfielder Fred Lynn singled with one out in the sixth inning and first baseman Tony Perez hit a run-scoring double off the center-field wall and scored on outfielder Jim Rice's single.

In Parrott's complete game loss to Minnesota in Game 2 (April 20), Smalley hit a home run in the eighth inning to provide the winning run in the 4–3 loss at home. Seattle led in only three of Parrott's starts and never after the fourth inning.

After his final 1980 start, an 8–0 loss to Milwaukee in Game 14 (September 13), Parrott was employed only in relief. He was credited with saves in three of his next four outings, although he pitched only one-third of an inning on September 17 and again on September 21, and one inning on September 24.

In Game 15 (September 30) at Kansas City, Parrott came on at the start of the home tenth and blanked the Royals on three hits and one walk through the thirteenth inning. In the top of the fourteenth, a squeeze bunt by third baseman Dave Edler brought in outfielder Kim Allen to give Seattle a 5–4 lead. In the home fourteenth, however, outfielder Willie Wilson and shortstop U. L. Washington singled, and third baseman George Brett hit a game-winning home run with none out to right field.

In the final game in the streak, Game 16 (October 5) at Texas, Parrott relieved with two out in the sixth inning when the Rangers tied the score, 2–2. Texas then won with one out in the ninth, as outfielder Johnny Grubb doubled to score outfielder Jim Norris from first base for a 3–2 victory in the final game of the season.

Parrott thus finished the season with a 1–16 record and a 7.28 earned run average in twenty-seven games.

In 1981 Parrott started and lost his first two decisions before finally beating Milwaukee, 12–1, at home on May 6. He finished that season with a 3–6 record, and the following March 5 he was traded to Milwaukee. Twenty-four days later, on March 29, 1981, the Brewers released him, and that was his last major league connection. He pitched a couple of years in the minor leagues and then retired.

Parrott finished his major league career with a 19–39 record, two shutouts, and a 4.88 earned run average in 119 games.

Bob Groom
1909 Washington Senators

15 Consecutive Losses

Bob Groom became acquainted with losing at an early age in his professional career. The six-foot two-inch, 175-pound right-hander, who was born September 12, 1884, in Belleville, Illinois, posted an 8–26 record for Fort Scott (Kansas) of the Missouri Valley League in 1904, his first pro season.

With Springfield (Missouri) of the same league, Groom had a 21–21 record in 1905 and a 20–18 log in 1906, then earning promotion to Portland of the Pacific Coast League. He had a 20–26 record in 1907 but bounced back to win twenty-nine games while losing fifteen in 1908, and before the 1909 season he was sold to the Washington Senators for $1,750.

With Washington, which had only once finished as high as sixth and needed plenty of help, Groom moved right into the starting rotation. He made his first major league start on April 15, 1909, and was routed in the first inning, losing 4–1. He beat Philadelphia, 3–2, pitching a complete ten-inning game for his first win, on April 28.

Groom beat St. Louis, 5–1, in a rain-shortened game on June 17 for his fifth win against seven defeats, then lost his next four decisions. In the morning game on July 5 at Boston, Groom won, 7–6, in relief to make his record 6–11. His fifteen-game losing streak began the next day at Boston's Huntington Avenue Grounds, with Washington in last place with a 22–45 record, twenty-three and one-half games behind first-place Detroit.

Some record books still list Groom's losing streak as nineteen games because the American League's official records did not credit him with the July 5 victory. In that game Groom relieved right-hander Long Tom Hughes in the third inning as Boston took a 5–3 lead. The Senators tied the score in the fifth and scored two more in the sixth for the 7–6 win. In the official records Hughes was charged with a loss in that game although his team won. Actually the win had to go to Groom, snapping his four-game losing streak.

1. Tuesday, July 6[2]

Washington	000 000 000	0	4	2
Boston	110 000 00x	2	4	1

WP **Pape**; LP **Groom**

2. Saturday, July 10

Washington	000 000 000	0	4	4
Cleveland	001 100 02x	4	4	2

WP **Young**; LP **Groom**, Hovlik (8)

3. Monday, July 19

Washington	000 002 000	2	4	5
Chicago	031 006 02x	12	13	2

WP **Scott**, Smith (6), Suter (8); LP **Groom**, Hovlik (6), Witherup (7)

4. Thursday, July 22

Washington	000 001 000	1	9	0
St. Louis	210 100 10x	5	5	1

WP **Waddell**; LP **Groom**, Witherup (7), Collins (8)

5. Saturday, July 24

Washington	020 000 100	3	10	2
St. Louis	500 100 12x	9	16	1

WP **Powell**; LP **Groom**

6. Wednesday, July 28[1]

Philadelphia	021 010 300	7	10	2
Washington	001 000 000	1	8	3

WP **Plank**; LP **Groom**, Oberlin (8)

7. Saturday, July 31[2]

Chicago	021 000 100	4	9	1
Washington	000 000 000	0	5	0

WP **Smith**; LP **Groom**, Ohl (7)

8. Wednesday, August 18

Philadelphia	000 020 000	2	11	0
Washington	000 000 001	1	8	0

WP **Plank**; LP **Groom**

9. Thursday, August 26

Washington	100 010 000	2	12	2
Cleveland	002 401 10x	8	12	1

WP **Young**; LP **Groom**, Oberlin (5)

10. Monday, August 30

Washington	000 000 000	0	7	3
St. Louis	211 001 30x	8	11	3

WP **Bailey**; LP **Groom**

11. Monday, September 6

Washington	000 003 002 0	5	8	4
Philadelphia	002 000 003 1	6	11	2

WP Plank, **Dygert** (10); LP **Groom** (10 innings) (afternoon game)

12. Saturday, September 11[1]

New York	000 200 010	3	6	3
Washington	000 000 000	0	1	2

WP **Brockett**; LP **Groom**, Reisling (9)

[1]*First game of a doubleheader.* [2]*Second game of a doubleheader.*

13. Thursday, September 16[2]

St. Louis	000 300 010	4	9	0
Washington	110 000 000	2	5	2

WP **Gilligan** LP **Groom**

14. Thursday, September 23

Detroit	120 030 020	8	10	0
Washington	001 000 000	1	10	1

WP **Donovan**; LP **Groom**, Gray (1), Reisling (6)

15. Saturday, September 25[1]

Chicago	000 020 000	2	2	1
Washington	010 000 000	1	5	0

WP **White**; LP **Groom**

The losing streak ended four days later at Washington's National Park.

Wednesday, September 29[2]

Cleveland	010 000 002	3	7	7
Washington	600 000 01x	7	8	2

WP **Groom**; LP **Winchell**, Otis (1), Falkenberg (2)

Washington, which had scored as many as three runs in a game only once in the previous ten games, exploded for six runs in the first inning after Cleveland second baseman Nap Lajoie had tripled and had been stranded in the top of the first. Two errors, a single by outfielder Clyde Milan, outfielder George Browne's double, which brought on left-hander Harry Otis in relief, a walk, singles by second baseman Germany Schaefer and shortstop George McBride, and a sacrifice fly by first baseman Tom Crooks gave Washington its six runs in the first, and outfielder Red Killefer scored the seventh run in the eighth. Groom, who walked five and struck out eight, gave up a run in the second and two in the ninth, when catcher Ted Easterly batted for right-hander Cy Falkenberg, singled, and scored.

Groom appeared in twenty-one games during his streak, starting sixteen games and relieving in five. He pitched seven complete games, losing six and tying one in twelve innings.

In his streak Groom got little offensive support. Washington scored a total of only nineteen runs in the fifteen defeats. Washington was shut out five times, scored one run five times, and two runs three times.

Three of the games were decided by a one-run margin, and the first two of them were the only games in the streak won in the final inning.

In Game 8 (August 18), which Philadelphia won, 2-1, the A's scored twice in the fifth inning on catcher Paddy Livingston's single, outfielder Danny Murphy's single two outs later, and a single by second baseman Eddie Collins. Washington muffed a chance to win in the ninth after Schaefer led off with a double, took third on first baseman Bob Unglaub's single to center, and scored on Killefer's single past shortstop. The rally fizzled when third baseman Wid Conroy bunted to the mound into a force at third, pinch-hitter Cliff Blankenship bunted toward third for the second out, and McBride struck out to end the game.

Game 11 (September 6) was the only one Groom lost in extra innings. Washington had a 5-2 lead in the last of the ninth when Philadelphia tied on two walks, a two-out pop double by third baseman Frank Baker, and a run-scoring single by first baseman Harry Davis. In the tenth, Livingston singled, advanced on a sacrifice, and scored on outfielder Heinie Heitmuller's double to center for a 6-5 victory.

In Game 15 (September 25) Washington scored in the second in a bunt single by Schaefer, on which left-hander Doc White made a wild throw, and McBride's pop single behind second. Chicago came back to win, 2-1, with two runs in the fifth that began with a walk to outfielder Patsy Dougherty. He was sacrificed to second, took third on shortstop Freddie Parent's single for the first hit off Groom, and scored the tying run on third baseman Lee Tannehill's out. The winning run scored on catcher Billy Sullivan's single over first for the only other Chicago hit.

Some of Groom's best pitching was done in three tie games during the streak, particularly in the 0-0 July 16 game at Detroit that lasted eighteen innings. Detroit right-hander Ed Summers went the route, allowing only seven hits and one walk, while left-hander Dolly Gray started for Washington and gave up one hit and one walk until relieved by Groom with one out in the ninth. He allowed five hits and five walks in the last nine and two-thirds innings before the game was called because of darkness.

On August 10 at Washington, third baseman Hobe Ferris homered in the seventh for St. Louis, and Washington tied in the ninth when outfielder Jack Lelivelt bunted safely and scored on pinch-hitter Jiggs Donahue's double to the right-field fence. Neither team scored again, and the game ended after twelve innings in a 1-1 tie.

Tall right-hander Bob Groom made his major league debut with the Washington Senators in 1909, and suffered twenty-six of his team's 110 defeats. Fifteen of the losses came in a row and the Nats scored only nineteen runs in the fifteen defeats. (Courtesy of National Baseball Library, Cooperstown, New York.)

On August 14 at Washington, Groom relieved Gray in the eighth and blanked Detroit on three hits over the last three and two-thirds innings of the 3–3 tie in eleven innings. Both August ties were called to allow the visiting teams to make train connections.

After Groom's fifteenth straight loss, Washington was in eighth place with a 39–105 record, fifty-four games behind first-place Detroit. The Senators finished fifty-six games out, twenty games from seventh-place St. Louis. Groom, who did not pitch again after ending his losing streak, finished the season with seven victories, a still-standing American League record of twenty-six defeats, and a creditable 2.87 earned run average.

Groom proved to be an accomplished pitcher in his ten-year career. In 1912 he posted a 24–13 record for Washington in his most successful season. He jumped to the St. Louis club of the Federal League in 1914 and returned to the American League with St. Louis in 1916. In 1917 he pitched a no-hit, no-run game against Chicago.

Groom was sold to Cleveland for the waiver price prior to the start of spring training in 1918, pitched in only fourteen games for the Indians, compiling a 2–2 record. Groom, who attended the St. Louis College of Physicians and Surgeons in 1909 and St. Louis University in 1910, retired from baseball with a record of 120 wins, 150 losses, twenty-two shutouts and an earned run average of 3.10.

Groom operated two coal companies and coached youth baseball teams in the Belleville area, where he died on February 19, 1948.

HITTING STREAKS

56 Games • Joe DiMaggio, 1941

44 Games • Pete Rose, 1978

41 Games • George Sisler, 1922

40 Games • Ty Cobb, 1911

39 Games • Paul Moliter, 1987

37 Games • Tommy Holmes, 1945

Hitting Streaks

Player	Team	Year	Games	Times at Bat	Runs Scored	Base Hits	Two-Base Hits	Three-Base Hits	Home Runs	Multiple Hit Games	On-Base Average in Streak	Batting Average in Streak
Joe DiMaggio	Yankees	1941	56	223	56	91	16	4	15	22	.463	.408
Pete Rose	Reds	1978	44	182	30	70	14	0	0	18	.423	.385
George Sisler	Browns	1922	41	174	43	79	14	7	0	24	.474	.454
Ty Cobb	Tiger	1911	40	167	40	80	12	8	1	26	.516	.479
Paul Molitor	Brewers	1987	39	164	43	68	17	3	7	19	.495	.415
Tommy Holmes	Braves	1945	37	156	43	66	11	3	9	21	.492	.423

Joe DiMaggio
1941 New York Yankees

56 Consecutive Games

Joe DiMaggio grew up in the San Francisco area and came east to become one of the game's great players. Born on November 25, 1914, in Martinez, California, he was one of nine children, with three of the boys becoming big-league ballplayers.

At age seventeen, DiMaggio made his pro debut with the San Francisco Seals of the Pacific Coast League and played with them through 1935. In 1933 he hit safely in sixty-one consecutive games. In 1934 he suffered a knee injury that turned off some major league teams, but not the New York Yankees, who bought him on November 22, 1934, for the bargain price of $25,000. He joined them for spring training in 1936 after hitting thirty-four homers and batting .398 with the Seals in 1935.

Injuries hampered DiMaggio early in his major league career, but the six-foot two-inch, 193-pound right-handed batter hit .323 as a rookie in 1936, and in 1937 led the league with forty-six homers, his career high. In 1939 he won the Most Valuable Player Award when he won the batting title with a .381 average. He won the batting title again the next year with a .352 average, and in each of these seasons he batted in at least 125 runs.

In 1941 both DiMaggio and the Yankees got away slowly. On May 14, 1941, Cleveland right-hander Mel Harder held DiMaggio hitless in three at bats and pitched his team to a 4–1 victory at Yankee Stadium. After that game DiMaggio's average was .306, and New York was in fourth place in the American League with a 14–14 record, five and one-half games behind first-place Cleveland.

DiMaggio started his historic fifty-six-game hitting streak the next afternoon at Yankee Stadium.

1. Thursday, May 15

Chicago	201 110 422	13	14	0
New York	100 000 000	1	9	2

	AB	R	H	
DiMaggio	4	0	1	(1B)

WP **Smith**; LP **Bonham**, Stanceu (5), Branch (8)

2. Friday, May 16

Chicago	000 005 000	5	7	0
New York	211 000 002	6	9	1

	AB	R	H	
DiMaggio	4	2	2	(3B, HR)

WP Breuer, **Murphy** (6); LP **Lee**

3. Saturday, May 17

Chicago	010 001 001	3	9	0
New York	000 010 001	2	5	3

	AB	R	H	
DiMaggio	3	1	1	(1B)

WP **Rigney**; LP **Chandler**

4. Sunday, May 18

St. Louis	110 000 000	2	6	1
New York	220 410 30x	12	16	0

	AB	R	H	
DiMaggio	3	3	3	(2-1B, 2B)

WP **Gomez**; LP **Harris**, Niggeling (5)

5. Monday, May 19

St. Louis	300 200 000	5	8	0
New York	000 000 010	1	4	2

	AB	R	H	
DiMaggio	3	0	1	(2B)

WP **Galehouse**; LP **Russo**, Peek (7)

6. Tuesday, May 20

St. Louis	020 012 031	9	13	6
New York	001 041 031	10	10	1

	AB	R	H	
DiMaggio	5	1	1	(1B)

WP Ruffing, Murphy (7), **Branch** (9); LP Auker, **Caster** (8)

7. Wednesday, May 21

Detroit	010 000 210 0	4	7	2
New York	100 100 002 1	5	14	1

	AB	R	H	
DiMaggio	5	0	2	(2-1B)

WP Donald, **Stanceu** (9); LP Rowe, **Benton** (7) (10 innings)

8. Thursday, May 22

Detroit	100 101 101	5	11	1
New York	201 002 01x	6	12	2

	AB	R	H	
DiMaggio	4	0	1	(1B)

WP **Peek**, Branch (8); LP **Newsom**, McKain (6)

9. Friday, May 23

Boston	200 021 022	9	13	2
New York	221 010 120	9	10	1

	AB	R	H	
DiMaggio	5	0	1	(1B)

Boston–Dobson, Harris (2), Dickman (6), D. Newsome (8), Ryba (9); New York–Chandler, Stanceu (6), Breuer (7), Murphy (9) (**tie game** 9 innings, darkness)

10. Saturday, May 24

Boston	002 110 200	6	9	4
New York	000 201 40x	7	9	1

	AB	R	H	
DiMaggio	4	2	1	(1B)

WP Gomez, **Branch** (7), Murphy (8); LP **Johnson**, Fleming (7), Wilson (8)

11. Sunday, May 25

Boston	013	000	420	10	14	4
New York	000	300	000	3	7	1

	AB	R	H	
DiMaggio	4	0	1	(1B)

WP **Grove**; LP **Russo**, Sanceu (7), Bonham (8)

12. Tuesday, May 27

New York	101	412	010	10	18	2
Washington	001	005	200	8	12	3

	AB	R	H	
DiMaggio	5	3	4	(3-1B, HR)

WP **Ruffing**, Murphy (6), Chandler (7); LP Chase, **Anderson** (2), Carrasquel (6), Zuber (7), Masterson (9)

13. Wednesday, May 28

New York	000	001	050	6	7	0
Washington	201	000	011	5	11	2

	AB	R	H	
DiMaggio	4	1	1	(3B)

WP **Peek**, Breuer (9); LP **Hudson**, Carrasquel (8)

14. Thursday, May 29

New York	000	11	2	7	2
Washington	001	01	2	6	0

	AB	R	H	
DiMaggio	3	1	1	(1B)

New York–Russo; Washington–Sundra (**tie game** 5 innings, rain)

15. Friday, May 30[1]

New York	000	100	003	4	5	2
Boston	001	001	010	3	10	1

	AB	R	H	
DiMaggio	2	1	1	(1B)

WP Donald, **Breuer** (8); LP **Johnson**

16. Friday, May 30[2]

New York	000	000	000	0	2	6
Boston	302	520	10x	13	16	1

	AB	R	H	
DiMaggio	3	0	1	(2B)

WP **Harris**; LP **Stanceu**, Chandler (3), Branch (4)

17. Sunday, June 1[1]

New York	011	000	000	2	7	0
Cleveland	000	000	000	0	8	0

	AB	R	H	
DiMaggio	4	1	1	(1B)

WP **Ruffing**; LP **Milnar**, Heving (9)

18. Sunday, June 1[2]

New York	000	010	040	5	7	1
Cleveland	100	000	002	3	6	0

	AB	R	H	
DiMaggio	4	0	1	(1B)

WP **Gomez**, Breuer (9); LP **Harder**, Brown (9)

19. Monday, June 2

New York	020	100	020	5	7	1
Cleveland	210	022	00x	7	10	0

	AB	R	H	
DiMaggio	4	2	2	(1B, 2B)

WP **Feller**; LP **Russo**, Stanceu (6), Chandler (8)

20. Tuesday, June 3

New York	000	100	100	2	8	1
Detroit	400	000	00x	4	7	0

	AB	R	H	
DiMaggio	4	1	1	(HR)

WP **Trout**; LP **Peek**

---

[1]*First game of a doubleheader.* [2]*Second game of a doubleheader.*

21. Thursday, June 5

New York	000 002 002 0	4	8	1
Detroit	000 003 010 1	5	10	2

	AB	R	H	
DiMaggio	5	1	1	(3B)

WP Newhouser, **Newsom** (9); LP Donald, **Breuer** (8), Murphy (10) (10 innings)

22. Saturday, June 7

New York	015 000 005	11	15	2
St. Louis	102 010 030	7	8	1

	AB	R	H	
DiMaggio	5	2	3	(3-1B)

WP Gomez, Chandler (5), **Stanceu** (8); LP Muncrief, Kramer (3), Caster (6), **Allen** (9), Trotter (9)

23. Sunday, June 8[1]

New York	003 001 032	9	11	0
St. Louis	100 110 000	3	7	0

	AB	R	H	
DiMaggio	4	3	2	(2-HR)

WP **Ruffing**; LP **Auker**, Ostermueller (9)

24. Sunday, June 8[2]

New York	520 000 1	8	9	2
St. Louis	201 000 0	3	8	1

	AB	R	H	
DiMaggio	4	1	2	(2B, HR)

WP Russo, **Breuer** (3); LP **Harris**, Caster (1), Muncrief (3), Kramer (7) (7 innings, darkness)

25. Tuesday, June 10

New York	000 005 300	8	14	1
Chicago	000 000 003	3	6	0

	AB	R	H	
DiMaggio	5	1	1	(1B)

WP **Peek**; LP **Rigney**, Haynes (8)

26. Thursday, June 12

New York	000 001 001 1	3	8	1
Chicago	010 010 000 0	2	9	0

	AB	R	H	
DiMaggio	4	1	2	(1B, HR)

WP Chandler, **Murphy** (9); LP **Lee** (10 innings)

27. Saturday, June 14

Cleveland	000 010 000	1	3	0
New York	101 020 00x	4	6	0

	AB	R	H	
DiMaggio	2	0	1	(2B)

WP **Donald**; LP **Feller**, Eisenstat (8)

28. Sunday, June 15

Cleveland	000 000 020	2	6	0
New York	111 000 00x	3	5	1

	AB	R	H	
DiMaggio	3	1	1	(HR)

WP **Ruffing**; LP **Bagby**, Smith (4)

29. Monday, June 16

Cleveland	100 200 100	4	12	2
New York	001 200 03x	6	10	1

	AB	R	H	
DiMaggio	5	0	1	(2B)

WP Gomez, **Murphy** (8), Russo (9); LP **Milnar**, Brown (8)

30. Tuesday, June 17

Chicago	020 010 401	8	11	0
New York	002 000 320	7	9	2

	AB	R	H	
DiMaggio	4	1	1	(1B)

WP Rigney, **Hallett** (8), Smith (9); LP Peek, Stanceu (7), **Murphy** (8)

[1]*First game of a doubleheader.* [2]*Second game of a doubleheader.*

31. Wednesday, June 18

Chicago	010 000 020	3	5	1
New York	020 000 000	2	10	2

	AB	R	H	
DiMaggio	3	0	1	(1B)

WP **Lee** LP **Chandler**

32. Thursday, June 19

Chicago	000 100 100	2	5	1
New York	000 510 01x	7	9	1

	AB	R	H	
DiMaggio	3	2	3	(2-1B, HR)

WP **Breuer**; LP **Smith**, Ross (5)

33. Friday, June 20

Detroit	100 000 012	4	7	2
New York	403 070 00x	14	17	1

	AB	R	H	
DiMaggio	5	3	4	(3-1B, 2B)

WP **Russo**; LP **Newsom**, McKain (3)

34. Saturday, June 21

Detroit	022 000 300	7	12	0
New York	100 000 100	2	8	1

	AB	R	H	
DiMaggio	4	0	1	(1B)

WP **Trout**, Benton (7); LP **Donald**, Bonham (7), Branch (8)

35. Sunday, June 22

Detroit	010 100 020	4	6	0
New York	002 001 002	5	8	1

	AB	R	H	
DiMaggio	5	1	2	(2B, HR)

WP Ruffing, **Murphy** (9); LP Newhouser, **Newsom** (7)

36. Tuesday, June 24

St. Louis	000 000 001	1	5	0
New York	201 100 05x	9	10	1

	AB	R	H	
DiMaggio	4	1	1	(1B)

WP **Gomez**; LP **Muncrief**, Kramer (8)

37. Wednesday, June 25

St. Louis	010 002 020	5	11	1
New York	000 220 03x	7	8	1

	AB	R	H	
DiMaggio	4	1	1	(HR)

WP Chandler, **Murphy** (6); LP Galehouse, **Allen** (5)

38. Thursday, June 26

St. Louis	000 000 100	1	1	1
New York	010 011 01x	4	6	0

	AB	R	H	
DiMaggio	4	0	1	(2B)

WP **Russo**; LP **Auker**

39. Friday, June 27

New York	110 001 102	6	10	1
Philadelphia	110 102 011	7	13	2

	AB	R	H	
DiMaggio	3	1	2	(1B, HR)

WP Dean, **Ferrick** (9); LP Breuer, Stanceu, **Branch** (9)

40. Saturday, June 28

New York	121 001 200	7	14	1
Philadelphia	000 130 000	4	8	0

	AB	R	H	
DiMaggio	5	1	2	(1B, 2B)

WP **Donald**, Murphy (9); LP **Babich**, Harris (7)

41. Sunday, June 29[1]

New York	000 033 012	9	12	0
Washington	000 004 000	4	6	1

	AB	R	H	
DiMaggio	4	1	1	(2B)

WP **Ruffing**, Murphy (6); LP **Leonard**, Carrasquel (7)

42. Sunday, June 29[2]

New York	210 102 100	7	11	4
Washington	102 100 001	5	12	1

	AB	R	H	
DiMaggio	5	1	1	(1B)

WP **Stanceu**, Peek (6), Bonham (9); LP Hudson, **Anderson** (5), Masterson (7), Kennedy (9)

43. Tuesday, July 1[1]

Boston	000 002 000	2	7	1
New York	000 402 01x	7	15	1

	AB	R	H	
DiMaggio	4	0	2	(2-1B)

WP **Russo**, Chandler (7); LP **Harris**, Ryba (4), Potter (8)

44. Tuesday, July 1[2]

Boston	000 20	2	4	3
New York	304 20	9	10	0

	AB	R	H	
DiMaggio	3	1	1	(1B)

WP **Bonham**; LP **Wilson**, Dobson (3) (5 innings, rain and darkness)

45. Wednesday, July 2

Boston	000 003 100	4	9	1
New York	011 060 00x	8	11	1

	AB	R	H	
DiMaggio	5	1	1	(HR)

WP **Gomez**, Murphy (6); LP **Newsome**, Wilson (5), Potter (6)

46. Saturday, July 5

Philadelphia	002 201 000	5	9	1
New York	210 022 12x	10	11	0

	AB	R	H	
DiMaggio	4	2	1	(HR)

WP **Ruffing**; LP **Marchildon**

47. Sunday, July 6[1]

Philadelphia	010 300 000	4	7	0
New York	420 010 01x	8	17	1

	AB	R	H	
DiMaggio	5	2	4	(3-1B, 2B)

WP Donald, **Bonham** (4); LP **Babich**, Hadley (2)

48. Sunday, July 6[2]

Philadelphia	000 000 001	1	5	1
New York	101 000 10x	3	9	0

	AB	R	H	
DiMaggio	4	0	2	(1B, 3B)

WP **Breuer**; LP **Knott**, Ferrick (5)

49. Thursday, July 10

New York	010 00	1	3	1
St. Louis	000 00	0	5	1

	AB	R	H	
DiMaggio	2	0	1	(1B)

WP **Gomez**; LP **Niggeling** (5 innings, rain)

50. Friday, July 11

New York	200 001 012	6	14	1
St. Louis	200 000 000	2	7	0

	AB	R	H	
DiMaggio	5	1	4	(3-1B, HR)

WP **Russo**; LP **Harris**, Kramer (9)

---

[1]*First game of a doubleheader.*   [2]*Second game of a doubleheader.*

51. Saturday, July 12

		R	H	
New York	000 502 000	7	8	1
St. Louis	000 100 301	5	10	2

	AB	R	H	
DiMaggio	5	1	2	(1B, 2B)

WP **Bonham**, Murphy (8); LP **Auker**, Muncrief (4), Ostermueller (8)

52. Sunday, July 13[1]

		R	H	
New York	000 600 002	8	13	2
Chicago	001 000 000	1	5	4

	AB	R	H	
DiMaggio	4	2	3	(3-1B)

WP **Chandler**; LP **Lyons**, Hallett (4)

53. Sunday, July 13[2]

		R	H	
New York	000 000 000 01	1	6	0
Chicago	000 000 000 00	0	3	0

	AB	R	H	
DiMaggio	4	0	1	(1B)

WP **Ruffing**; LP **Lee** (11 innings)

54. Monday, July 14

		R	H	
New York	001 000 000	1	8	1
Chicago	020 100 04x	7	9	1

	AB	R	H	
DiMaggio	3	0	1	(1B)

WP **Rigney**; LP **Breuer**, Stanceu (8), Branch (8)

55. Tuesday, July 15

		R	H	
New York	104 000 000	5	10	0
Chicago	020 110 000	4	12	1

	AB	R	H	
DiMaggio	4	1	2	(1B, 2B)

WP Peek, **Branch** (5); LP **Smith**

56. Wednesday, July 16

		R	H	
New York	200 140 012	10	11	0
Cleveland	110 001 000	3	8	1

	AB	R	H	
DiMaggio	4	3	3	(2-1B, 2B)

WP **Donald**; LP **Milnar**, Krakauskas (6)

The next night the teams moved from Cleveland's small League Park to Municipal Stadium, and 67,468, the largest crowd at that time for a major league night game, saw the streak end.

Thursday, July 17

		R	H	
New York	100 000 120	4	8	0
Cleveland	000 100 002	3	7	0

	AB	R	H
DiMaggio	3	0	0

WP **Gomez**, Murphy (9); LP **Smith**, Bagby (8)

Two outstanding plays by Cleveland third baseman Ken Keltner helped end the longest hitting streak in major league history.

In the first inning third baseman Red Rolfe singled with one out and scored on outfielder Tommy Henrich's double. DiMaggio then hit

[1]*First game of a doubleheader.* [2]*Second game of a doubleheader.*

a hard smash that Keltner gloved across the foul line and threw to first for the out. DiMaggio walked in the fourth, and in Cleveland's half of the inning outfielder Gee Walker hit an inside-the-park homer to tie the score.

In the seventh Keltner made another fine play on DiMaggio's wicked grounder near the foul line and threw him out. Second baseman Joe Gordon followed with a homer into the left-field seats to give New York a 2–1 lead.

DiMaggio came up for his final time in the eighth after outfielder Charlie Keller tripled, pitcher Lefty Gomez singled one out later, first baseman Johnny Sturm singled, Rolfe doubled for a 4–1 New York lead, and Henrich walked to load the bases. Right-hander Jim Bagby then relieved left-hander Al Smith and on a 1–1 pitch got DiMaggio to hit a hard grounder to shortstop, where Lou Boudreau fielded it on a nasty high hop and threw to second baseman Ray Mack to start an inning- and streak-ending double play.

That was DiMaggio's last chance, but there was still some suspense in the last of the ninth inning. Walker and first baseman Oscar Grimes opened with singles, and right-hander Johnny Murphy relieved Gomez. Pinch-hitter Larry Rosenthal tripled, and Cleveland had the tying run on third with none out. If the score were tied, DiMaggio might get another chance to bat in the tenth. However, Murphy didn't let the run score. He got pinch-hitter Hal Trosky to ground out to first as Rosenthal held third, induced pinch-hitter Soup Campbell to bounce to the mound with Rosenthal being trapped and run down, and then ended the game by getting outfielder Roy Weatherly to ground out to short-stop Phil Rizzuto.

After DiMaggio hit in his fifty-sixth straight game, New York was in first place with a 55–27 record and held a six-game lead over second-place Cleveland. New York won forty-one of the fifty-six games, lost thirteen and tied two.

During his streak, DiMaggio collected ninety-one hits in 223 at bats, had sixteen doubles, four triples and fifteen home runs. He scored fifty-six runs, batted in fifty-five runs, drew twenty-one walks, was hit by the pitcher twice, and reached base once on catcher's interference, striking out only seven times. He batted .408 during the streak to raise

Opposite: **Center fielder Joe DiMaggio of the New York Yankees shows off his classic swing during his all-time record fifty-six-game hitting streak that lasted for more than two months in 1941. (Courtesy of AP/Wide World Photos.)**

his season's average sixty-nine points to .375, and had an on-base percentage of .463.

Four times DiMaggio had four hits in a game. He also had five three-hit games, thirteen two-hit games and thirty-four one-hit games. After being held hitless July 17, DiMaggio began another streak the next day that lasted through sixteen games.

DiMaggio feasted on the pitching of the sixth-place St. Louis Browns, hitting .458 with five homers and seventeen runs batted in for twelve games. He hit .524 in five games against Philadelphia, and .422 against Chicago in twelve games. His lowest average was .300 against Boston, but he batted in nine runs in eight games. He hit .385 against Cleveland, .381 against Washington, and .375 against Detroit.

Seven times DiMaggio kept his streak alive on his last time at bat, and five of those games were early in the streak.

In Game 8 (May 22) DiMaggio hit a run-scoring fly in the first inning but went hitless three times before hitting a single in his last at bat in the seventh inning of a 6–5 New York win over Detroit. The next day in Game 9 (May 23), Joe singled in the eighth in his last at bat of a 9–9 tie game with Boston that was called because of darkness after nine innings. He also waited until his fourth and last at bat before hitting a single to drive in the tying and winning runs in the seventh inning in Game 10 (May 24), to help New York beat Boston, 7–6.

In Game 14, DiMaggio opened the fourth inning with a single and struck out in the fifth before the game was halted by rain in the top of the sixth, ending in a 2–2 five-inning tie at Washington.

In Game 15 (May 30) New York's only hits off Boston left-hander Earl Johnson until the ninth inning were a single and a game-tying home run in the fourth inning by Rolfe. With one out in the top of the ninth, pinch-hitter Red Ruffing singled off the left-field wall, and DiMaggio, who had been walked twice and retired once, singled. With two out, an error by third baseman Jim Tabor loaded the bases before Keller walked to force in one run and shortstop Frankie Crosetti hit a two-run single to help New York win, 4–3, at Boston.

That Memorial Day doubleheader (Games 15 and 16) produced the worst defensive day in DiMaggio's career. In the opener he dropped a fly ball in center field to give Boston the run that put the Red Sox in front, 3–1, in the eighth, but redeemed himself with his hit in the ninth. In the second game DiMaggio hit a wind-blown fly that outfielder Pete Fox lost in the sun in right field in the fourth inning. The ball fell for a double, Joe's only hit in three trips to the plate and one of only two hits New York got off left-hander Mickey Harris in a 13–0 Boston victory in which DiMaggio made three more errors. He fumbled a single by outfielder Ted Williams and made two wild throws, committing half of New York's six errors in the Fenway Park rout.

DiMaggio was 0-for-3 in Game 18 (June 1) when he faced right-hander Mel Harder in his last at bat in the eighth inning at Cleveland. This time Joe singled off the glove of Keltner, the third baseman who helped stop the streak more than a month and one-half later.

Against St. Louis in Game 36 (June 24), DiMaggio grounded out to third, fouled out, and flied out in his first three trips to the plate against rookie right-hander Bob Muncrief. In his last at bat in the five-run eighth, DiMaggio singled to left and scored as New York won at home, 9–1.

The seventh and final time DiMaggio kept his streak alive with a hit in his last at bat was in Game 38 (June 26), and in this one he got help from a teammate and from St. Louis manager Luke Sewell, who had replaced Fred Haney as pilot of the Browns three weeks before.

Against right-hander Eldon Auker, DiMaggio flied to left in the second, was safe on shortstop Johnny Berardino's fumble in the fifth, and grounded out weakly to third in the sixth. New York had a 3–1 lead in the bottom of the eighth when Rolfe walked with one out.

Fearful of hitting into a double play that would prevent DiMaggio coming to bat, Henrich got manager Joe McCarthy's permission to bunt. Henrich sacrificed successfully, and now DiMaggio was the batter with two out and first base open. With St. Louis trailing by only two runs, an intentional walk certainly seemed in order for the hot-hitting DiMaggio, but that didn't happen.

When he came to bat, DiMaggio was batting .378 during his streak, .424 against St. Louis, and .333 against Auker. Keller, a left-handed batter who would be the batter if DiMaggio walked, was 0-for-2 in this game at that point. He had batted only .246 during Joe's streak, .300 against St. Louis, and .111 against Auker. While both were power hitters, Keller struck out five times as often in 1941 as did DiMaggio, who fanned only seven times in the streak and thirteen times for the season.

Allowed to hit in this situation, DiMaggio slammed the first pitch past third into the left-field corner for a run-scoring double and New York won, 4–1. The only St. Louis run was also the the only hit off Yankee left-hander Marius Russo, a home run by first baseman George McQuinn.

In Game 25 (June 10) at Chicago, DiMaggio's only hit in five at bats was a grounder in the seventh that third baseman Dario Lodigiani knocked down, and what may have been the most controversial hit in the streak happened against Chicago in Game 30 (June 17). In the seventh inning of an 8–7 Chicago win, he hit a routine grounder to shortstop that took a bad hop off Luke Appling's shoulder, and DiMag beat the throw to first. After a long delay the official scorer ruled a hit, and that set a New York club record. The next day in Game 31 (June 18), DiMaggio's only hit was a grounder to the shortstop that Appling knocked down and didn't bother to throw to first as New York lost, 3–2.

DiMaggio tied the modern major league record, set at forty-one games by St. Louis Browns first baseman George Sisler in 1922, with a sixth-inning double off knuckleballing right-hander Dutch Leonard in the first game of the June 29 doubleheader at Washington, then broke the record with a seventh-inning single off right-hander Red Anderson in the second game, despite the fact that his favorite bat was stolen by a souvenir hunter between games. New York won the twin bill by scores of 9–4 and 7–5.

DiMaggio's next target was the forty-four-game streak for the all-time record by Baltimore outfielder Willie Keeler in 1897. In Game 44 (July 1) against Boston, DiMaggio lined a single to center in the first inning of a 9–2 New York win called because of rain and darkness after five innings. He broke the record the next day in Game 45 (July 2), when his only hit in five at bats was a two-run homer deep into the left-field stands in the six-run fifth inning off right-hander Dick Newsome in an 8–4 Yankee rout.

The third and last night game New York played during the streak was Game 49 (July 10), and it was a 1–0 New York win at St. Louis that was halted by rain after five innings. In the first inning DiMaggio hit a hard grounder that shortstop Alan Strange got his glove on but could not hold. He flied out in his other time at bat.

His least impressive hit in the streak came in Game 54 (July 14), when he beat out a slow roller to third base in the sixth inning for his only hit in New York's 7–1 win at Chicago.

In his final game in the streak on July 16 at Cleveland's League Park, a crowd of 15,000 saw DiMaggio single up the middle on the first pitch to him after Henrich had walked with two out in the first inning. Later in the game, DiMaggio walked, singled, and doubled. A ground-out was all that prevented a perfect day at bat.

When DiMaggio broke Sisler's modern record of forty-one games, he said, "Sure, I'm tickled. Who wouldn't be? It's a great thing. I've realized an ambition. I'm glad the strain is over. Now, I'm going after that forty-four-game streak and I'll keep right on swinging and hitting as long as I can.

"I never really was concerned about the mark until around the thirty-third game. Yesterday in Philly, I think was the first time I was really nervous. I was tense out there today, too."

When the streak finally ended two and one-half weeks later, DiMaggio said, "I can't say that I'm glad it's over. Of course, I wanted to go on as long as I could. Now that the streak is over, I just want to go out there and keep helping to win ball games.

"That play Ken [Keltner] made on me in the first inning when he went behind third for a backhand stop of that hard smash was a beautiful piece of work. When they take 'em away from you like that, there's nothing a fellow can do about it. Anyway, it's all over now."

The day after the streak stopped, DiMaggio started a sixteen-game streak that lasted from July 18 through August 2 before he went 0-for-4 in both games of an August 3 doubleheader against St. Louis. In those sixteen games he batted .426, and from the start of the fifty-six-game streak through August 2 he hit .408 for the seventy-three games. In addition he reached base safely in eighty-four straight games by hit or walk from May 14 through August 2, before St. Louis right-hander Johnny Niggeling stopped him in his 2–0 win in the August 4 opener when Joe went 0-for-4.

DiMaggio batted .357 that season, and finished third in batting, in hits (193) and runs (177). He was fourth in homers (30) and first in runs batted in (125), and won the second of three Most Valuable Player Awards as New York won the pennant by seventeen games over Boston with a 101–53 record.

When DiMaggio retired after the 1951 season, his thirteen-year major league career average was .325. Twice he led the league in batting, homers, and runs batted in, and finished with 361 homers and 1,537 RBIs. In ten World Series he batted .271 with eight homers in fifty-one games. In eleven All-Star Games he batted .225 with one homer. He was elected to the Hall of Fame in 1955.

Pete Rose
1978 Cincinnati Reds
44 Consecutive Games

Pete Rose came by his athletic ability naturally. Born in Cincinnati on April 14, 1941, he grew up in that area idolizing his father, who was still playing organized team sports past the age of forty.

Not blessed with an outstanding arm or great speed, Rose still managed to star in high school sports. He was signed June 18, 1960, to a pro contract without much enthusiasm by the Cincinnati Reds. His greatest asset was desire and hustle, which helped him win a job with the Reds in spring training in 1963, after three years in the low minors.

The switch-hitting Rose played second base for the Reds that year and was named National League Rookie of the Year. In his first fifteen seasons with Cincinnati, he played regularly at second base, left field, right field and third base; won three batting titles; and had more than 200 hits in nine seasons.

On May 5, 1978, Rose collected his three-thousandth hit three weeks after turning thirty-seven. However, as Cincinnati beat Chicago, 1–0, on June 13, Rose went hitless in three times at bat against right-hander Dennis Lamp and left-hander Willie Hernandez, and his batting average was only .267.

At that point Rose had had only six hits in his last fifty-one at bats, but the next afternoon at Cincinnati's Riverfront Stadium, he started his National League record-tying streak with the Reds in second place in the Western Division with a 36–25 record, two games behind San Francisco.

1. Wednesday, June 14

Chicago	000 100 000	1	4	0
Cincinnati	300 000 00x	3	6	2

	AB	R	H	
Rose	4	1	2	(2-1B)

WP **Sarmiento**, Tomlin (6), Bair (9); LP **Roberts**, Moore (9)

2. Friday, June 16

St. Louis	000 000 000	0	0	2
Cincinnati	000 031 00x	4	7	1

	AB	R	H	
Rose	4	1	2	(1B, 2B)

WP **Seaver**; LP **Denny**, Schultz (7)

3. Saturday, June 17

St. Louis	012 000 200	5	10	1
Cincinnati	200 000 121	6	11	1

	AB	R	H	
Rose	4	2	2	(2-1B)

WP Bonham, Hume (2), **Borbon** (8); LP Vuckovich, Littell (8), **Schultz** (9)

4. Sunday, June 18

St. Louis	110 000 000	2	9	1
Cincinnati	021 000 10x	4	7	1

	AB	R	H	
Rose	4	1	1	(1B)

WP **Norman**, Sarmiento (6); LP **Martinez**, Urrea (7)

5. Tuesday, June 20

Cincinnati	200 001 012	6	12	1
San Francisco	003 000 000	3	10	4

	AB	R	H	
Rose	5	2	2	(1B, 2B)

WP Moskau, **Borbon** (7), Bair (8), Tomlin (9); LP Montefusco, **Lavelle** (7), Moffitt (9), Curtis (9)

6. Wednesday, June 21

Cincinnati	000 000 000	0	3	0
San Francisco	000 300 00x	3	5	1

	AB	R	H	
Rose	4	0	1	(1B)

WP **Halicki**; LP **Seaver**, Sarmiento (8)

7. Thursday, June 22

Cincinnati	200 100 200	5	13	0
San Francisco	000 000 000	0	3	2

	AB	R	H	
Rose	4	0	1	(1B)

WP **Bonham**, Sarmiento (7); LP **Knepper**, Williams (7), Curtis (8), Moffitt (9)

8. Friday, June 23

Cincinnati	000 000 000	0	3	1
Los Angeles	000 001 000	1	7	0

	AB	R	H	
Rose	4	0	1	(1B)

WP **Hooton**; LP **Norman**, Bair (8)

9. Saturday, June 24

Cincinnati	010 010 010	3	13	0
Los Angeles	010 102 00x	4	9	0

	AB	R	H	
Rose	5	1	4	(3-1B, 2B)

WP **Sutton**, Hough (7), Welch (8); LP **Hume**, Borbon (6), Sarmiento (7)

10. Sunday, June 25

Cincinnati	010 000 202	5	12	1
Los Angeles	210 000 001	4	8	2

	AB	R	H	
Rose	3	1	2	(2-1B)

WP Moskau, **Borbon** (7), Bair (9); LP **John**, Rautzhan (9)

11. Monday, June 26

| Cincinnati | 003 000 001 | 4 | 4 | 0 |
| Houston | 200 000 010 | 3 | 7 | 2 |

	AB	R	H	
Rose	5	1	1	(1B)

WP **Seaver**, Bair (9), Tomlin (9); LP **Lemongello**

12. Tuesday, June 27

| Cincinnati | 001 000 300 | 4 | 8 | 0 |
| Houston | 220 200 01x | 7 | 10 | 0 |

	AB	R	H	
Rose	4	1	1	(1B)

WP **Niekro**, Sambito (8); LP **Bohnam**, Borbon (5), Tomlin (7), Sarmiento (8)

13. Wednesday, June 28

| Cincinnati | 000 000 000 | 0 | 4 | 1 |
| Houston | 000 000 30x | 3 | 8 | 0 |

	AB	R	H	
Rose	4	0	1	(1B)

WP **Dixon**; LP **Norman**, Borbon (8)

14. Thursday, June 29

| Cincinnati | 000 000 000 | 0 | 4 | 0 |
| Houston | 201 000 02x | 5 | 11 | 1 |

	AB	R	H	
Rose	3	0	1	(2B)

WP **Bannister**; LP **Hume**, Tomlin (7)

15. Friday, June 30[1]

| Los Angeles | 000 000 230 | 5 | 8 | 0 |
| Cincinnati | 300 000 000 | 3 | 9 | 1 |

	AB	R	H	
Rose	4	1	1	(1B)

WP **John**, Rautzhan (8); LP Moskau, **Bair** (8)

16. Friday, June 30[2]

| Los Angeles | 000 013 010 | 5 | 7 | 3 |
| Cincinnati | 000 000 020 | 2 | 11 | 0 |

	AB	R	H	
Rose	5	1	3	(3-1B)

WP **Welch**, Forster (7), Hough (9); LP **Sarmiento**, Borbon (8)

17. Saturday, July 1

| Los Angeles | 000 000 101 | 2 | 6 | 1 |
| Cincinnati | 000 000 000 | 0 | 6 | 1 |

	AB	R	H	
Rose	5	0	1	(2B)

WP **Rhoden**; LP **Seaver**

18. Sunday, July 2

| Los Angeles | 010 130 001 | 6 | 14 | 0 |
| Cincinnati | 300 000 40x | 7 | 11 | 1 |

	AB	R	H	
Rose	4	1	1	(2B)

WP Bonham, Borbon (5), **Bair** (7); LP **Rau**, Hough (7), Rautzhan (8)

19. Monday, July 3

| Houston | 203 000 002 00 | 7 | 10 | 1 |
| Cincinnati | 302 002 000 01 | 8 | 15 | 0 |

	AB	R	H	
Rose	5	1	3	(2-1B, 2B)

WP Norman, Sarmiento (7), Tomlin (9), **Bair** (10); LP Bannister, McLaughlin (5), **Sambito** (9) (11 innings)

20. Tuesday, July 4

| Houston | 101 000 100 | 3 | 9 | 0 |
| Cincinnati | 100 000 000 | 1 | 4 | 2 |

	AB	R	H	
Rose	4	1	1	(1B)

WP **Richard**; LP **Hume**, Tomlin (7), Borbon (9)

[1]*First game of a doubleheader.* [2]*Second game of a doubleheader.*

21. Wednesday, July 5

Houston	000 001 000	1	7	1
Cincinnati	020 000 00x	2	7	1

	AB	R	H	
Rose	4	0	1	(1B)

WP **Moskau**, Bair (9); LP **Niekro**

22. Friday, July 7[1]

San Francisco	020 030 020	7	11	0
Cincinnati	000 020 103	6	13	2

	AB	R	H	
Rose	5	1	3	(3-1B)

WP **Blue**, Williams (6), Curtis (8), Moffitt (9), Lavelle (9); LP **Seaver**, Borbon (6), Sarmiento (7), Tomlin (9)

23. Friday, July 7[2]

San Francisco	000 000 100	1	9	0
Cincinnati	000 020 00x	2	8	1

	AB	R	H	
Rose	4	0	1	(1B)

WP **Bonham**, Bair (7); LP **Barr**, Curtis (7)

24. Saturday, July 8

San Francisco	020 000 020	4	7	0
Cincinnati	000 002 000	2	4	1

	AB	R	H	
Rose	4	1	1	(1B)

WP Montefusco, **Lavelle** (6); LP Norman, **Sarmiento** (7), Tomlin (8), Borbon (8)

25. Sunday, July 9

San Francisco	000 200 000	2	10	1
Cincinnati	000 003 50x	8	8	0

	AB	R	H	
Rose	4	1	3	(3-1B)

WP Moskau, **Hume** (6), Borbon (7), Tomlin (7); LP **Halicki**, Curtis (6), Moffitt (7), Knepper (8)

26. Thursday, July 13

New York	020 010 010	4	5	0
Cincinnati	001 000 100	2	9	2

	AB	R	H	
Rose	5	0	2	(1B, 2B)

WP **Koosman**, Lockwood (7); LP **Seaver**, Sarmiento (8)

27. Friday, July 14

New York	110 100 000	3	7	2
Cincinnati	001 200 30x	6	10	0

	AB	R	H	
Rose	5	0	2	(2-1B)

WP Norman, Borbon (4), Sarmiento (6), **Bair** (7); LP **Zachry**, Siebert (7), Bernard (7)

28. Saturday, July 15

New York	020 200 010	5	13	0
Cincinnati	010 002 40x	7	12	1

	AB	R	H	
Rose	2	2	1	(1B)

WP Moskau, Borbon (4), **Tomlin** (6), Sarmiento (8); LP Swan, Siebert (6), **Murray** (6), Lockwood (7), Bernard (8)

29. Sunday, July 16

New York	000 010 010	2	6	3
Cincinnati	510 300 00x	9	12	2

	AB	R	H	
Rose	5	1	1	(2B)

WP **Hume**; LP **Kobel**, Bernard (5), Siebert (7)

30. Monday, July 17

Montreal	320 100 000	6	15	2
Cincinnati	000 240 20x	8	10	3

	AB	R	H	
Rose	4	0	1	(1B)

WP Norman, Borbon (2), **Sarmiento** (6), Bair (8); LP Grimsley, **Bahnsen** (5), Pirtle (8)

[1]*First game of a doubleheader.* [2]*Second game of a doubleheader.*

31. Tuesday, July 18

Montreal	001 001 010	3	8	0
Cincinnati	000 000 001	1	6	1

	AB	R	H	
Rose	4	0	2	(1B, 2B)

WP **Dues**, Knowles (7), Garman (9); LP **Seaver**, LaCoss (8), Borbon (9)

32. Wednesday, July 19

Cincinnati	000 000 340	7	8	0
Philadelphia	000 110 000	2	10	1

	AB	R	H	
Rose	4	1	1	(1B)

WP Moskau, **Tomlin** (6), Bair (7); LP **Carlton**, McGraw (8), Reed (8)

33. Thursday, July 20

Cincinnati	020 031 000	6	9	1
Philadelphia	102 212 00x	8	15	0

	AB	R	H	
Rose	5	1	1	(1B)

WP Kaat, **Brusstar** (5), McGraw (7); LP Hume, **Sarmiento** (4), Tomlin (6), Borbon (8)

34. Friday, July 21

Cincinnati	010 006 300	10	14	2
Montreal	010 000 002	3	7	0

	AB	R	H	
Rose	3	1	1	(1B)

WP **LaCoss**, Borbon (9); LP **Grimsley**, Pirtle (6), Bahnsen (7)

35. Saturday, July 22

Cincinnati	000 001 100	2	5	1
Montreal	000 001 000	1	8	1

	AB	R	H	
Rose	3	0	1	(1B)

WP **Norman**, Bair (8); LP **Schatzeder**, Knowles (8)

36. Sunday, July 23

Cincinnati	001 003 000 000 01	5	9	0
Montreal	000 003 010 000 00	4	13	0

	AB	R	H	
Rose	6	0	2	(1B, 2B)

WP Seaver, Tomlin (8), Bair (9), **Sarmiento** (11), Borbon (14); LP Rogers, Garman (7), Knowles (8), Bahnsen (11), **Twitchell** (14) (14 innings)

37. Monday, July 24

Cincinnati	010 001 102	5	12	0
New York	011 000 100	3	5	1

	AB	R	H	
Rose	5	2	2	(2-1B)

WP Moskau, Borbon (7), Tomlin (7), **Sarmiento** (8); LP Zachry, Kobel (7), **Lockwood** (8)

38. Tuesday, July 25

Cincinnati	000 110 000	2	7	3
New York	000 500 22x	9	12	0

	AB	R	H	
Rose	4	1	3	(2-1B, 2B)

WP **Swan**; LP **Hume**, Borbon (4), Tomlin (7)

39. Wednesday, July 26

Cincinnati	000 200 001	3	10	0
New York	303 033 00x	12	11	0

	AB	R	H	
Rose	3	0	1	(2B)

WP **Espinosa**, Bernard (9); LP **LaCoss**, Sarmiento (6), Bair (7)

40. Friday, July 28[1]

Philadelphia	200 701 020	12	14	1
Cincinnati	001 010 000	2	8	1

	AB	R	H	
Rose	2	1	1	(2B)

WP **Lerch**; LP **Norman**, Borbon (4)

[1]*First game of a doubleheader.* [2]*Second game of a doubleheader.*

41. Friday, July 28[1]

Philadelphia	000 000 001	1	8	0
Cincinnati	000 010 10x	2	7	0

	AB	R	H	
Rose	4	0	1	(1B)

WP **Seaver**, Bair (9); LP **Carlton**

42. Saturday, July 29

Philadelphia	000 000 002	2	7	0
Cincinnati	231 000 00x	6	9	1

	AB	R	H	
Rose	4	1	3	(3-1B)

WP **Moskau**, Bair (9); LP **Lonborg**, Kaat (2), Eastwick (6), Brusstar (8)

43. Sunday, July 30

Philadelphia	000 001 002	3	14	1
Cincinnati	020 020 10x	5	11	0

	AB	R	H	
Rose	5	0	2	(2-1B)

WP **Hume**, Sarmiento (8), Bair (9); LP **Christenson**, Reed (7)

44. Monday, July 31

Cincinnati	010 000 002	3	9	2
Atlanta	000 100 001	2	10	0

	AB	R	H	
Rose	4	0	1	(1B)

WP **LaCoss**, Bair (9); LP **Niekro**

The streak ended the next night before 31,159 at Atlanta–Fulton County Stadium.

Tuesday, August 1

Cincinnati	300 010 000	4	7	3
Atlanta	200 150 35x	16	21	1

	AB	R	H
Rose	4	0	0

WP **McWilliams**, Campbell (6), Garber (7); LP Norman, **Borbon** (1), Hume (6), Sarmiento (7), Tomlin (8)

Despite getting away to a three-run lead, Cincinnati was badly beaten as Atlanta came from behind to win easily, helped by home runs by third baseman Bob Horner, first baseman Dale Murphy, and outfielder Barry Bonnell.

Rose hit the ball hard twice in his five trips to the plate but came up empty. After drawing a walk on a 3–2 pitch in the first inning, he came closest to a hit in the second when he hit the first pitch for a vicious liner to the mound, which left-hander Larry McWilliams reached across his body and caught ankle high as he fell to the ground. Rose hit a hard routine grounder to shortstop Jerry Royster in the fifth. Against right-hander Gene Garber in the seventh, Rose came up with outfielder

[1]*Second game of a doubleheader.*

Dave Collins on first and hit a liner right to third that Horner gloved and threw to first for a double play.

Rose came up for his last chance with two out in the ninth. He bunted foul toward third on the first pitch, took two balls, foul-tipped the next pitch, and then struck out on Garber's change-up to end the game and his record streak. Atlanta catcher Joe Nolan said after the game that Rose barely tipped the final pitch, "and it just stuck in my glove."

After Rose hit in his forty-fourth straight game, Cincinnati was in second place in the Western Division with a 62–43 record, one-half game behind San Francisco as the Reds won twenty-six games and lost eighteen during the streak.

Rose collected seventy hits in 182 times at bat during the streak for a .385 average, with fifty-six singles and fourteen doubles. He scored thirty runs, had eleven runs batted in, twelve bases on balls, was hit by the pitcher once, had five sacrifices, one sacrifice fly, and only five strikeouts. His on-base percentage was .423. During his streak he lifted his average for the season forty-nine points to .316. The leadoff batter in every game, he drew his first walk in the streak in Game 7 (June 22), when he played left field in his only start at any position except third base during the streak.

Rose had one four-hit game, six three-hit games, eleven two-hit games, and twenty-six one-hit games. Six of his singles were bunts, and four times a bunt was his only hit of the game, twice in his last at bat. He hit safely in the first inning fifteen times and hit safely six times in his last time at bat. The sixth time was in Game 32 (July 19) at Philadelphia, when he came up with two out in the ninth and bunted safely down the third-base line. Against right-handed pitchers, he batted .397 with forty-six hits in 116 at bats, and .364 against left-handed pitchers with twenty-four hits in 66 bats.

Rose faced every team in the league except San Diego and Pittsburgh, and only against Atlanta failed to hit .300, playing only one game against the Braves. He batted .433 against Los Angeles, .417 against St. Louis, .414 against New York, .400 against San Francisco, .375 against Philadelphia, .350 against Montreal, .310 against Houston, and .500 against Chicago, a team he faced only in Game 1 (June 14), when he began his historic streak with two singles off left-hander Dave Roberts.

When right-hander Tom Seaver pitched a 4–0 no-hitter in Game 2 (June 16), Rose doubled in the first two runs. In Game 3 (June 17), with the score tied, Rose singled for his second hit, stole second, and scored the winning run with two out in the ninth.

In his most productive game in the streak, Rose doubled in the first inning and added three singles in Game 9 (June 24), but Cincinnati lost at Los Angeles, 4–3. More satisfying was Game 19 (July 3), one of Rose's three-hit games, in which he doubled and scored in the three-run first and singled twice and knocked in a run to help the Reds beat Houston, 8–7, at home in eleven innings.

In Game 28 (July 15) Rose singled in the third to break the Cincinnati club record of 27, set by outfielder Edd Roush in 1920, equaled by him in 1924, and then matched by outfielder Vada Pinson in 1965. He broke the record for a switch-hitter in Game 29 (July 16) with a double to right center on his fourth time at bat and set a modern National League record for an infielder with a single on the game's first pitch in Game 34 (July 21). The record had been set in 1922 by St. Louis second baseman Rogers Hornsby.

Three nights later Rose singled in the seventh, then singled and scored the winning run in the ninth in a 5–3 victory at New York in Game 37 (July 24). The next night in Game 38 (July 25), Rose flied out in the first, then singled between shortstop and third base in the third for the first of his three hits to break the modern National League record, set in 1945 by Boston outfielder Tommy Holmes. As the New York crowd of 38,158 gave Rose a long ovation after his hit in the third, Holmes came out of the stands and went to first base to congratulate the new record holder.

Doubles in the fifth inning and the third inning in the next two games extended the streak. In Game 41 (July 28) Rose hit the ball hard on his first two times at bat, but was 0-for-3 when he bunted toward third in the sixth and beat it out for his only hit in four trips.

Rose singled on his first three times at bat in Game 42 (July 29) and singled in the fifth and again in the sixth in Game 43 (July 30), enabling him to surpass the streak Chicago shortstop Bill Dahlen put together in 1894.

On July 31, the largest crowd of the season at Atlanta, 45,077, saw Rose walk in the first inning and line out to shortstop in the third. In the sixth he hit a hard ground single right past diving second baseman Rod Gilbreath for his only hit, but it was the one that tied the all-time National League record of forty-four games, set in 1897 by Baltimore outfielder Willie Keeler.

After the streak ended the next night, twelve games short of Joe

DiMaggio's all-time record, Rose was a little upset. "If I had any guts, I'd have bunted that last change-up," Rose said. "Garber was pitching like it was the seventh game of the World Series. . . . I'm not saying anything about him bearing down, I just said he should challenge somebody. I had one pitch to swing at that was a strike."

Of the catch McWilliams made in the second inning, Rose said, "I hit a ball that was halfway into center field and the guy caught it. . . . I hit two on the nose. He made a helluva play."

Asked if he was relieved now that the pressure was off, Rose said, "No, I'm not relieved. I'm teed off [but] I guess it is a load off my shoulders. . . . It's been exciting. I really enjoyed it. It's better for it to end in a 16–4 game than a 2–1 game."

Rose said the next day, "I was disappointed because I felt I could have gone on." After watching the last pitch on television on the night of the game he said that it might have been a ball. "The last one might have been too close to take. You don't want to end the streak arguing with the umpire. Besides, Jim Quick was doing a good job back there. It was too close to take and put the pressure on him."

Summing up, Rose said it was a streak without luck. "Almost every night, I've hit shots," he said. "I've said all along I could have had twenty more hits in the streak. I've been getting the meat of the bat on the ball a lot. You would think a guy would get lucky one time in forty-four games. But all my hits were clean hits. There wasn't one off somebody's glove."

Rose finished the 1978 season with a .302 average, led the National League with a career-high fifty-one doubles and was second in the league with 103 runs scored and with 198 hits as Cincinnati finished second in the West, two and one-half games behind Los Angeles.

Rose became a free agent after this season and signed with Philadelphia. He switched to first base, where he played his final eight seasons, and enjoyed his tenth 200-hit season in 1979. He played with the Phillies through 1983, became a free agent, and joined Montreal. On August 16, 1984, he was traded to Cincinnati and became player-manager of the Reds. On September 11, 1985, he singled for his 4,192nd hit, breaking Ty Cobb's all-time record.

Earlier that season Rose set a National League record for runs scored. He holds a flock of major league and National League records and had his final time at bat on August 17, 1986. He finished with 4,256 hits and a .303 career batting average in 3,562 games. He played in six World Series and in sixteen All-Star Games.

George Sisler
1922 St. Louis Browns

41 Consecutive Games

George Sisler was such an accomplished hitter and fielder he earned the nickname "Gorgeous George." Born March 24, 1893, in Manchester, Ohio, Sisler grew up in Akron and signed a pro contract as a pitcher with Akron of the Ohio-Pennsylvania League while in high school. Since he had received no money to sign, Sisler decided, on his high school graduation, to attend the University of Michigan, where Branch Rickey was coach.

Rickey also served as a St. Louis Browns scout, becoming their manager at the end of the 1913 season. During Sisler's senior year in college he attempted to void the contract George had signed as a minor. Akron had sold the contract to Columbus, which sold it to Pittsburgh, and a bitter battle between the Pirates and Browns ensued.

The National Commission ruled in favor of St. Louis, and Sisler reported to the Browns on graduation, appearing in eighty-one games as pitcher, first baseman, and outfielder. He became the regular first baseman in 1916, and in 1917 batted .353 to finish second to Detroit's Ty Cobb in the batting race. He followed that by batting .341, .352, .407, with a still-standing-record 257 hits in 1920, and .371 in 1921.

In 1920 the Browns finished fourth, their first first-division finish in twelve years, climbed to third in 1921, and made a real run for the pennant in 1922. St. Louis had a 54–39 record and a lead of one and one-half games after losing to New York, 11–6, on July 26, and Sisler went 0-for-5 against right-handers Waite Hoyt and Joe Bush, dropping his average for the season to .412, two points behind Cobb.

Sisler began his then record forty-one-game batting streak the next afternoon on his home field, Sportsman's Park, St. Louis.

1. Thursday, July 27

New York	000 100 040 01	6	14	2
St. Louis	000 200 003 00	5	9	2

	AB	R	H	
Sisler	5	1	1	(2B)

WP Shawkey, Mays (9), **Bush** (10); LP Vangilder, Kolp (8), Danforth (10), **Wright** (10) (11 innings)

2. Friday, July 28

New York	141 000 100	7	8	2
St. Louis	200 010 000	3	6	0

	AB	R	H	
Sisler	3	1	1	(1B)

WP **Jones**; LP **Kolp**

3. Saturday, July 29

Boston	000 000 100	1	9	2
St. Louis	000 400 00x	4	6	0

	AB	R	H	
Sisler	2	1	1	(1B)

WP **Shocker**; LP **Pennock**, Fullerton (7)

4. Saturday, August 5

Philadelphia	001 000 000	1	8	0
St. Louis	020 001 10x	4	8	1

	AB	R	H	
Sisler	4	1	2	(1B, 3B)

WP **Kolp**; LP Rettig, **Eckert** (1), Heimach (4)

5. Sunday, August 6

Washington	102 000 010	4	9	3
St. Louis	205 000 10x	8	13	1

	AB	R	H	
Sisler	4	1	3	(3-1B)

WP **Shocker**; LP **Johnson**, Brillheart (3)

6. Monday, August 7

Washington	000 010 000	1	8	1
St. Louis	000 029 50x	16	19	1

	AB	R	H	
Sisler	3	2	2	(2-1B)

WP **Wright**; LP **Mogridge**, Erickson (6)

7. Tuesday, August 8

Washington	000 110 010	3	8	1
St. Louis	000 000 010	1	7	2

	AB	R	H	
Sisler	4	0	2	(1B, 2B)

WP **Zachary**; LP **Davis**, Pruett (9)

8. Wednesday, August 9

Washington	400 011 001	7	14	2
St. Louis	203 010 20x	8	12	2

	AB	R	H	
Sisler	5	1	1	(1B)

WP Vangilder, Kolp (1), **Pruett** (6); LP Francis, Brillheart (3), **Johnson** (3)

9. Saturday, August 12

St. Louis	000 403 000	7	12	1
Chicago	100 000 014	6	18	1

	AB	R	H	
Sisler	4	1	3	(1B, 2-2B)

WP **Shocker**, Pruett (9), Wright (9); LP **Courtney**, Hodge (4), Blankenship (7)

10. Sunday, August 13

St. Louis	101 100 000	3	10	2
Chicago	060 100 02x	9	11	0

	AB	R	H	
Sisler	4	1	1	(2B)

WP **Leverett**, Faber (5); LP **Vangilder**, Bayne (2), Pruett (3)

11. Tuesday, August 15[1]

St. Louis	000 000 010	1	11	1
Washington	201 000 21x	6	10	0

	AB	R	H	
Sisler	4	1	3	(2-1B, 2B)

WP **Zachary**; LP **Wright**, Pruett (7)

12. Tuesday, August 15[2]

St. Louis	011 002 210	7	12	0
Washington	000 000 001	1	7	2

	AB	R	H	
Sisler	5	0	2	(1B, 3B)

WP **Davis**; LP **Francis**

13. Wednesday, August 16[1]

St. Louis	020 000 410	7	13	1
Washington	110 010 000	3	10	0

	AB	R	H	
Sisler	4	0	1	(1B)

WP **Shocker**; LP **Brillheart**

14. Wednesday, August 16[2]

St. Louis	000 201 000	3	10	4
Washington	061 101 02x	11	14	1

	AB	R	H	
Sisler	5	1	1	(1B)

WP **Johnson**; LP **Kolp**, Bayne (2), Meine (5)

15. Thursday, August 17

St. Louis	000 000 008	8	14	2
Washington	000 011 003	5	5	1

	AB	R	H	
Sisler	5	1	1	(1B)

WP **Davis**, Wright (9); LP **Mogridge**, Francis (9)

16. Friday, August 18

St. Louis	011 000 110	4	13	4
Philadelphia	033 001 01x	8	13	0

	AB	R	H	
Sisler	5	0	1	(1B)

WP **Naylor**; LP **Vangilder**, Kolp (3)

17. Saturday, August 19[1]

St. Louis	102 041 100	9	13	2
Philadelphia	020 101 010	5	8	1

	AB	R	H	
Sisler	4	1	3	(2-1B, 3B)

WP **Shocker**; LP Heimach, **Harriss** (4), Ketchum (6)

18. Saturday, August 19[2]

St. Louis	301 100 000	5	12	2
Philadelphia	200 110 11x	6	10	1

	AB	R	H	
Sisler	3	1	1	(1B)

WP **Rommel**; LP **Wright**

19. Monday, August 21

St. Louis	000 030 030	6	13	1
Philadelphia	500 100 10x	7	11	0

	AB	R	H	
Sisler	5	0	2	(2-1B)

WP **Heimach**, Harriss (9); LP **Davis**, Kolp (1), Vangilder (8)

20. Tuesday, August 22

St. Louis	100 032 030	9	16	1
Boston	003 100 000	4	7	4

	AB	R	H	
Sisler	5	0	3	(3-1B)

WP **Shocker**; LP **Pennock**

[1]*First game of a doubleheader.* [2]*Second game of a doubleheader.*

21. Wednesday, August 23

St. Louis   310 000 200   6 10 0
Boston   001 100 010   3 8 2

	AB	R	H	
Sisler	4	1	3	(2-1B, 2B)

WP Wright, **Vangilder** (4); LP **Ferguson**, Piercy (2), Fullerton (8)

22. Thursday, August 24

St. Louis   360 100 030 13 20 2
Boston   000 000 110   2 6 3

	AB	R	H	
Sisler	6	3	4	(3-1B, 2B)

WP **Kolp**; LP **Karr**, Ferguson (1), Piercy (3)

23. Friday, August 25[1]

St. Louis   010 002 000   3 10 1
New York   000 000 001   1 7 0

	AB	R	H	
Sisler	3	1	2	(2-1B)

WP **Shocker**; LP **Hoyt**, Murray (9)

24. Friday, August 25[2]

St. Louis   001 010 102   5 10 1
New York   301 200 00x   6 10 0

	AB	R	H	
Sisler	5	0	1	(1B)

WP **Bush**, Jones (9); LP **Davis**, Vangilder (1), Pruett (4), Bayne (6)

25. Saturday, August 26

St. Louis   000 000 011   2 10 3
New York   020 121 12x   9 13 2

	AB	R	H	
Sisler	4	0	1	(1B)

WP **Mays**; LP **Wright**, Bayne (7)

26. Monday, August 28

St. Louis   000 010 000 00   1 4 0
New York   010 000 000 01   2 8 0

	AB	R	H	
Sisler	5	0	1	(1B)

WP **Shawkey**; LP **Shocker** (11 innings)

27. Tuesday, August 29

St. Louis   001 000 050   6 5 1
Cleveland   010 000 101   3 9 2

	AB	R	H	
Sisler	4	1	1	(1B)

WP **Kolp**, Vangilder (8); LP **Uhle**, Edwards (8)

28. Wednesday, August 30

St. Louis   000 140 006 11 13 3
Cleveland   200 100 000   3 10 1

	AB	R	H	
Sisler	4	2	3	(2-1B, 3B)

WP **Wright**, Vangilder (8); LP **Boone**, Mails (9)

29. Thursday, August 31

St. Louis   011 020 020   6 15 2
Cleveland   002 000 005   7 11 1

	AB	R	H	
Sisler	5	0	3	(1B, 2-2B)

WP Winn, **Edwards** (9); LP Davis, **Vangilder** (9)

30. Friday, September 1

St. Louis   000 200 020   4 9 0
Detroit   000 000 001   1 8 0

	AB	R	H	
Sisler	4	1	2	(2-1B)

WP **Shocker**; LP **Ehmke**

[1]*First game of a doubleheader.* [2]*Second game of a doubleheader.*

31. Saturday, September 2

St. Louis	040 000 010	5	9	2
Detroit	011 110 000	4	8	0

	AB	R	H	
Sisler	4	0	2	(2-1B)

WP Kolp, **Pruett** (6); LP Oldham, **Johnson** (2)

32. Sunday, September 3

St. Louis	000 000 300 00	3	13	1
Detroit	100 101 000 01	4	11	2

	AB	R	H	
Sisler	5	0	1	(1B)

WP **Davis**; LP Wright, **Pruett** (8) (11 innings)

33. Monday, September 4

Cleveland	020 000 100	3	8	0
St. Louis	400 040 20x	10	16	2

	AB	R	H	
Sisler	4	3	4	(1B, 2-2B, 3B)

WP **Shocker**; LP **Lindsey**, Edwards (7) (morning game)

34. Monday, September 4

Cleveland	000 100 000	1	12	3
St. Louis	203 100 51x	12	15	2

	AB	R	H	
Sisler	5	4	3	(2-1B, 2B)

WP **Vangilder**; LP **Winn**, Mails (5), Edwards (9) (afternoon game)

35. Tuesday, September 5

Cleveland	000 105 030	9	14	2
St. Louis	202 400 02x	10	15	0

	AB	R	H	
Sisler	4	2	2	(2-1B)

WP Kolp, Pruett (6), **Shocker** (7), Wright (9); LP Boone, Lindsey (5), Winn (6), **Edwards** (8), Morton (8)

36. Wednesday, September 6

Cleveland	000 001 200	3	7	3
St. Louis	122 401 01x	11	14	1

	AB	R	H	
Sisler	5	2	2	(2-1B)

WP **Davis**; LP **Uhle**, Middleton (4)

37. Friday, September 8

Detroit	300 200 201	8	13	2
St. Louis	000 000 300	3	5	2

	AB	R	H	
Sisler	3	1	2	(2-1B)

WP **Johnson**, Olsen (7); LP **Shocker**, Wright (9)

38. Saturday, September 9

Detroit	000 000 000	0	5	1
St. Louis	520 210 42x	16	20	0

	AB	R	H	
Sisler	5	3	3	(2-1B, 3B)

WP **Vangilder**; LP **Pillette**, Hilling (1), Moore (3)

39. Monday, September 11

Detroit	000 130 000	4	7	1
St. Louis	010 100 012	5	10	3

	AB	R	H	
Sisler	5	2	2	(1B, 3B)

WP Davis, **Pruett** (6); LP **Ehmke**

40. Saturday, September 16

New York	011 000 000	2	9	0
St. Louis	000 001 000	1	7	1

	AB	R	H	
Sisler	4	0	1	(2B)

WP **Shawkey**; LP **Shocker**

41. Sunday, September 17

| New York | 000 001 000 | 1 | 5 | 0 |
| St. Louis | 000 003 02x | 5 | 12 | 1 |

	AB	R	H	
Sisler	3	2	1	(1B)

WP **Pruett**; LP **Hoyt**, Jones (8)

Sisler's streak, an American League record at the time, ended the next afternoon at Sportsman's Park, St. Louis.

Monday, September 18

| New York | 000 000 012 | 3 | 6 | 0 |
| St. Louis | 000 010 100 | 2 | 5 | 3 |

	AB	R	H
Sisler	4	0	0

WP **Bush**; LP Davis, **Pruett** (9), Shocker (9)

Sisler grounded out to second base in the first inning, grounded out to shortstop in the fourth, fouled out to third with a runner on base to end the sixth, and grounded out to second again for the first out of the St. Louis ninth.

This was a key game in the American League pennant race. The three-game series began with New York in first place, half a game in front of St. Louis, and ended with the Yankees one and one-half games ahead. They were never headed the rest of the way.

In this final meeting of the teams that season, New York trailed, 2–1, going into the ninth inning but loaded the bases in the ninth on a single, a passed ball, a safe fielder's choice, and a walk. After right-hander Urban Shocker relieved left-hander Hub Pruett, and after a force-out at the plate, outfielder Whitey Witt lined a single to bring home the tying and winning runs. Witt had been hit in the head by a pop bottle thrown by a fan as he was chasing a fly ball in the ninth inning of the first game of the series and had to be carried off the field. He returned to play well in the last two games of the series.

After Sisler hit in his forty-first straight game, St. Louis was in second place with an 87–57 record, one-half game behind New York. St. Louis won twenty-five of the forty-one games in Sisler's streak, but the first baseman was sidelined twice by injuries after starting the streak.

St. Louis Browns first baseman George Sisler was equally adept with bat or glove. He batted over .400 twice and hit .420 in 1922 when he had a forty-one game hitting streak. (Courtesy of National Baseball Library, Cooperstown, New York.)

In Game 3 (July 29), a 4–1 win over Boston, Sisler was retired in the first inning, then led off the fourth with a ground ball to first baseman George Burns. Both batter and fielder slid into first, Sisler winning for a single, but Burns spiked him below the left knee. Later in that four-run inning, Sisler scored the game's first run, but then left the lineup and missed the next six games, not returning until August 5.

In a 5–4 victory over Detroit in Game 39 (September 11), Sisler struck out twice, flied to left, singled to left, and scored in the eighth, then tripled to right center field to send home the tying run in the ninth and came home with the winning run on a line single to center by second baseman Marty McManus with two out and the bases loaded.

During that game, however, Cobb grounded to shortstop, and Sisler, reaching for the throw from Wally Gerber, suffered a severe strain of the deltoid muscle in his right shoulder. That injury kept him out of the lineup for the next four games. The team physician wanted Sisler to give up playing for the rest of the season, but Sisler insisted on having his shoulder taped so that he could play, and he returned September 16 for the key series with the Yankees.

The injury affected his hitting as well as his fielding, as he had to use his bare left hand to lift his gloved hand to catch throws above his waist. "I should not have been in there," Sisler said, "but we so desperately wanted to win the pennant." St. Louis did win five of the six games he missed in August, and three of the four in September.

Sisler tied Cobb's then major league record in Game 40 (September 16), in the 2–1 loss to the Yankees in the series opener. Batting with just one good arm, he bounced a double off the shins of New York second baseman Aaron Ward in the fourth inning for his only hit in four at bats. With the tying and winning runs on base in the sixth, Sisler grounded to second into a double play.

The next day in Game 41 (September 17), when St. Louis beat New York, 5–1, Sisler broke Cobb's record in the sixth inning after grounding out in both the first and third innings. After outfielder Babe Ruth hit his thirty-third homer of the season over the right-field stands in the top of the sixth inning to give the Yankees a 1–0 lead, the Browns scored three times in the home sixth on a walk, Sisler's single to center, a run-scoring single by outfielder Ken Williams, a stolen base, and a two-out single by catcher Hank Severeid. Sisler walked in the eighth and scored ahead of Williams, who hit his thirty-eighth homer of the season into the right-field stands.

During the streak Sisler collected four hits in two games, had three hits in ten games, two hits in twelve games, and one hit in seventeen games. Only once did he go to the ninth inning before extending his streak. That was in Game 15 (August 17), when he went hitless in four at bats until St. Louis, trailing at Washington, 2-0, rallied for eight runs and won, 8-5. Sisler was scheduled to be the eighth batter in that ninth inning, and five reached base when Sisler came up with two out and the bases loaded and hit a run-scoring single to left to put St. Louis ahead, 3-2.

In two other games Sisler got his only hit in his last at bat in the eighth inning. In Game 2 (July 28), a 7-3 loss to New York, Sisler batted in a run in the fifth with a sacrifice fly and singled in the eighth in his third official at bat. In Game 27 (August 29) at Cleveland, St. Louis trailed, 2-1, until the five-run eighth, when Sisler singled to left to knock in the third run of the rally, the eventual winning run.

Although an accomplished bunter, Sisler was proud that he never bunted to extend his streak. He didn't hit a homer, either, but he did have twenty-one extra-base hits. He had fifty-eight singles, fourteen doubles and seven triples, and scored forty-three runs in 174 times at bat for a .454 average, lifting his season's average twelve points to .424. He drew eleven walks, was hit by the pitcher once, and had six sacrifice flies.

Sisler's best day was in Game 33 (September 4) in a 10-3 win over Cleveland. He had a single, two doubles, a triple, a walk, and scored three runs in five trips. He doubled home the game's first two runs in the four-run first inning. In his other four-hit game, Sisler singled three times, doubled, and scored three runs in six at bats as St. Louis won Game 22 (August 24) at Boston, 13-2.

Against New York Sisler batted only .281 with nine hits in thirty-two at bats, but hit .647 against Boston, .581 against Cleveland, .500 against Chicago, and over .400 against Philadelphia, Washington, and Detroit. His on-base percentage was .474.

Sisler finished 1922 with a .420 average, the third highest in this century, and beat Cobb for the batting title by nineteen points. He was never that dominant a player again. A violent sinus attack sidelined him in 1923, and his .345 average in 1925 was his highest after that. He hit .361 before the sinus problem, only .320 afterward.

Before the 1924 season, Sisler was named manager of the St. Louis Browns and held the job through 1926, with a third-place finish in 1925 his best. After the club finished seventh in 1926 he was replaced, although he remained the first baseman and hit .327 in 149 games in 1927. He was then sold to Washington for $25,000, but played only twenty games before the Senators sold him to the Boston Braves for $7,500 in late May. He hit a combined .331 that year, then .326 and .309 in 1930, before joining Rochester of the International League for the 1931 season.

In 1932 Sisler was the player-manager of the Shreveport-Tyler club of the Texas League; then he retired. More than a decade later, he became a scout for Branch Rickey with several clubs and also served as batting instructor for the Pittsburgh Pirates through 1961.

Sisler finished his major league playing career of 2,055 games with 2,812 hits, a .340 average, and two batting titles. He was elected to the Hall of Fame in 1939. He died on March 26, 1973, two days after his eightieth birthday, in St. Louis.

Ty Cobb
1911 Detroit Tigers

40 Consecutive Games

Fierce desire to excel helped Ty Cobb become the greatest player of his era and one of the greatest players of all time. Born December 18, 1886, in Narrows, Georgia, Cobb was pushed by his father, who was a teacher, politician, and newspaper editor, to make something of himself. Ty once thought he might become a doctor, but baseball held a special appeal for him.

Cobb made his professional baseball debut in 1904 with Augusta of the Sally League, and showed little. However, after hitting .326 in 104 games for Augusta in 1905, he was sold to Detroit in time to play in 41 American League games that season and bat .240. The six-foot one-inch, 175-pound left-handed hitter and right-handed thrower, who hit with his hands slightly apart on the bat, hit .320 in 97 games in his first full major league season in 1906, and never batted that low again.

Cobb won the first of his twelve league batting titles in a span of thirteen years with a .350 average in 1907, when he also won the first of his six base-stealing championships with forty-nine thefts. Cobb hit .384 in 1910, and was batting .393 after going hitless in four times at bat against left-hander Ray Collins of Boston in a 6–5 Detroit victory at home on May 14, 1911.

Cobb's then modern major league record forty-game hitting streak began the next afternoon in Detroit's Bennett Park, with the Tigers in first place with a 23–5 record and a seven-game lead over second-place Boston.

1. Monday, May 15

Boston	000	210	000	1	4	7	1
Detroit	111	000	000	2	5	10	2

	AB	R	H	
Cobb	4	0	2	(1B, 2B)

WP **Covington**; LP **Wood** (10 innings)

2. Tuesday, May 16

Boston	000	301	020	6	10	1	
Detroit	000	231	001	7	16	2	

	AB	R	H	
Cobb	5	2	3	(1B, 2-2B)

WP **Lafitte**; LP Karger, **Cicotte** (6)

3. Thursday, May 18

Philadelphia	101	200	000	4	8	4	
Detroit	022	103	01x	9	15	2	

	AB	R	H	
Cobb	4	1	1	(1B)

WP **Mullin**; LP **Plank**

4. Friday, May 19

Philadelphia	003	203	000	8	19	4	
Detroit	301	220	01x	9	8	3	

	AB	R	H	
Cobb	3	2	1	(3B)

WP Lively, Covington (4), **Works** (7); LP
Coombs, **Russell** (1)

5. Saturday, May 20

Philadelphia	206	040	011	14	16	2	
Detroit	220	000	440	12	14	3	

	AB	R	H	
Cobb	5	2	3	(3-1B)

WP **Coombs**, Plank (8); LP **Donovan**,
Willett (4), Lafitte (9)

6. Sunday, May 21

Philadelphia	120	000	030	6	10	4	
Detroit	020	000	000	2	4	3	

	AB	R	H	
Cobb	3	0	1	(1B)

WP **Krause**; LP **Lively**

7. Monday, May 22

Washington	001	112	002	7	18	1	
Detroit	000	011	010	3	6	3	

	AB	R	H	
Cobb	4	1	2	(1B, 2B)

WP **Walker**; LP **Lafitte**

8. Tuesday, May 23

Washington	100	010	510	8	13	3	
Detroit	100	111	05x	9	12	3	

	AB	R	H	
Cobb	4	2	3	(2-1B, 2B)

WP **Mullin**; LP **Gray**, Johnson (8)

9. Wednesday, May 24

Washington	112	000	001	00	5	11	2	
Detroit	000	020	120	01	6	10	4	

	AB	R	H	
Cobb	5	0	2	(1B, 2B)

WP **Works**; LP Groom, **Hughes** (9) (11
innings)

10. Thursday, May 25

Washington	000	103	011	6	11	1	
Detroit	000	000	011	2	8	2	

	AB	R	H	
Cobb	4	0	2	(1B, 2B)

WP **Johnson**; LP **Willett**, Covington (9)

11. Saturday, May 27

St. Louis	000 001 011	3 8 5
Detroit	011 001 42x	9 14 2

	AB	R	H
Cobb	5	2	2 (2-1B)

WP **Lafitte**; LP **Bailey**

12. Sunday, May 28

St. Louis	203 040 012	12 13 2
Detroit	020 002 020	6 11 3

	AB	R	H
Cobb	5	1	2 (1B, 3B)

WP **Hamilton**; LP **Covington**, Works (3), Willett (8)

13. Monday, May 29

Detroit	200 020 110	6 10 2
Cleveland	112 011 001	7 15 3

	AB	R	H
Cobb	5	1	2 (2-1B)

WP Blanding, **Gregg** (8); LP **Mullin**

14. Tuesday, May 30

Detroit	000 000 101 1	3 8 0
Cleveland	000 000 101 0	2 7 5

	AB	R	H
Cobb	5	0	1 (2B)

WP **Summers**; LP **Mitchell** (10 innings) (morning game)

15. Tuesday, May 30

Detroit	200 002 002	6 8 0
Cleveland	010 020 002	5 10 2

	AB	R	H
Cobb	3	2	1 (1B)

WP Works, **Donovan** (6); LP **Gregg** (afternoon game)

16. Thursday, June 1

Detroit	310 020 001 1	8 19 4
Washington	100 000 402 0	7 10 1

	AB	R	H
Cobb	4	0	3 (2-1B, 2B)

WP **Lively**; LP Walker, **Otey** (3) (10 innings)

17. Friday, June 2

Detroit	200 121 001	7 9 2
Washington	216 010 04x	14 17 7

	AB	R	H
Cobb	5	2	3 (3-1B)

WP **Hughes**; LP **Willett**, Works (3), Covington (3), Mitchell (8)

18. Saturday, June 3

Detroit	300 010 021	7 13 0
Washington	010 000 010	2 6 3

	AB	R	H
Cobb	5	2	3 (1B, 2-3B)

WP **Mullin**; LP **Johnson**

19. Monday, June 5

Detroit	120 000 200	5 10 1
Washington	100 000 000	1 6 4

	AB	R	H
Cobb	4	1	3 (3-1B)

WP **Lafitte**; LP **Groom**, Gray (9)

20. Wednesday, June 7

Detroit	000 010 200	3 10 0
Philadelphia	000 100 012	4 9 2

	AB	R	H
Cobb	4	1	2 (1B, 3B)

WP **Coombs**; LP **Summers**

21. Thursday, June 8

| Detroit | 100 100 222 | 8 | 15 | 1 |
| Philadelphia | 000 020 100 | 3 | 8 | 3 |

| | AB | R | H | |
| **Cobb** | 3 | 2 | 3 | (3-1B) |

WP **Donovan**; LP **Plank**

22. Friday, June 9

| Detroit | 001 020 001 | 4 | 11 | 2 |
| Philadelphia | 002 010 11x | 5 | 10 | 0 |

| | AB | R | H | |
| **Cobb** | 5 | 0 | 1 | (1B) |

WP **Krause**; LP **Mullin**

23. Saturday, June 10

| Detroit | 000 010 112 0 | 5 | 13 | 3 |
| Boston | 003 200 000 1 | 6 | 11 | 1 |

| | AB | R | H | |
| **Cobb** | 4 | 1 | 1 | (1B) |

WP **Wood**; LP Works, Willett (5), **Lafitte** (8) (10 innings)

24. Monday, June 12

| Detroit | 001 011 200 | 5 | 14 | 2 |
| Boston | 100 010 200 | 4 | 10 | 1 |

| | AB | R | H | |
| **Cobb** | 4 | 0 | 4 | (2-1B, 2-2B) |

WP **Willett**; LP **Hall**

25. Wednesday, June 14

| Detroit | 101 100 000 | 3 | 10 | 4 |
| New York | 030 000 02x | 5 | 6 | 3 |

| | AB | R | H | |
| **Cobb** | 5 | 0 | 2 | (2-1B) |

WP **Ford**; LP Lively, **Summers** (3)

26. Thursday, June 15

| Detroit | 000 000 000 | 0 | 4 | 3 |
| New York | 200 010 02x | 5 | 12 | 1 |

| | AB | R | H | |
| **Cobb** | 4 | 0 | 2 | (1B, 2B) |

WP **Fisher**; LP **Mullin**

27. Saturday, June 17

| Detroit | 001 010 000 | 2 | 10 | 0 |
| New York | 000 000 021 | 3 | 8 | 2 |

| | AB | R | H | |
| **Cobb** | 4 | 0 | 1 | (1B) |

WP **Warhop**; LP **Donovan**

28. Sunday, June 18

| Chicago | 700 330 200 | 15 | 16 | 2 |
| Detroit | 010 043 053 | 16 | 21 | 4 |

| | AB | R | H | |
| **Cobb** | 6 | 3 | 5 | (4-1B, 3B) |

WP Summers, Works (1), Covington (6), **Mitchell** (8); LP White, Olmstead (7), **Walsh** (8)

29. Monday, June 19

| Chicago | 001 002 011 | 5 | 12 | 3 |
| Detroit | 024 002 00x | 8 | 10 | 0 |

| | AB | R | H | |
| **Cobb** | 4 | 1 | 2 | (2-1B) |

WP **Willett**; LP **Young**, Lange (3), Baker (7)

30. Tuesday, June 20

| Cleveland | 001 001 100 | 3 | 10 | 4 |
| Detroit | 250 010 00x | 8 | 10 | 3 |

| | AB | R | H | |
| **Cobb** | 4 | 1 | 1 | (1B) |

WP **Lively**; LP **Mitchell**, Krapp (2)

31. Wednesday, June 21

Cleveland	000 201 000	3	8	2		
Detroit	200 210 00x	5	9	5		

	AB	R	H	
Cobb	4	1	1	(HR)

WP **Lafitte**; LP **Blanding**

32. Thursday, June 22

Cleveland	000 001 210	4	8	2
Detroit	000 200 100	3	6	4

	AB	R	H	
Cobb	3	0	1	(1B)

WP **West**; LP **Summers**

33. Friday, June 23

Cleveland	100 000 100	2	4	2
Detroit	000 003 10x	4	8	1

	AB	R	H	
Cobb	4	1	2	(2-1B)

WP **Works**; LP **Young**

34. Sunday, June 25

Detroit	110 002 000	4	11	2
Chicago	000 060 20x	8	12	1

	AB	R	H	
Cobb	5	1	2	(2-1B)

WP **White**, Walsh (6); LP **Willett**, Lafitte (6)

35. Monday, June 26

Detroit	000 100 410	6	12	0
Chicago	102 000 000	3	8	1

	AB	R	H	
Cobb	3	2	2	(2-1B)

WP **Summers**; LP **Young**, Lange (7), Olmstead (8)

36. Tuesday, June 27

Detroit	000 000 000	0	4	1
Chicago	011 000 01x	3	10	2

	AB	R	H	
Cobb	4	0	1	(1B)

WP **Walsh**; LP **Donovan**, Lively (8)

37. Wednesday, June 28

St. Louis	200 000 000	2	6	3
Detroit	000 000 03x	3	4	2

	AB	R	H	
Cobb	4	1	2	(1B, 3B)

WP **Lafitte**; LP **Hamilton**, Mitchell (8)

38. Thursday, June 29

St. Louis	101 200 200	6	11	1
Detroit	121 000 010	5	9	4

	AB	R	H	
Cobb	4	0	1	(1B)

WP **Powell**; LP **Works**, Summers (7)

39. Saturday, July 1

St. Louis	000 000 000	0	4	0
Detroit	001 003 40x	8	10	1

	AB	R	H	
Cobb	3	1	1	(1B)

WP **Willett**; LP **Hamilton**, Mitchell (7)

40. Sunday, July 2

Cleveland	101 020 020	6	11	2
Detroit	060 102 50x	14	16	1

	AB	R	H	
Cobb	4	3	3	(2-1B, 3B)

WP **Summers**; LP **Krapp**, West (2), James (7)

After an open date, Cobb's streak ended the next day at Detroit's Bennett Park.

Tuesday, July 4

| Chicago | 120 110 011 | 7 | 15 | 1 |
| Detroit | 000 000 012 | 3 | 10 | 1 |

	AB	R	H
Cobb	4	0	0

WP **Walsh**; LP **Lively**, Lafitte (8) (morning game)

Cobb went hitless in four trips to the plate against Chicago right-hander Ed Walsh, a spitball pitcher who went on to win twenty-seven games in 1911. Once Cobb grounded to first base into a double play. He came up for his last chance in the eighth inning after outfielder Davy Jones had doubled and taken third on an infield out. Cobb grounded out to shortstop as Jones scored Detroit's first run of the game, but the streak was over. Detroit scored twice in the ninth but Cobb did not come to bat.

Outfielder Ping Bodie led the fifteen-hit Chicago attack as every White Sox player hit safely. The defeat dropped Detroit into second place behind Philadelphia.

After Cobb hit safely in his fortieth straight game, Detroit had a 46–22 record and was in first place, one-half game in front of Philadelphia, having won twenty-three games and lost seventeen, starting in mid–May.

During his streak Cobb scored forty runs, collected eighty hits in 167 times at bat — including twelve doubles, eight triples, and one home run — and batted .479, raising his season's average fifty-two points to .445. He also had nine walks, was hit by the pitcher five times, had one sacrifice and one sacrifice fly, and his on-base average was a record .516, the highest for any streak of thirty-five or more games. His twenty-six multiple-hit games is also a record. He had one five-hit game, one four-hit game, nine three-hit games, fifteen two-hit games, and fourteen one-hit games.

Cobb batted .600 in eight games against Washington, hit .588 against Boston, .545 against Chicago, .444 against Philadelphia, .385 against New York, .381 against St. Louis, and .375 against Cleveland.

Cobb hit safely in the first inning in eighteen games and waited just three times until his last at bat to get his only hit.

Outfielder Ty Cobb of the Detroit Tigers won twelve American League batting titles in a thirteen-year span, including one in 1911 when he batted a career high of .420 and hit safely in forty consecutive games. (Courtesy of National Baseball Library, Cooperstown, New York.)

One of the latter was Game 3 (May 18) in which Detroit was leading by five runs going into the last of the eighth inning against Philadelphia. With two out, shortstop Donie Bush singled to give Cobb another chance, and Ty singled to right. Cobb then purposely allowed himself to be picked off first by left-hander Eddie Plank, and Bush raced home to make the final score 9-4 before Ty was run down and tagged out.

With Detroit holding a 2-0 lead at New York after seven innings in Game 27 (June 17), Cobb, who had walked once and been retired three times, singled off first baseman Hal Chase's glove with one out in the eighth. He failed to score, however, and New York scored twice in the eighth and once in the ninth to win, 3-2.

In Game 32 (June 22) Detroit trailed Cleveland, 3-2, before tying the score in the seventh when right-hander Ed Summers singled, advanced on two outs, and scored on a single by Cobb, who had reached base previously only in the fifth when he was hit by a pitch. Cleveland then won, 4-3, with a run in the eighth on singles by outfielders Joe Jackson and Joe Birmingham around a sacrifice and an infield out.

In three of his fourteen one-hit games, the speedy Cobb extended his streak with an infield single. He singled to shortstop in the second inning of Game 30 (June 20); singled to third base in the first inning of Game 36 (June 27), and singled to the mound in the sixth inning of Game 39 (July 1). His only hit in three games was an extra-base hit.

The home run he hit in the streak was in Game 31 (June 21) off Cleveland right-hander Fred Blanding. In the first inning after a walk and a force-out, Cobb hit a smash over first base that bounced into the stands beyond the bag for a homer, one of eight he hit in 1911.

In his biggest game in the streak, Cobb pounded out five hits in six at bats to help Detroit edge Cleveland, 16-15, in Game 28 (June 18). He tripled once and singled four times, the fourth being a bouncer to third that drove in the first of three runs in the bottom of the ninth. Cobb then scored the winning run on outfielder Sam Crawford's double to center. This was Cobb's only five-hit game of the season.

Cobb also helped Detroit win when he got four hits in Game 24 (June 12) at Boston. He singled and was stranded in the first inning, doubled home a third-inning run to tie the score, singled to start the one-run sixth, and doubled off the left-field fence to drive in the final two runs in the seventh of a 5-4 Tiger victory.

No mention was made of the fact that Cobb broke the league record for hitting in consecutive games, set by Cleveland third baseman Bill Bradley in 1902 when he hit in twenty-nine straight games. In fact, not until Ty hit in his fortieth straight game was the streak noted.

Although Cobb finished the 1911 season with the best performance of his career, Detroit finished second to Philadelphia by thirteen and one-half games, winning eighty-nine games and losing sixty-five.

Cobb led the league that year with 147 runs, 248 hits, forty-seven doubles, twenty-four triples, a .420 average, 144 runs batted in, 367 total bases, and a slugging percentage of .621, all career highs. He was second in the league with eight homers. The batting title was the fifth of the twelve Cobb won during his twenty-four-year career in the major leagues.

Cobb was player-manager of Detroit from 1921 through 1926, then played for the Philadelphia Athletics in 1927 and 1928, after twenty-two years with Detroit. In his career he collected 4,191 hits for a record that lasted until 1985, and hit for a career batting average of .367, a record that has never been seriously threatened. Cobb, who was elected to the Hall of Fame in 1936, died in Atlanta on July 17, 1961.

Paul Molitor
1987 Milwaukee Brewers
39 Consecutive Games

Paul Molitor was one of the nation's finest amateur athletes in the 1970s. Born on August 22, 1956, at St. Paul, Minnesota, Molitor starred at his St. Paul high school for three years in soccer, basketball, and baseball, and at the University of Minnesota in baseball for three years before signing with the Milwaukee Brewers in June 1977, after being selected in the first round of the free-agent draft.

The six-foot, 175-pound, right-hand-hitting infielder batted .364 in sixty-four games for Milwaukee's Class A Midwest League farm club at Burlington, Iowa, and was named the league's most valuable player in that first pro season in 1977.

In 1978 Molitor played 125 games as a rookie for the Brewers. He took over at shortstop when Robin Yount was injured, moved to second base when Yount returned, and batted .273. Over the years with the Brewers, he has been a regular at second and third, and a designated hitter as well as playing shortstop and the outfield.

Molitor's aggressive style of play has led to a succession of injuries to his ankles, ribs, elbows, wrists, and hamstring muscles that have prevented him from playing in more than 125 games in six of his first eleven seasons.

On June 26, 1987, Molitor played third base in a 10–5 Milwaukee victory and went hitless in three times at bat against Toronto left-hander Jimmy Key before leaving the game with a hamstring pull. After that game his average was .323, and the Brewers were three games over .500.

Molitor did not play again until after the All-Star Game break, when Milwaukee was in fourth place in the American League's Eastern Division with a 42–43 record, eleven games behind first-place New York. He played on July 16 in the first game after the break as the designated hitter, and that day began his hitting streak in Milwaukee County Stadium.

1. Thursday, July 16

		R	H	E
California	010 001 200	4	9	4
Milwaukee	041 000 01x	6	10	1

	AB	R	H	
Molitor	4	2	1	(2B)

WP **Higuera**, Clear (7), Plesac (8); LP **McCaskill**, Lazorko (4), Buice (8)

2. Friday, July 17

		R	H	E
California	020 000 000	2	5	0
Milwaukee	001 500 60x	12	20	0

	AB	R	H	
Molitor	5	0	3	(3-1B)

WP **Wegman**, Mirabella (8), Aldrich (9); LP **Witt**, Finley (4), Lucas (7), Minton (8)

3. Saturday, July 18

		R	H	E
California	002 003 034	12	15	1
Milwaukee	030 012 000	6	6	1

	AB	R	H	
Molitor	4	0	1	(1B)

WP Sutton, **Buice** (6); LP Bosio, Mirabella (6), Crim (6), **Plesac** (7), Clear (9)

4. Sunday, July 19

		R	H	E
California	003 000 050	8	10	2
Milwaukee	001 040 000	5	10	0

	AB	R	H	
Molitor	4	0	1	(1B)

WP Reuss, **Lazarko** (5), Minton (8); LP Nieves, **Aldrich** (8), Mirabella (8), Crim (8)

5. Monday, July 20

		R	H	E
Seattle	101 240 300	11	17	1
Milwaukee	315 031 00x	13	13	2

	AB	R	H	
Molitor	5	2	3	(3-1B)

WP Kundson, Madrid (5), **Crim** (7), Clear (9); LP **Morgan**, Thomas (3), Reed (5), Clarke (8)

6. Wednesday, July 22

		R	H	E
Seattle	100 000 100	2	8	0
Milwaukee	000 001 000	1	4	0

	AB	R	H	
Molitor	3	0	1	(1B)

WP **Langston**; LP **Wegman**

7. Thursday, July 23

		R	H	E
Oakland	110 100 110	3	10	1
Milwaukee	004 401 03x	12	16	2

	AB	R	H	
Molitor	5	2	3	(2-1B, HR)

WP **Bosio**, Crim (8), Plesac (9); LP **Andujar**, Nelson (4), Leiper (5), Caudill (8)

8. Friday, July 24

		R	H	E
Oakland	000 100 010	2	8	0
Milwaukee	000 112 42x	10	17	2

	AB	R	H	
Molitor	4	1	1	(2B)

WP **Nieves**, Clear (8); LP **Ontiveros**, Cadaret (6), Howell (8)

9. Saturday, July 25

Oakland	100	511	500	13	19	0
Milwaukee	020	000	002	4	7	1

	AB	R	H	
Molitor	4	1	2	(1B, HR)

WP **Young**, Eckersley (6), Caudill (8); LP **Knudson**, Madrid (4), Aldrich (7)

10. Sunday, July 26

Oakland	000	000	040	4	10	3
Milwaukee	121	201	00x	7	12	1

	AB	R	H	
Molitor	5	2	3	(1B, 2B, 3B)

WP **Higuera**, Plesac (8); LP **Lamp**, Leiper (4), Nelson (7)

11. Monday, July 27

Milwaukee	000	101	110	4	7	0
Texas	000	200	102	5	11	0

	AB	R	H	
Molitor	5	0	1	(1B)

WP Witt, Russell (7), **Williams** (8); LP Wegman, **Plesac** (8)

12. Tuesday, July 28

Milwaukee	002	040	201	9	13	0
Texas	100	000	001	2	8	1

	AB	R	H	
Molitor	3	3	1	(HR)

WP **Bosio**, Clear (7); LP **Guzman**, Creel (7), Mohoric (9)

13. Wednesday, July 29

Milwaukee	110	002	022	001	9	17	2
Texas	205	000	001	000	8	16	3

	AB	R	H	
Molitor	7	2	2	(2B, 3B)

WP Nieves, Madrid (3), Aldrich (4), Crim (8), **Plesac** (9); LP Harris, Russell (6), Mohoric (8), Williams (9), **Kilgus** (12), Loynd (12) (12 innings)

14. Thursday, July 30

Chicago	000	000	100	1	10	0
Milwaukee	000	002	22x	6	10	0

	AB	R	H	
Molitor	3	1	2	(2-2B)

WP **Knudson**, Crim (7); LP **Allen**, Thigpen (7)

15. Friday, July 31

Chicago	110	030	102	8	15	0
Milwaukee	110	000	103	6	10	0

	AB	R	H	
Molitor	4	2	2	(2-1B)

WP **Dotson**, Nielsen (9), Searage (9), Thigpen (9); LP **Higuera**, Burris (5), Clear (8)

16. Saturday, August 1

Chicago	002	100	000	3	6	2
Milwaukee	000	000	020	2	6	0

	AB	R	H	
Molitor	4	1	1	(1B)

WP **LaPoint**, DeLeon (7), Thigpen (8), Searage (9); LP **Wegman**

17. Sunday, August 2

Chicago	004	100	200	7	16	1
Milwaukee	002	100	000	3	5	2

	AB	R	H	
Molitor	3	1	1	(HR)

WP **Long**, Thigpen (7); LP **Bosio**, Aldrich (3), Crim (5), Clear (8), Plesac (9)

18. Tuesday, August 4

Baltimore	230	000	003	000	8	14	1
Milwaukee	105	100	100	001	9	12	0

	AB	R	H	
Molitor	6	2	3	(1B, 2B, HR)

WP Nieves, Crim (6), Plesac (9), **Knudson** (12); LP McGregor, Habyan (4), **Williamson** (9) (12 innings)

19. Wednesday, August 5

Baltimore	100 000 000	1	6	0
Milwaukee	000 220 01x	5	12	0

	AB	R	H	
Molitor	2	0	1	(2B)

WP **Higuera**; LP **Bell**, Griffin (7)

20. Thursday, August 6

Baltimore	013 200 002	8	14	0
Milwaukee	120 510 02x	11	12	2

	AB	R	H	
Molitor	4	3	2	(1B, 2B)

WP Wegman, **Aldrich** (4), Crim (7); LP Flanagan, **Griffin** (4), Habyan (5), Niedenfuer (8)

21. Friday, August 7

Milwaukee	000 010 210 3	7	10	1
Chicago	101 000 200 0	4	12	1

	AB	R	H	
Molitor	5	0	1	(2B)

WP Knudson, **Clear** (7), Plesac (10); LP LaPoint, **Thigpen** (7), Searage (10), Winn (10) (10 innings)

22. Saturday, August 8[1]

Milwaukee	101 003 000	5	10	0
Chicago	003 000 000	3	10	1

	AB	R	H	
Molitor	4	2	2	(2-1B)

WP **Burris**, Crim (6); LP **DeLeon**, Long (6), Searage (7)

23. Saturday, August 8[2]

Milwaukee	101 000 220	6	10	2
Chicago	010 121 30x	8	13	2

	AB	R	H	
Molitor	3	2	1	(1B)

WP **Bannister**, Winn (7), Thigpen (8); LP **Bosio**, Aldrich (8)

24. Sunday, August 9

Milwaukee	410 000 003	8	13	1
Chicago	000 003 010	4	7	0

	AB	R	H	
Molitor	4	2	1	(2B)

WP **Nieves**, Clear (7), Plesac (9); LP **Allen**, Long (1), Searage (8), Winn (8)

25. Monday, August 10

Texas	011 010 000 000	3	5	0
Milwaukee	003 000 000 001	4	9	1

	AB	R	H	
Molitor	4	1	2	(2-1B)

WP Higuera, **Aldrich** (12); LP Guzman, Howe (7), **Russell** (9) (12 innings)

26. Tuesday, August 11

Texas	230 000 020	7	10	1
Milwaukee	000 010 000	1	8	2

	AB	R	H	
Molitor	4	0	3	(2-1B, 3B)

WP **Harris**, Williams (8), Mohorcic (9); LP **Knudson**, Clear (7)

27. Wednesday, August 12

Texas	202 006 110	12	16	0
Milwaukee	000 000 210	3	9	0

	AB	R	H	
Molitor	4	1	3	(2-1B, 2B)

WP **Kilgus**, Williams (7), Russell (8); LP **Burris**, Aldrich (6), Crim (8), Plesac (9)

28. Thursday, August 13

Milwaukee	000 002 011	4	6	0
Baltimore	000 401 00x	5	10	1

	AB	R	H	
Molitor	4	1	1	(HR)

WP **Boddicker**, Niedenfuer (8); LP **Bosio**, Clear (8)

---

[1]*First game of a doubleheader.* [2]*Second game of a doubleheader.*

29. Friday, August 14

Milwaukee	005 001 000	6	9	2
Baltimore	100 000 100	2	9	0

	AB	R	H	
Molitor	5	0	1	(1B)

WP **Nieves**, Crim (7); LP **Bell**, O'Connor (7), Griffin (8)

30. Saturday, August 15

Milwaukee	000 010 000	1	6	2
Baltimore	000 002 00x	2	6	1

	AB	R	H	
Molitor	3	0	1	(1B)

WP **Flanagan**; LP **Higuera**

31. Sunday, August 16

Milwaukee	000 200 022	6	12	0
Baltimore	000 011 000	2	6	1

	AB	R	H	
Molitor	5	0	2	(1B, 2B)

WP Barker, **Crim** (6), Plesac (8); LP **Schmidt**, Williamson (8)

32. Monday, August 17

Milwaukee	101 003 000	5	11	0
Cleveland	000 000 012	3	9	3

	AB	R	H	
Molitor	3	1	1	(1B)

WP **Knudson**; LP **Bailes**, Gordon (6)

33. Tuesday, August 18

Milwaukee	031 003 010 000	8	14	2
Cleveland	100 007 000 001	9	14	2

	AB	R	H	
Molitor	6	0	2	(2-1B)

WP Akerfelds, Easterly (6), Jones (8), **Farrell** (12); LP Bosio, Crim (6), Clear (7), Aldrich (7), Plesac (9), **Burris** (12) (12 innings)

34. Wednesday, August 19

Milwaukee	030 810 100	13	15	1
Cleveland	000 020 000	2	9	4

	AB	R	H	
Molitor	6	2	4	(2-1B, 2B, HR)

WP **Nieves**; LP **Candiotti**, Gordon (2), Easterly (7), Vande Berg (9)

35. Thursday, August 20

Milwaukee	035 006 000	14	13	0
Cleveland	000 002 000	2	4	0

	AB	R	H	
Molitor	5	1	3	(1B, 2-2B)

WP **Higuera**, Burris (7), Aldrich (9); LP **Schrom**, Vande Berg (4), Akerfelds (7), Jones (9)

36. Friday, August 21

Kansas City	000 000 000	0	6	1
Milwaukee	000 012 00x	3	6	2

	AB	R	H	
Molitor	3	1	1	(2B)

WP **Barker**, Crim (7); LP **Jackson**

37. Saturday, August 22

Kansas City	200 005 010	8	12	1
Milwaukee	202 000 300	7	11	2

	AB	R	H	
Molitor	4	1	2	(2-1B)

WP Saberhagen, J. Davis (7), **Gleaton** (7); LP Wegman, **Knudson** (6), Burris (8)

38. Sunday, August 23

Kansas City	102 101 000	5	11	2
Milwaukee	000 412 21x	10	17	1

	AB	R	H	
Molitor	4	1	1	(1B)

WP Bosio, **Aldrich** (6); LP Leibrandt, **Stoddard** (5), Farr (6), Quisenberry (8)

39. Tuesday, August 25

Cleveland	010	003	032	9	10	1
Milwaukee	050	032	00x	10	11	2

	AB	R	H	
Molitor	4	2	1	(1B)

WP **Nieves**, Burris (8), Crim (9); LP
Schrom, Easterly (2), Gordon (6), Vande
Berg (8)

The streak ended the next night at Milwaukee County Stadium.

Wednesday, August 26

Cleveland	000	000	000	0		0	3	1
Milwaukee	000	000	000	1		1	4	0

	AB	R	H
Molitor	4	0	0

WP **Higuera**; LP Farrell, **Jones** (10) (10
innings)

Molitor failed to get the ball out of the infield in four at bats against rookie right-hander John Farrell, making his second major league start. He struck out in the first inning, grounded to shortstop into a double play in the third, and grounded out to shortstop in the sixth. With two out and a runner on second in the eighth, he hit a slow roller to third. Brook Jacoby charged in to field the ball and threw to first baseman Pat Tabler. First-base umpire Mike Reilly called Molitor out, then changed the call to safe when Tabler juggled the ball for an error.

The crowd of 11,246 on a rainy night was rooting for Molitor to get another chance, since the game was scoreless after nine innings. With right-hander Doug Jones pitching in the Milwaukee tenth, outfielder Rob Deer was hit by a pitch and outfielder Mike Felder ran for him. Felder took second on an infield out by third baseman Ernest Riles, and shortstop Dale Sveum was walked intentionally before outfielder Rick Manning came up to bat for second baseman Juan Castillo. With the fans hoping Manning would walk or make the second out to give Molitor another chance, Manning hit an 0–1 pitch to center field for a single to score Felder from second base with the winning run. From the on-deck circle, Molitor raced to first base to congratulate Manning on his game-winning hit.

After Molitor hit in his thirty-ninth straight game, Milwaukee was in fourth place in the East with a 67–58 record, seven and one-half games behind first-place Detroit, and the Brewers won twenty-four and lost fifteen of the thirty-nine games.

The streak was interrupted for one game after Molitor had hit in five straight games on July 20. He then sat out Milwaukee's 6–4 win over Seattle on July 21 with a tender elbow. He started the season as Milwaukee's third baseman, but two hamstring injuries and elbow problems put him on the disabled list for three weeks. He returned July 16 to begin his streak and served as the designated hitter after that. He was the leadoff batter in every game during the streak except for July 19, 22, 24, 25, and 27, batting third in those games.

During the streak Molitor collected sixty-eight hits in 164 times at bat for a .415 average, raising his season's average forty-seven points to .370. He had seventeen doubles, three triples, and seven home runs. He scored forty-three runs, batted in thirty-three, drew twenty-five walks, was hit by the pitcher once, had two sacrifices, and an on-base percentage of .495. He also stole fifteen bases in sixteen attempts and struck out twenty-three times. Only one of his hits was a bunt.

Molitor batted .500 against Seattle in two games and .500 against Oakland in four games. He hit .458 against Cleveland, .444 against Texas, .379 against Baltimore, .367 against Chicago, .364 against Kansas City, and .353 against California. He did not face the other five clubs. He batted in a high of six runs against three teams and hit two homers against two teams.

In one game Molitor had four hits. He had three hits in eight games, two hits in ten games, and one hit in twenty games. In Game 10 (July 26) Molitor accomplished something that had not been done in the league since 1974. In Milwaukee's 7–4 win at home over Oakland, he singled in the first inning, then stole second, third, and home. Later in that game he doubled and tripled.

His biggest night was in Game 34 (August 19) in Milwaukee's 13–2 win at Cleveland. After grounding out his first two times up, Molitor hit a three-run homer in the eight-run fourth inning, had a leadoff double, and scored in the fifth and then added two singles before being removed for a pinch-runner.

The next night in Game 35 (August 20) in Milwaukee's most one-sided victory of the season, a 14–2 win at Cleveland, Molitor again batted in three runs and a two-run double in the three-run second, a one-run double in the five-run third, and then a leadoff single in the sixth to start a six-run rally.

Molitor extended his streak in his first time at bat nine times, in his second at bat thirteen times, in his third seven times, in his fourth seven times, and in his fifth three times. Only three times did he keep his streak alive in his last at bat.

The first of those was in Game 16 (August 1), when Molitor went hitless in his first three at bats, then singled off right-hander Jose DeLeon in the eighth inning of Chicago's 3-2 win at Milwaukee.

In Game 24 (August 9) in Milwaukee's 8-4 victory at Chicago, Molitor walked and scored in the four-run first, then went hitless three times before looping a double to right field off right-hander Jim Winn in the three-run ninth.

The closest Molitor came to having his streak snapped was in a 5-4 loss at Baltimore in Game 28 (August 13). He walked once and was hitless in three times at bat against right-hander Mike Boddicker. Right-hander Tom Niedenfuer relieved in the eighth and had two out in the ninth, when Molitor hit his tenth homer of the season.

Molitor singled in the fifth inning and scored in Milwaukee's 10-5 win over Kansas City for his lone hit in Game 38 (August 23), and singled in the sixth inning and scored in a 10-9 win over Cleveland for his only hit in Game 39 (August 25), the streak finale.

At the end of his streak, Molitor said, "It's impossible not to be a little split, but there is no way you can be disappointed when the guy in front of you drives in the winning run."

Of Farrell, the Cleveland pitcher who stopped him, Molitor said, "It was one of those nights when he had a good enough fastball. I couldn't keep up with him and what he was trying to do. He kept me confused."

As for his compiling the fifth longest batting streak in modern baseball history, Molitor said, "I'm not sure if it's set in to the degree it will. It's hard to imagine going six weeks without an 0-for. I'm sure as time goes by, I'll appreciate it more."

After the thirty-ninth game in the streak, Molitor went hitless in nine of the next thirteen games, but he finished the season at .353, the second highest batting average in the league and the highest of his career. He led the league with 114 runs and 41 doubles.

Milwaukee finished strong to finish third in the East with a 91-71 record, seven games behind first-place Detroit.

Tommy Holmes
1945 Boston Braves

37 Consecutive Games

Tommy Holmes was an accomplished hitter and outfielder, but he lacked the power the pre–World War II New York Yankees wanted their outfielders to have. As a result Holmes became a star in the National League.

Born in Brooklyn, New York, on March 29, 1918, Holmes was signed by the Yankees and made his professional debut with their Piedmont League farm club at Norfolk in 1937. The five-foot ten-inch, 180-pound left-handed hitter and outfielder batted .320 his first year, then led the Eastern League in 1938 with a .368 average for Binghamton. While he hit 25 home runs at Norfolk, he never hit more than nine in his last four years in New York's farm system, the last three with Newark of the International League.

Although he batted over .300 each year in the minor leagues, the Yankees sold Holmes to the Boston Braves after the 1941 season, and he became a regular right away. He batted .278, .280, and .309 in his first three seasons as Boston's center fielder.

Homes moved to right field in 1945 when he emerged as one of baseball's best, with many stars having gone into military service. As the Braves divided a doubleheader with the Chicago Cubs on June 3, 1945, winning the opener, 2–1, and losing the second game, 3–1, Holmes went hitless twice in the first game and three times in the nightcap against right-hander Claude Passeau, who pitched a two-hitter.

Holmes, who had gone hitless only three times that season before the doubleheader, was batting .378 after the twin bill, second in the league. After an open date and the rainout of a doubleheader at Philadelphia, Holmes began his streak in the opener of a twilight-night doubleheader at Philadelphia's Shibe Park, with Boston in seventh place with a 15–21 record, nine games behind first-place New York.

1. Wednesday, June 6[1]

Boston	027 022 002	15	15	0
Philadelphia	100 000 000	1	9	0

	AB	R	H	
Holmes	6	2	3	(2-1B, 3B)

WP **Cooper**; LP **Sproull**, Coffman (3), Monteagudo (6)

2. Wednesday, June 6[2]

Boston	030 001 201	7	10	1
Philadelphia	010 110 000	3	9	3

	AB	R	H	
Holmes	5	2	2	(1B, 2B)

WP **Hutchings**, Hutchinson (9); LP **Wyatt**

3. Thursday, June 7[1]

Boston	003 000 000	3	9	3
Philadelphia	000 100 000	1	7	2

	AB	R	H	
Holmes	5	1	2	(2-1B)

WP **Tobin**; LP **Lee**, Lucier (9)

4. Thursday, June 7[2]

Boston	100 122 100	7	12	1
Philadelphia	011 000 001	3	7	0

	AB	R	H	
Holmes	5	1	3	(1B, 2B, 3B)

WP **Earley**; LP **Barrett**, Kennedy (6)

5. Saturday, June 9

New York	000 000 000	0	7	2
Boston	000 000 13x	4	9	3

	AB	R	H	
Holmes	4	1	1	(1B)

WP **Logan**; LP **Feldman**, Adams (8)

6. Sunday, June 10[1]

New York	100 200 110	5	13	1
Boston	004 000 40x	8	9	2

	AB	R	H	
Holmes	4	1	1	(1B)

WP **Cooper**; LP **Vioselle**, Emmerich (8)

7. Sunday, June 10[2]

New York	000 001 000	1	5	0
Boston	100 011 00x	3	7	2

	AB	R	H	
Holmes	4	1	2	(1B, 2B)

WP **Tobin**; LP **Hansen**, Fischer (7)

8. Tuesday, June 12

Philadelphia	000 000 000	0	4	1
Boston	023 120 11x	10	12	0

	AB	R	H	
Holmes	4	2	1	(1B)

WP **Hutchings**; LP **Wyatt**, Judd (5)

9. Wednesday, June 13[1]

Philadelphia	011 001 000	3	6	3
Boston	001 700 00x	8	10	2

	AB	R	H	
Holmes	3	2	3	(2-1B, HR)

WP **Cooper**; LP **Barrett**, Lucier (4)

10. Wednesday, June 13[2]

Philadelphia	001 001 010 000 002	5	9	0
Boston	000 200 001 000 001	4	11	8

	AB	R	H	
Holmes	4	1	2	(2-1B)

WP **Lee**, Mauney (9), **Barrett** (14), Judd (15); LP **Logan**, **Hutchinson** (9) (15 innings)

---

[1]*First game of a doubleheader.* [2]*Second game of a doubleheader.*

11. Thursday, June 14

Philadelphia	502	400	200	13	13	0
Boston	140	012	000	8	14	0

	AB	R	H	
Holmes	4	1	1	(HR)

WP Sproull, **Coffman** (2), Judd (6); LP Earley, **Fette** (1), Cozart (4), Schacker (7), Hutchinson (9)

12. Friday, June 15

Brooklyn	010	021	230	9	16	2
Boston	010	014	020	8	8	1

	AB	R	H	
Holmes	4	1	1	(2B)

WP Pfund, **King** (6); LP Tobin, **Hutchinson** (7)

13. Saturday, June 16

Brooklyn	100	000	202	000	5	12	3
Boston	020	300	000	001	6	11	2

	AB	R	H	
Holmes	5	0	2	(2-1B)

WP Pyle, Tobin (7), **Hutchings** (11); LP Herring, Rudolph (4), Buker (7), Pfund (9), King (10), **Davis** (12) (12 innings)

14. Sunday, June 17[1]

Brooklyn	010	042	200	9	14	1
Boston	000	003	030	6	8	3

	AB	R	H	
Holmes	5	0	1	(2B)

WP **Gregg**, Buker (8), King (9); LP **Cooper**, Hutchinson (7), Earley (8), Fette (9)

15. Sunday, June 17[2]

Brooklyn	001	000	000	1	7	3
Boston	200	000	20x	4	5	0

	AB	R	H	
Holmes	3	0	1	(1B)

WP **Logan**; LP Lombardi, Buker (7), Seats (7)

16. Tuesday, June 19

Boston	001	104	021	9	13	0
New York	000	002	000	2	8	1

	AB	R	H	
Holmes	5	1	1	(1B)

WP **Tobin**; LP **Emmerich**, Fischer (6), Voiselle (8)

17. Wednesday, June 20

Boston	033	501	210	15	16	0
New York	321	102	001	10	16	2

	AB	R	H	
Holmes	5	3	3	(3-1B)

WP Hutchings, **Hutchinson** (2), Logan (8); LP Brewer, **Fischer** (3), Harrell (4), Adams (8)

18. Friday, June 22

Boston	000	301	003	7	11	1
Brooklyn	210	040	001	8	11	0

	AB	R	H	
Holmes	3	2	2	(2-1B)

WP Gregg, King (6), **Seats** (9); LP Cooper, Pyle (3), Hutchings (5), Fette (6), **Earley** (8)

19. Saturday, June 23

Boston	302	002	032	12	15	1
Brooklyn	050	000	54x	14	15	2

	AB	R	H	
Holmes	3	2	2	(2-1B)

WP Pfund, Seats (1), Herring (3), Rudolph (8), **Buker** (8), King (9), Gregg (9); LP Logan, Hutchinson (7), **Pyle** (8), Hutchings (8)

20. Sunday, June 24[1]

Boston	000	200	202	6	12	1
Brooklyn	000	410	04x	9	11	1

	AB	R	H	
Holmes	5	1	1	(1B)

WP **Lombardi**; LP **Tobin**, Hutchings (8)

[1]*First game of a doubleheader.* [2]*Second game of a doubleheader.*

21. Sunday, June 24[2]

Boston	010 000 020	3	6	0
Brooklyn	000 001 000	1	6	3

	AB	R	H	
Holmes	4	1	1	(1B)

WP **Andrews**; LP **Davis**

22. Wednesday, June 27[1]

Cincinnati	110 002 000 1	5	11	1
Boston	000 100 300 0	4	9	2

	AB	R	H	
Holmes	5	1	2	(1B, HR)

WP **Kennedy**; LP Cooper, **Hutchinson**
(8), Hutchings (10) (10 innings)

23. Wednesday, June 27[2]

Cincinnati	000 003 100	4	7	0
Boston	000 000 200	2	5	1

	AB	R	H	
Holmes	3	0	1	(2B)

WP **Fox**; LP **Logan**, Hutchings (8)

24. Thursday, June 28

Cincinnati	131 000 001	6	10	0
Boston	101 200 003	7	10	2

	AB	R	H	
Holmes	4	0	1	(1B)

WP **Tobin**; LP Dasso, **Lisenbee** (8)

25. Friday, June 29

Cincinnati	002 100 100	4	11	0
Boston	000 100 000	1	8	0

	AB	R	H	
Holmes	4	0	2	(2-1B)

WP **Walters**; LP **Andrews**

26. Saturday, June 30

St. Louis	001 300 000	4	9	1
Boston	006 002 00x	8	11	1

	AB	R	H	
Holmes	3	2	3	(1B, 3B, HR)

WP Pyle, **Hutchings** (5); LP **Creel**,
Dockins (3), Jurisich (8)

27. Sunday, July 1[1]

St. Louis	100 000 002 0	3	9	1
Boston	110 000 100 3	6	11	0

	AB	R	H	
Holmes	4	1	2	(1B, HR)

WP Logan, **Cooper** (9); LP Wilks, Byerly
(7), **Dockins** (9), Jurisich (10) (10 innings)

28. Sunday, July 1[2]

St. Louis	200 020 210	7	12	2
Boston	140 000 30x	8	11	2

	AB	R	H	
Holmes	3	2	2	(2-HR)

WP **Tobin**, Hutchings (8); LP **Donnelly**,
Byerly (7), Barrett (8)

29. Tuesday, July 3

Chicago	301 503 426	24	28	1
Boston	010 001 000	2	10	2

	AB	R	H	
Holmes	4	1	3	(3-1B)

WP **Passeau**; LP **Andrews**, Hutchinson
(4), Javery (6), Heving (7), Wietelmann (9)

30. Wednesday, July 4[1]

Chicago	110 020 010	5	11	1
Boston	100 000 020	3	10	3

	AB	R	H	
Holmes	5	1	2	(1B, 2B)

WP **Erickson**, Derringer (8); LP **Logan**,
Hendrickson (8), Cooper (9)

[1]*First game of a doubleheader.* [2]*Second game of a doubleheader.*

31. Wednesday, July 4[2]

Chicago	210 030 001	7	10	0
Boston	211 000 020	6	14	1

	AB	R	H	
Holmes	5	1	2	(2-1B)

WP **Vandenberg**, Derringer (9); LP Hutchings, Hendrickson (7), **Logan** (9), Cooper (9)

32. Thursday, July 5

Chicago	000 102 000	3	9	1
Boston	100 000 100	2	7	0

	AB	R	H	
Holmes	4	0	1	(1B)

WP **Wyse**; LP **Tobin**

33. Friday, July 6[1]

Pittsburgh	110 000 300	5	9	3
Boston	021 200 62x	13	12	0

	AB	R	H	
Holmes	5	2	3	(1B, 2B, HR)

WP **Andrews**, Cooper (8); LP Gerheauser, Beck (5), **Rescigno** (7)

34. Friday, July 6[2]

Pittsburgh	200 001 005	8	13	2
Boston	370 020 02x	14	19	2

	AB	R	H	
Holmes	5	2	3	(3-2B)

WP **Hendrickson**; LP **Roe**, Beck (2), Gables (4)

35. Saturday, July 7

Pittsburgh	010 001 040	6	10	1
Boston	100 500 01x	7	9	2

	AB	R	H	
Holmes	3	1	1	(1B)

WP Hutchings, **Cooper** (8); LP Sewell, Cuccurullo (5), **Gerheauser** (8)

36. Sunday, July 8[1]

Pittsburgh	000 340 030	10	12	3
Boston	303 000 200	8	11	1

	AB	R	H	
Holmes	4	2	1	(1B)

WP Strincevich, Rescigno (3), **Gables** (4), Sewell (8); LP Logan, Hendrickson (5), **Andrews** (8), Hutchinson (8)

37. Sunday, July 8[2]

Pittsburgh	100 000 000	1	5	4
Boston	100 701 04x	13	14	0

	AB	R	H	
Holmes	5	1	1	(HR)

WP **Tobin**; LP **Butcher**, Strincevich (4), Rescigno (5)

After a three-day break in the schedule for the All-Star Game, which was cancelled to reduce wartime travel, the league record streak of Holmes ended in Chicago's Wrigley Field.

Thursday, July 12[1]

Boston	000 000 010	1	3	1
Chicago	031 002 00x	6	14	0

	AB	R	H	
Holmes	4	0	0	

WP **Wyse**; LP **Tobin**

[1]*First game of a doubleheader.* [2]*Second game of a doubleheader.*

Against Chicago right-hander Hank Wyse, Holmes went to bat four times and hit only one ball out of the infield as his streak came to an end. Wyse, posting his eleventh win against five losses, allowed only three hits — singles by outfielder Bill Ramsey and first baseman Vince Shupe, who scored the only Boston run in the eighth, and a triple by second baseman Eddie Joost. Wyse had a no-hitter until the sixth inning, while Chicago pounded out 14 hits to win its 11th game in a row. That streak ended in the second game won by Boston, 3–1. After Holmes hit safely in his 37th straight game, Boston was in sixth place with a 36–36 record, seven games behind first-place Chicago, although the second game of June 17 was suspended in the top of the eighth because of the Sunday law and was not finished or added to Boston's win total until it was completed on August 4. The Braves won 22 of the 37 games and averaged almost 7 runs per game.

During his streak Holmes had 66 hits in 156 at bats for a .423 average, with 43 singles, 11 doubles, three triples, and nine home runs. He scored 43 runs, batted in 41, had 18 walks, was hit by the pitcher three times and had one sacrifice while striking out only twice. His on-base percentage was .492, and he lifted his season's batting average to .401. He batted second in the order through 23 games, then batted third, and he played left field for the first 12 games and then switched back to right. Brooklyn's pitching gave Holmes the most trouble. He batted .344 against the Dodgers, .364 against New York, .375 against Cincinnati, .409 against Pittsburgh, .444 against Chicago, .472 against Philadelphia, and .700 against St. Louis, playing three games against the Cards, with four of his seven hits against them being homers. In five games Holmes kept his streak alive with a hit in the ninth inning or in his last time at bat.

In Game 6 (June 10) Holmes hit a two-run single in the four-run seventh inning for his only hit in his last at bat, as Boston beat New York, 8–4. Holmes singled in the ninth and scored the tying run on a single and a fly ball in Game 10 (June 13). The game went 15 innings, and Philadelphia scored twice in the final inning to win, 5–4, before Holmes hit his second single of the game to drive in Boston's fourth run.

In Game 16 (June 19) Holmes grounded out twice, then hit a wicked grounder that bounced off the forearm of first baseman Phil Weintraub but was scored an error in the fifth. In the seventh he popped out but extended his streak with a single up the middle off right-hander Bill Voiselle in the ninth, as Boston won, 9–2, at New York.

The streak was in real jeopardy in both ends of the June 24 doubleheader (Games 20 and 21) in Brooklyn. Holmes singled for his only hit in the ninth inning of a 9–6 loss in the opener and looped a single to right on his last time at bat in the eighth and scored in Boston's 3–1 win in the nightcap. Holmes had 8 three-hit games, 13 two-hit games, and 16 one-hit games in the streak. His best showing was in Game 26 (June 30), when he was hit by the pitcher in the first, singled and tripled home two runs in the six-run third, and hit a two-run homer in the sixth inning of an 8–4 win over St. Louis.

In two other games Holmes batted in four runs. In Game 28 (July 1) he capped the four-run second with a homer and hit a two-run homer in the three-run seventh for an 8–7 win over St. Louis. In Game 34 (July 6), in a 14–8 victory over Pittsburgh, he had three doubles to knock in four runs, taking the major league lead in runs batted in, with 66. Holmes broke the National League record for hitting in consecutive games, set by St. Louis second baseman Rogers Hornsby in 1922.

In Game 35 (July 7) Holmes singled and scored in the five-run fourth for his lone hit in a 7–6 win over Pittsburgh. His last hit in the streak was a two-run homer in the seven-run fourth, to help Boston beat Pittsburgh, 13–1, in Game 37 (July 8).

The only two strikeouts Holmes had in his streak came in consecutive games. In Game 23 (June 27) he drove in Boston's only runs with a double in the seventh for his lone hit, then looked at the third strike with a runner on base on a three-two pitch thrown by right-hander Howie Fox as Cincinnati beat Boston, 4–2. In Game 24 (June 28), he singled home a run in the third for his only hit, but he also struck out, and in the ninth he popped out with a man on base shortly before third baseman Chuck Workman's three-run homer gave Boston a 7–6 win over Cincinnati.

In the final 80 games of the season, Holmes batted .306 to finish the season at .352, second in the league, but he led the league with 224 hits, 47 doubles, 28 homers, 367 total bases, and a .577 slugging percentage. Holmes batted over .300 for the next three seasons, helping the Braves win the 1948 pennant with a .325 average. That was his last year as a full-time regular. In 1951 he became player-manager of Boston's Eastern League farm club at Hartford, until he took over the same job with the Braves on June 19, 1951. He lost that job on June 1, 1952, and signed as a pinch-hitter at Brooklyn on June 17.

Holmes served as a minor league manager and scout for the next six years. He ended his eleven-year playing career in the big leagues with a .302 average and 88 home runs in 1,320 games.

Conclusion

Streaks have always drawn the most interest from devotees of baseball, and streaks have generally determined how teams or individuals fare in the rankings.

For instance, of the nine teams which won seventeen or more consecutive games in a season, six finished in first place, one finished second and two finished fourth. The most curious of the nine was the 1916 New York Giants, who won seventeen games in a row early in the season, all on the road, then won an all-time record twenty-six straight games, all at home, in the season's final month, and still managed to finish no better than fourth.

In contrast to that is the record of the 1935 Chicago Cubs. Third with less than a month left in the season, the Cubs won twenty-one consecutive games, and clinched the pennant with their twentieth victory in a row, three games from the season's end.

Of the nine teams which lost nineteen or more games in a season, every one finished last in its league or division.

Of the nine pitchers who won sixteen or more straight games in a season, only Pittsburgh's Roy Face failed to win more than twenty games, but the relief pitcher's 18–1 record was the highest winning percentage in the group. Five of the nine pitchers led his league in wins, and six of the nine led his team to the pennant.

Four of the six pitchers who lost fifteen or more consecutive games lost at least twenty games that season, and every one of the teams involved finished with the league's worst record.

Of the six batters who compiled hitting streaks of thirty-seven or more games, five finished the season with batting averages over .350. The exception was Pete Rose, who hit .302, a far cry from the .420 compiled by both Ty Cobb in his 1911 streak and George Sisler in his 1922 streak.

Pitching may be more important than hitting as illustrated by the fact that only Joe DiMaggio, with his fifty-six-game streak in 1941, led his team to a pennant.

Gene Mauch, a major league manager with four different clubs for more than a quarter century, had more than a nodding acquaintance with streaks—both good and bad.

Of losing streaks, Mauch used to say, "They're funny. If you lose at the beginning of a season, you just got off to a bad start. If you lose in the middle of the season, you're in a slump. If you lose at the end, you're choking.

"When you're winning, you get to feeling you're never going to lose again. When you're losing, you think you'll never win another game."

Index

255